SPRUNG FROM DIVINE INSANITY

SPRUNG FROM DIVINE INSANITY

The Harmonious Madness of Byron, Keats and Shelley

ANDREW KEANIE

Greenwich Exchange
London

Acknowledgements
Thanks to Janet Davidson and Patrick Ramsey for making this book.
Thanks too to James Hodgson, who has been encouraging and inspiring
since the beginning of the project.

Greenwich Exchange, London

First published in Great Britain in 2018
All rights reserved

Sprung from Divine Insanity:
The Harmonious Madness of Byron, Keats and Shelley
© Andrew Keanie, 2018

Printed and bound by imprintdigital.com
Cover design by December Publications
Tel: 07951511275

Greenwich Exchange Website: www.greenex.co.uk

Cataloguing in Publication Data is available
from the British Library

ISBN: 978-1-910996-14-0

to Eleanor and Emma,
and in memory of Granny Doris

Teach me half the gladness
    That thy brain must know,
Such harmonious madness
    From my lips would flow
The world should listen then – as I am listening now.

                        – Shelley, 'To a Skylark'

There are several kinds of divine madness. That which proceeds from the Muses taking possession of a tender and unoccupied soul, awakening, and bacchically inspiring it towards songs and other poetry, adorning myriads of ancient deeds, instructs succeeding generations; but he who, without this madness from the Muses, approaches the poetical gates, having persuaded himself that by art alone he may become sufficiently a poet, will find in the end his own imperfections, and see the poetry of his cold prudence vanish into nothingness before the light of that which has sprung from divine insanity.

                        – *Shelley Letters*, II, 29

CONTENTS

Preface

IN THE EIGHTEENTH CENTURY, THE POET, painter and printmaker, William Blake (1757-1827) opened up a whole new vista of vision and clarity in poetry that would be almost entirely unwelcome during his lifetime. However, despite the lack of encouragement, this vista would be explored further by other, younger English poets. They too would find themselves ignored or maligned. They came to be known as the English 'Romantics'. Their works show that they were often in strong conflict with the way things were, and also inspired with visions of the way things should be.

Anyone who is young, or remembers being young, knows what it feels like to have an intellect that is new and a nervous system that is tenderly sensitive, and knows how unavoidable it is to fire up in anger at, or shrink back in disgust from, badness and stupidity. But by maturity, one finds oneself marked if one has not assimilated to the prevailing sensibility, the prevailing acceptance of wrongness.

> The Priest sat by and heard the child,
> In trembling zeal he seiz'd his hair:
> He held him by his little coat,
> And all admired the Priestly care.
>
> — 'A little Boy Lost', Blake

The world we keep getting reminded is real – the world we keep getting reminded, therefore, to be getting on with – is, obviously, wrong.

> The weeping child could not be heard,
> The weeping parents wept in vain;
> They strip'd him to his little shirt,
> And bound him in an iron chain;
>
> And burn'd him in a holy place,
> Where many had been burn'd before:
> The weeping parents wept in vain.
> Are such things done on Albion's shore?
>
> — 'A Little Boy Lost', Blake

The answer to Blake's question is, of course, yes. Such things were done and passively accepted then, and such things are done and passively accepted now. Parents, educators, politicians, counsellors and other authorities constantly get things wrong. They continue to insist that theirs are the voices worth listening to, the lights worth being guided by.

The oceans have already been radiated. Incandescent nuclear high-noon looks more likely now (2018) than it ever did. You are expected to continue consuming and polluting. If you are young, you are normally expected to let go of your airy soul and put your actual shoulder to someone else's wheel. They will punish or reward you – or at any rate the bit of you left – on their terms. No wonder so many people, who would otherwise feel so orphaned, uninformed, alienated, maddened and held in contempt, become instead what Blake called 'sleepers':

> England! awake! awake! awake!
> Jerusalem thy sister calls!
> Why wilt thou sleep the sleep of death,
> And close her from thy ancient walls?

> *– Jerusalem*

If you insist on being awake, if you will not even pretend to be asleep – that is, if you refuse to join the 'throng,/Just skilled to know the right and choose the wrong' (as Byron put it in *English Bards and Scotch Reviewers*) – you will make an open wound of yourself, which is widely considered unwise in a world where wellness and compliance are two sides of the same coin. Hence, many involved in the arts wisely conform to the rules of the pundits. Blake saw it, and said it:

> The enquiry in England is not whether a man has talents or genius, but whether he is passive and polite, a virtuous ass, and obedient to noblemen's opinions in art and science. If he is, he is a good man; if not, he must be starved.
> – lines from Blake's 'Annotations to Sir Joshua Reynolds's *Discourses*', written *c.* 1808

Despite – or rather because of – putting things so clearly, Blake was regarded (if regarded at all) as something of a fantasist, not to be taken seriously. The last thing placemen and cronies want is a précis as clear as Blake's on the dishonourable science of place-hunting and cronyism.

The three poets discussed in this book were held, like Blake, in contempt by placemen and pundits. They, like Blake, told the truth. They could tell it with the frankness and naivety of Hans Andersen's inconvenient boy on seeing the Emperor's new clothes.

'Those who will not reason are bigots,' said Byron, 'those who cannot, are fools, and those who dare not, are slaves.' Byron, Keats and Shelley protested so eloquently and urgently against the wrong turns being taken by the dominators of their country's culture and civilization. But all the wrong turns have by now of course been taken.

> I am sure my bones would not rest in an English grave, or my clay mix with the earth of that country. I believe the thought would drive me mad on my deathbed, could I suppose that any of my friends would be base enough to convey my carcass back to your soil.
>
> – Byron, letter to publisher John Murray, 7 June 1819

There seems no way back from the unreal world we have been coerced and muddled into getting on with as if it were the real one. Those of us who are not bigots, fools or slaves – and have still not been calumniated – have been characterised by the majority as crucially lacking in substantiality. In his teenage years Shelley saw the dominating social and political legerdemain making a ghost of the good life. He would remain undeceived for the rest of his life.

> Where Athens, Rome, and Sparta stood,
> There is a moral desert now;
> The mean and miserable huts,
> The yet more wretched palaces
> Contrasted with those ancient fanes,
> Now crumbling to oblivion
> The long and lonely colonnades,
> Through which the ghost of Freedom stalks.
>
> – *Queen Mab*

As (pre-Christian) Plato taught, Freedom exists, really and eternally. However, as freedom is (in Shelley's Christian England) merely an abstract noun, it can be looked straight through by tyrants and their messengers as easily as any non-existent ghost.

Great poetry can bring near the far bright beauty of what should have been, of what should be. In this sense, great poetry is protest. Byron, Keats and Shelley still can stir the heart because they can put us back in touch with our buried or exiled selves – the sincerest and noblest parts of oneself one is expected to forfeit in order to purchase a half-life relatively unmolested in this naughty world. The poets' ideas and hopes, which constitute our true inheritance, never became our organising principles, and we still suffer silently the same 'acceptable' level of bamboozlement that Blake perceived in

> The land of darkness flamed, but no light & no repose:
> The land of snows of trembling & of iron hail incessant:
> The land of earthquakes, and the land of woven labyrinths:
> The land of snares & traps & wheels & pit-falls & dire mills
> *– Jerusalem*

Poetry, as deadpan Auden put it, makes nothing happen. *Romantic* poetry (merely a 'lie in the brain', as Auden, again, so influentially put it) has been diminished in the jolts and jars of disillusionment, and has melted almost entirely into amorphous post-modernism. Poetry is now so far off from elemental, essential passions that it has no presence in people's imaginations anymore. But

> A spirit and a Vision are not, as the modern philosophy supposes, a cloudy vapour, or a nothing: they are organized and minutely articulated beyond all that the mortal and perishing nature can produce. He who does not imagine in stronger and better lineaments, and in stronger and better light than his perishing and mortal eye can see, does not imagine at all. (Blake)

Like Keats and Shelley, Byron can bring poetry home to us,
and with his words he can bring about the kind of traction that
makes possible the bringing to us of truth from elsewhere –
whether that be from our lost selves or the other side of time.
When the supposedly worldly, jaded Byron says that what will
remain of us

> will one day be found
> When this world shall be *former* underground,
> Thrown topsy-turvy, twisted, crisp'd, and curl'd,
> Baked, fried, and burnt, turn'd inside out or drown'd
> – Don Juan, IX, xxxvii

he is as soaring and visionary as the otherworldly author of *Queen
Mab*. He is as 'Far from the shore' and as 'far from the trembling
throng' as Keats, the subject of Shelley's *Adonais*.

These poets knew as teenagers what was wrong with the world.
They felt it. They suffered it. They wished they could change it.
They wanted to fight. In this, they were like many young people.
So what was so special about their scribbling and singing about
it? What was the point of their using language at all? This is a
reasonable question. Asked with bad intent, however, it beats all
the lies you can invent. Language is not just for communication.
It is not just for sending messages. It is a form of action. There are
statements such as 'You're under arrest' or 'I name this ship' which
are performative – their speaker can perform the action only by
uttering the words. For such acts, knowing in advance what will
be said does not change anything. Everyone at a wedding
anticipates the words 'I now pronounce you husband and wife',
but until the words are actually said, the ceremony does not count.
With performative language, saying equals doing.

> I will not cease from Mental Fight,

Nor shall my Sword sleep in my hand
Till we have built Jerusalem
In England's green & pleasant Land.

– Blake, *Milton*

For the poets, language is performative. They did not use it so much to inform as to actualise. In order for their knowledge to be true, the songs had to be sung.

As the world, in all its unhappily agreed 'reality', now bubbles to the point at which poetry, song, hope and ideas are about to be boiled away forever, perhaps the best way to spend the time that remains is in mourning the greatest (though so traduced) poets by listening to their songs and seeing their visions. The three poets in focus in this study uttered truth and beauty, and in doing so made them real. Their rules and regulations were not those of the placeman or the pundit. Had they conformed, their dazzling and life-changing works as we know them would have had to stay in outer space like repudiated UFOs. Little Cockney Keats would have kept his impertinent love of Greek culture to himself. Bad Lord Byron would not have conjured in words his own soul and the soul of the world as he wandered and meditated amongst decay. Mad Shelley would not have invoked his West Wind – that mysterious carrier to us of his troubled, truthful soul through time and space.

Introducing the Children
of the Revolution

WITH THE FRENCH REVOLUTION IN 1789, and the widespread revolutionary sympathies of the 1790s, came a whole new way of thinking about society and politics. Thinking about poetry in a new way became a part of the general optimism and unrest. The poetic revolution of William Wordsworth and Samuel Taylor Coleridge – one thinks of their joint *Lyrical Ballads* collection of 1798 – was the driving force behind the new thinking. By the end of the Napoleonic wars, during 1812-1815 – when England was about to cease hostilities with France – Wordsworth had become a tax collector and Coleridge was reinventing himself as a safe political animal. Having been made Poet Laureate in 1813 the other Lake poet, Robert Southey, had taken to toadying to the King and the Prince of Wales:

> Lift up your heads, ye Gates; and ye everlasting portals,
> Be ye lift up! for lo! a glorified Monarch approacheth,
> One who in righteousness reigned, and religiously govern'd
> his people ...

> – *A Vision of Judgement*, VIII

For the younger poets, their predecessors' failure of courage was massively disappointing. Byron would make it clear in the Preface to his satirical poem *The Vision of Judgement* (1822) that he was writing in direct opposition to Southey's latest career-minded utterance, *A Vision of Judgement* (1821):

> If there is anything obnoxious to the political opinions of a portion of the public in the following poem, they may thank Mr Southey ... to attempt to canonise a monarch, who, whatever were his household virtues, was neither a successful nor a patriot king, – inasmuch as several years of his reign passed in war with America and Ireland, to say nothing of the aggression upon France, – like all other exaggeration, necessarily begets opposition.

The essayist William Hazlitt, staunchly republican all his life, was similarly revolted by the signs of self-interest in the older poets. The poets now known as the second generation English Romantics arrived. The terms 'second generation' (Byron, Keats and Shelley) and 'first generation' (Wordsworth and Coleridge) were not used at the time. The group associated with the radical editor, poet and publisher, Leigh Hunt, including Hazlitt and Keats, was called the 'Cockney' school, which was a snobbish label used by well-heeled Establishment reviewers. Byron and Shelley were supposed to head up the 'Satanic' school, which again was an expression of extreme disapproval of writers whose badness, madness or dangerousness was unwarranted by Anglican authority. Hence, at the time, Byron and Shelley were perceived to be in one group and Keats in another. But in terms of their poetic styles there are various and numerous overlaps. All three poets use elaborate poetic language, which is sumptuously metaphorical and full of classical allusions. The similarities can be appreciated after two centuries, but at the time 'Cockney' and 'Satanic' were supposed to be two totally different categories.

After the Battle of Waterloo (1815), there was a new tide of feeling carrying the new generation of poets forward. They sensed that Wordsworth and Coleridge had ceased to function as the vital force they once were in literature and society. Byron, Keats and Shelley (all born in the early 1790s) were children of the revolution of Wordsworth and Coleridge (both born in the early 1770s) as well as children of the French Revolution. What Wordsworth and Coleridge had already said about society had been profoundly important to the younger writers. Hazlitt's essay, 'My First Acquaintance With Poets' (1822), about Hazlitt's first meetings with Wordsworth and Coleridge in 1798, conveys a sense of a new era for English literature, and for England. In this essay, Hazlitt said of Wordsworth that 'There was ... a fire in his eye (as if he saw something in objects more than the outward appearance)', and of Coleridge that 'the light of his genius shone into my soul'.

Though routinely kicked aside even at that time, poetry did matter then more than it does now, and there were poets out to be useful to readers in search of real (if not material) nourishment for their inner lives. But as far as Byron, Keats and Shelley were concerned, two of their key sources of nourishment (as provided by Wordsworth and Coleridge) had run out. Their work is haunted by their yearning for a fresh replacement, and a fresh way forward. In *The Revolt of Islam* (1818), Shelley recalls how it felt to be shaken right through by the recognition of his calling in life – to oppose tyranny and transform society:

> I do remember well the hour which burst
> My spirit's sleep: a fresh May-dawn it was,
> When I walked forth upon the glittering grass,

And wept – I knew not why, until there rose,
From the near schoolroom, voices that, alas!
Were but one echo from a world of woes –
The harsh and grating strife of tyrants and of foes.

And then I clasped my hands, and looked around
(But none was near to mock my streaming eyes,
Which poured their warm drops on the sunny ground):
So without shame I spake – 'I will be wise,
And just, and free, and mild, if in me lies
Such power; for I grow weary to behold
The selfish and the strong still tyrannise
Without reproach or check.' I then controlled
My tears; my heart grew calm ...

Shaken and transformed by the strength of his own desire for freedom of thought and speech, the poet has to share the news. He knows that sharing such news in a largely unresponsive world will take a lifetime of thankless effort. But the fresh call to arms, arriving from somewhere deep within the poet's own heart, is a call that must be answered. The answer is the poet's life and work:

> ... a Poet hidden
>   In the light of thought,
> Singing hymns unbidden,
>   Till the world is wrought
> To sympathy with hopes and fears it heeded not
>   – 'To a Skylark'

On the whole, the younger poets were more cosmopolitan in attitude than the older poets. When Byron, Keats and Shelley were emerging into print, Wordsworth and Coleridge were becoming middle aged and really beginning to consider, in earnest, the benefits of Britain's often blinkered approach to national and international challenges. The younger poets were thinking about the Orient, and other broader European traditions of art and literature, and they were becoming infectiously excitable:

> The Isles of Greece, the Isles of Greece!
> Where burning Sappho loved and sung,
> Where grew the arts of War and Peace,
> Where Delos rose, and Phœbus sprung!
> Eternal summer gilds them yet ...
>
> – *Don Juan*, III, lxxxvi

In looking east, and in looking back in time, the younger poets saw brighter light and hitherto underexploited mental wealth, or 'realms of gold' as Keats put it. However, Keats – though just as open and excitable as Byron and Shelley – was not an aristocrat, and this would be held against him relentlessly by British reviewers whose fluency in the language of condescension was uniformly first-rate.

1

Keats, the Little Cockney Chancer

THE MAGAZINES THAT REVIEWED KEATS'S WORK were keen to uphold what they saw as the tenets of Augustan poetry – John Dryden, Alexander Pope and Dr Samuel Johnson. It was, in the end, a losing battle since the manners and fashions of the time were changing. Many of the magazine-reviewers had already resisted (in vain) what Hazlitt called Wordsworth's 'levelling genius'. Charles James Fox, a lover of classical literature, had said to Coleridge 'I am not of your party, Sir', which said a lot. It stated a position that was aristocratic and privileged. Wordsworth and Coleridge, and later Keats, were neither. Privilege also meant a classical education. A literary man was expected to have been classically educated.

People who read the works of Byron, Keats and Shelley – three of the greatest dreamers and poets who ever lived – have more often than not been influenced first by scientism, which is unpropitious to dreams and hostile to poetry. In such an ethos, dreams are the individual's and are un-recordable by technology, and are therefore of doubtful material status. Poetry full of imagery and feeling has few outlets unlike, say, the chopped up prose sentences that so often get published in the *TLS* and elsewhere.

Having trained as a doctor in Guy's Hospital, London, Keats knew about material existence in plenty of empirical ways (including anatomy, botany, chemistry and physiology), and could therefore be counted a 'man of the world'. He knew about suffering. He could explain precisely, for example, the difference between a sore throat and syphilis. As a trainee doctor, he would have had to work with the noises of children in agony. Patients had limbs amputated without anaesthetic. Away from the hospital, there was more, personal suffering for Keats. He nursed his consumptive brother Tom to the bitter end, in 1818. It would not be long after that before Keats would glean from coughing fits that he himself was consumptive, and would die like poor Tom.

Physical agony aside, in terms of emotional agony Keats experienced the sweetness of his feelings for the love of his life, Fanny Brawne, turning to bitterness and tears, even as his own tuberculosis drove him to Italy in search of better health, and finally to his own Roman deathbed in 1821. During his short and traumatic life he transformed himself into a great poet with much to say about what suffering is, and what can be done by the sufferer.

If the public understanding of Keats's work was flattened during his lifetime into reviews fit for a conformist readership, those very reviews can (and in this study will) be evoked to garland his prescience all the more. As Coleridge said, the most eloquent contemporary attacks on genius can become, in the fullness of time, encomia. (For about 150 years after his death, Shakespeare's achievement was considered disputable because of his works' lack of classical form.) However, one could add that neglect of Keats's work would hold back the rise of his reputation at least as much as the plainer hostility he encountered during his lifetime. For nearly two decades after his death, not one reprint of his poems was published in England. In 1835, his publisher John Taylor was loath to publish the poet's work again: 'but the world cares nothing for him – I fear that even 250 copies would not sell'. On this basis most poetry published in Britain today would not be published at all. A copy of his *Poems* (1817) that Keats had given to Wordsworth was found after Wordsworth's death over three decades later with its pages still uncut. (So, by his late forties the monumental forefather of English Romanticism had himself become as responsive to new poetry as an actual monument.)

The first biographical study of Keats – Richard Monckton Milnes's *Life, Letters, and Literary Remains* – was not published until 1848. It would take until a century after Keats's birth for him to be established as a major writer. In the meantime, the fact that his poetry was often a point of contention for the Victorians – such as Matthew Arnold, Gerard Manley Hopkins and Walter Pater – indicates the deepening sense of its significance and growing renown.

2

Keats's Humble Origins, Politics and Poetry

HE LOST HIS FATHER (WHO HAD been the head ostler at The Swan and Hoop, Finsbury, London) at the age of nine. He lost his mother at fourteen. Orphaned, and with no guardian in the world but the solicitor Richard Abbey, he had to look after his younger brothers, George and Tom, and his younger sister, Fanny. George's decision to emigrate to America in June 1818 affected him deeply. So did Tom's death later that same year. So too did his separation from Fanny, who had to stay with the Abbey family in Walthamstow. Keats and his sister were aggrieved by Abbey's stony attitude towards them, which involved restricting Fanny's freedom, giving them little money, and keeping them apart. (*Letters*, I, 62-3) Abbey actually denied Fanny Keats the opportunity to visit Tom in the final stages of his illness in November 1818. Keats could rarely get out of bed in the morning feeling happy and thinking of the day as his own. He could not listen to the nightingale on Hampstead Heath, nor visualise the Grecian urn, so much with a weekday poet's leisurely solicitude as with a longing for it. 'This is the world,' he told George in

March 1819, 'thus we cannot expect to give away many hours to pleasure – Circumstances are like Clouds continually gathering and bursting – While we are laughing the seed of some trouble is put into the wide arable land of events – while we are laughing it sprouts.. grows and suddenly bears a poison fruit which we must pluck.' (*Letters*, II, 79) His apostrophising was often ignored or ridiculed, and he never made any money from his writing.

He did visit Scotland, the north of Ireland and the Lake District, and found on his travels sublime scenery and savage poverty. More typically, though, he visited the sort of down-at-heel locations that were so un-poetically populated by budget holidaymakers during peak seasons. He holidayed at Margate, Shanklin (on the Isle of Wight), and Burford Bridge (Surrey). These venues seem a far cry from the awesome Alps that had been the backdrop to the young Wordsworth's search for himself, and they seem like standing water compared to the glittering and heaving Mediterranean that would be the backdrop to Byron's search for himself. Having lived in Britain all his short life, Keats's chief purpose in going to Italy was vainly to prolong his life, but actually to die.

Keats lived and worked in a land already considered claustrophobic by Byron and Shelley. They had become sick of an Englishness they saw as prescribed and life-limiting. They wanted nothing to do with Anglicanism other than to attack it. They wanted nothing to do with lowered horizons other than to attack or (at least in Shelley's case) raise them. They saw citizenship – at any rate, *their* citizenship – of a country with a literary culture now presided over by maturing, mortgage-sensible Lake Poets as deeply problematic. The young poets, in turn, were hated and despised for their attitudes. On 5 August 1822, the London *Courier* would pronounce that 'Shelley, the writer of some infidel poetry,

has been drowned; *now* he knows whether there is a God or no.'
Reactionary criticism seemed to be having the final say. In a land
where 'Satanic' Shelley could be consigned by journalists to his
'native' Hell, 'Cockney' Keats could not have been true to himself
as a writer and realistically expected to escape with a whole skin.

Keats's first big poetic romance, *Endymion* (1818), was
manhandled and mauled by reviewers because of his 'low' birth,
his second-rate education (we might call it a vocational education
– Shakespeare catches the mood in his reference to 'rude
mechanics'), his political radicalism, and the 'lax morality'
presumed to be the results of hereditary shortcomings. From 1815,
he was a friend of, and admired by, the controversial editor of the
weekly *Examiner*, Leigh Hunt: 'Mr Keats is no half-painter, who
has only distinct ideas occasionally, and fills up the rest with
commonplaces. He feels all as he goes. In his best pieces, every bit
is precious; and he knew it, and laid it on as carefully as Titian or
Giorgione ... There are stanzas, for which Persian kings would fill
a poet's mouth with gold' (*Leigh Hunt: Selected Writings*, 107-
8). Hunt had served time in Surrey Gaol (1813-14), and he had
had to pay a fine of £500 (and give a security of £750 for good
conduct during five years) for libelling the Prince Regent. Hunt's
offence had been to hit out at the monarchy and the sycophantic
mainstream press by complaining that English newspaper readers
would never know that such a '*delightful, blissful, wise,
pleasurable, honourable, virtuous, true and immortal* PRINCE,
was a violator of his word, a libertine over head and ears in debt
and disgrace, a despiser of domestic ties, the companion of
gamblers and demireps, a man who has just closed half a century
without one single claim on the gratitude of his country or the
respect of posterity!' (*Examiner*, 22 March, 1812) A friend of
Hunt's could hardly expect the indulgence of the Establishment.

Hunt's paternal lineage could be traced to West India, and his dark hair, dark skin and thick lips made a wonderful target of him for British journalists whose duty it was to fend off foreign influence.

Keats was eager to meet this arch-fiend of contemporary counterculture. His friend, Charles Cowden Clarke, had already spent time in Hunt's inspiring company, and when Clarke told Keats about it, the poet became, if anything, even keener to meet Hunt. Keats produced the following lines, 'Written On the Day That Mr Leigh Hunt Left Prison', in February 1815:

> What though for showing truth to flatter'd state,
>   Kind Hunt was shut in prison, yet has he,
>   In his immortal spirit, been as free
> As the sky-searching lark, and as elate.

During his time in prison, Hunt had the support of his family and friends. Liberal-mindedness characterised his visitors' attitudes to his incarceration. Visitors included (the by now famous) Byron (charmed by 'the wit in the dungeon') and Shelley ('boiling with indignation at the horrible injustice & tyranny of the sentence'). But Byron and Shelley were not in Keats's modest, and therefore vulnerable, position in society. They were aristocrats unattached to the strings of petty-bourgeois embarrassment that can be twitched with such hateful knowingness by reviewers (hired to encourage readers to look down on writers so much that they forget to look up). Keats told Benjamin Bailey in 1817 that he was 'disgusted with literary Men', and two years later he told his brother 'You see what it is to be under six foot and not a lord.' (*Letters*, II, 61)

Keats's impetuous and youthful support for Hunt was in some sense a forward-payment for Hunt's crucial support of him. The lines on Hunt (quoted above, and below) effected Keats's letter of application for membership of the Hunt coterie, which at the time included the historical painter and art critic Benjamin Haydon, the essayist Charles Lamb and the Irish poet (later to become Byron's biographer) Thomas Moore. It is possible that at this point Keats, like many young people, was high-minded and energised with enthusiasms he did not quite mean, and it may have been the case that he guessed going public with an initial commitment to Hunt's politics would help him on his own way as a poet:

> Minion of grandeur! think you [Hunt] did wait?
>> Think you he naught but prison walls did see,
>> Till, so unwilling, thou unturn'dst the key?
> Ah, no! far happier, nobler was his fate!
> In Spenser's halls he stray'd, and bowers fair,
>> Culling enchanted flowers; and he flew
> With daring Milton through the fields of air:
>> To regions of his own his genius true
> Took happy flights. Who shall his fame impair
>> When thou art dead, and all thy wretched crew?

Not yet having alchemised his own 'jumbled heap' of thoughts and feelings into poetic gold, Keats was admiring, and aspiring to, the dignity of inner riches that made Hunt superior to his persecutors, and essentially free despite his actual imprisonment. 'The busy time is just gone by,' said Keats to Clarke on leaving the medical profession to become a poet, 'and I can now devote any time you may mention to the pleasure of seeing Mr Hunt – 'twill be an Era in my existence.' (*Letters*, I, 113)

In an influential review article, the redoubtable Tory journalist, 'Z' (John Gibson Lockhart, who would also write a much admired biography of his father-in-law Sir Walter Scott), said that Hunt is the ideal of a Cockney Poet. He raves perpetually about 'green fields', 'jaunty streams', and 'o'er-arching leafiness', exactly as a Cheapside shop-keeper does about the beauties of his box on the Camberwell road. Mr Hunt is altogether unacquainted with the face of nature in her magnificent scenes; he has never seen any mountain higher than Highgate-hill, nor reclined by any stream more pastoral than the Serpentine River. But he is determined to be a poet eminently rural, and he rings the changes – till one is sick of him, on the beauties of the different 'high views' which he has taken of God and nature, in the course of some Sunday dinner parties, at which he has assisted in the neighbourhood of London.

– 'Cockney School I', *Blackwood's Edinburgh Magazine*

To a reactionary writer such as 'Z', any sympathiser with Hunt was either a typically minor irritant to be routinely eradicated or a full-scale menace to be seen off with heavier rhetoric – it depended on the offender's estimated capacity to challenge the spirit of defence or displace the Establishment. Keats's (perhaps rather naive, or shrewd, or a bit of both) advocacy of Hunt was treated as a minor irritant.

Writing to Charles Ollier, his publisher, about his new poem, *Adonais: an Elegy on the Death of John Keats* (1821), Shelley claimed that Keats's death was hastened by his treatment at the hands of vindictive reviewers. (*Letters*, II, 297) If Shelley's sense of solidarity with the imprisoned Hunt had been heartfelt, his empathy with the calumniated Keats was – and remains – vascular with admiration:

> He has outsoared the shadow of our night;
> Envy and calumny and hate and pain,
> And that unrest which men miscall delight,
> Can touch him not and torture not again;
> From the contagion of the world's slow stain
> He is secure ... (XL)

He is a portion of that loveliness
Which once he made more lovely ... (XLIII).

Despite the substantial quantity and magnificent quality of his tribute to Keats, Shelley's Preface to *Adonais* does, unfortunately, seem to reduce both Shelley's and Keats's visionary *raisons d'être* to a daftly defiant entrenchment in a dream of how things work in the world – a pair of ineffectual angels, perhaps. The following serves to illustrate how Shelley exposed both himself and his subject to further ridicule: 'The savage criticism of *Endymion*, which appeared in the *Quarterly Review*, produced the most violent effect on [Keats's] susceptible mind; the agitation thus originated ended in the rupture of a blood-vessel in the lungs; a rapid consumption ensued'. This kind of discourse is represented in the satirical novels of Thomas Love Peacock (Shelley's friend) as transcendental twaddle not untypical of the age. In *Headlong Hall* (1816) and *Nightmare Abbey* (1818), Peacock made (albeit affectionate) fun of the sort of mysticism that still seemed to find a way into some of his learned friends' accounts of life and death. Byron, however, did not upholster every satirical blow he delivered with the affection of a Peacock. He had little time for the scribbling of a former apothecary with pretensions, and he had scarcely more time for talk of medical matters coming from his notably unworldly friend, Shelley. In *Don Juan*, Byron would devote some lines to 'John Keats, who was killed off by one critique'. In saying as much, Byron was poking private fun at Shelley's sympathy with Keats as much as he was poking public fun at Keats: 'Poor fellow! His was an untoward fate;/'Tis strange the mind, that very fiery particle,/Should let itself be snuffed out by an article.' (*Don Juan*, XI, lx) Given Shelley's ostracisation, and given Byron's continuing projection of his own *enfant terrible* image (Byron had noted elsewhere that his own response to a bad review was to consume three bottles of claret), it would be a very long time before Keats's humorously smothered spark would mount into universally recognised starry brightness.

As already mentioned, the politics of Hunt and his 'Cockney' circle were often acidly expressed, and this elicited strong feelings in readers. Broadly speaking, the Cockneys' attitude was a continuation of the English Jacobinism of the 1790s (when even the most discreet nods of sympathy towards Revolutionary France would be exposed and excoriated in, for example, the pages of the *Edinburgh Review*). Many of Keats's earliest poems contain bluntly republican points of view. 'On Peace' is a call to the crowned heads of Europe to use their power and success for universal freedom:

> O Europe! let not sceptered tyrants see
>   That thou must shelter in thy former state;
> Keep thy chains burst, and boldly say thou art free;
>   Give thy kings law – leave not uncurbed the great
> So with the horrors past thou'lt win thy happier fate!

The poems to Tadeusz Kosciuszko, the general who led an unsuccessful revolt against the partitioning of his native Poland, express the view that Kosciuszko is part of a perennial political integrity traceable back to King Alfred, the founder of the Saxon Constitution of England:

> When some good spirit walks upon the earth,
>   Thy name with Alfred's, and the great of yore
> Gently commingling, gives tremendous birth
> To a loud hymn, that sounds far, far away ...
>
> – 'To Kosciusko'

The title page of Keats's first published collection, *Poems*, had a dedication to Hunt, and there was also a picture of Shakespeare and a few lines quoted from Edmund Spenser. This all combined to present an assertion of Keats's political sympathies. Hunt's leading articles for *The Examiner* regularly invoked writers like Chaucer, Shakespeare and Spenser as the custodians of English freedom, and now Keats's *Poems* was almost certainly going to irritate conventional readers in that it was published on 3 March 1817 (a Monday), which immediately followed Hunt's keen censure (in the Sunday's *Examiner*) of the Foreign Secretary Lord Castlereagh's part in trying to suspend the habeas corpus act. Hunt's article, 'On the Proposed Suspension of the Habeas Corpus Act', called Castlereagh 'a man, who is proved guilty in the House of Commons of violating the Constitution and setting at nought the representative rights of the people, coming forward and asking for a suspension of our most sacred privilege'. Furthermore, Hunt warned readers that 'The Suspension Bill, if it pass, will be an unconstitutional assumption of power by the House of Commons illegally constituted.' Given the timing, the publication of Keats's new *Poems* was tantamount to an announcement of the poet's concurrence with the author of the leader in *The Examiner*.

The first stanza of the poem, 'Written on 29 May, the Anniversary of the Restoration of Charles II', is delivered as a sort of alarm to politically sleepwalking British citizens, and the second stanza invokes again the individuals already championed by Hunt:

> Infatuate Britons, will you still proclaim
> His memory, your direst, foulest shame?
> Nor patriots revere?
>
> Ah! while I hear each traitorous lying bell,
> 'Tis gallant Sydney's, Russel's, Vane's sad knell,
> That pains my wounded ear.

The man mentioned in the second stanza, Algernon Sydney, the author of *Discourses Concerning Government*, was the English Whig politician beheaded for his supposed part in the Rye House Plot to assassinate Charles II. Keats had learned from reading Gilbert Burnet's *History of My Own Times* (2 volumes, 1724 and 1734) that Sydney was an exceptionally courageous republican. But now (according to Keats), in the nineteenth century, crowds of falsely conscious Britons were involved in festivities initiated by a corrupt Prince Regent.

How strongly did Keats really feel that his fellow-citizens' celebrations were morally wrong? Were his republican leopard-spots paint or did they go all the way through? The earlier poems are his most overtly political ones. They are accomplished and even stirringly subversive, but they are not what the poet is best remembered for. They were scarcely given any attention at the time. Clarke said that *Poems* 'might have emerged in Timbuktoo with far stronger chance of fame and approbation ... The whole community, as if by compact, seemed determined to know nothing about it.' In June 1817, there was an anonymous review in the *Anti-Gallican Monitor*: 'this dress is made by a great-grandchild of Milton, after the poet's mode; but the white crepe in his buttonhole, a token of grief for the loss of his liberty, is on the ground of Milton's political principles – Poor youth!' James Ollier, the publisher of *Poems*, would express in forthright terms his reasons for dropping the collection:

> By far the greater number of persons who have purchased it from us have found fault with it in such plain terms, that we have in many cases offered to take the book back rather than be annoyed with the ridicule which has, time after time, been showered upon it. In fact, it was only on Saturday last that we were under the mortification of having our own opinion of its merits flatly contradicted by a gentleman, who told us he considered it 'no

better than a take in'. These are unpleasant imputations for any one in business to labour under ...

A take-in is a deception, fraud or imposition. This would not be the last time the poet's work would be viewed so dimly by readers outside the magic Cockney circle. Hunt felt that these early offerings from Keats – 'the impatient workings of the younger god within him' (*Indicator*, August 1820) – were the forerunners of the best kind of royalty.

3

Keats and Chapman's Homer

K EATS'S SONNET, 'ON FIRST LOOKING INTO Chapman's Homer' (1816), shows two things about the poet: his lack of classical education and the burgeoning of his genius. It is also an epiphany – a conversion of a young man into a poet with a vision. Mundanely, he was not able to read the Greek poet Homer until his discovery of an English translation by the Elizabethan poet, George Chapman. Once introduced to ancient Greek poetry (albeit at a remove), Keats would retain and renew an extraordinary raptness with it for the rest of his life:

> Much have I travell'd in the realms of gold,
>   And many goodly states and kingdoms seen;
>   Round many western islands have I been
> Which bards in fealty to Apollo hold.
> Oft of one wide expanse had I been told
>   That deep-brow'd Homer ruled as his demesne;
>   Yet did I never breathe its pure serene
> Till I heard Chapman speak out loud and bold ...

Having in previous poems rather formally esteemed Hunt's ability to 'travel' in dreams and poetry, now Keats had begun to do some extravagant, inspirational, and unguarded travelling of his own. He had just discovered in himself, and was exploring, a heroic amplitude in a different dimension – the 'mental space' that Coleridge had appreciated in the poetry of Spenser. The sense of wonder is irresistible: 'Then felt I like some watcher of the skies/ When a new planet swims into his ken'. The joy of discovery is in these lines. The age of science and wonder in which he lived is undoubtedly part of the grounding of Keats's flourishing art. Galileo could only have found the moons of Jupiter by looking into another astronomer's (Copernicus's) telescope. Similarly, the teenage Keats found, through Chapman's translation of Homer, things he had 'been told' about, and had perhaps felt somehow, but had never actually seen or heard before. Crucially, he allowed them to continue to exist on their own twilit terms without trying to haul them with Herculean disrespect into the light of common day. Such mindfulness makes Keats's poetry something of a variant of the prevailing science of the age. He did not, so to speak, remove the 'swimming' new 'planet' from its element of dreams and poetry or fatally reduce it at the waking, worldly end of his 'telescope'. Denis Diderot may have proclaimed influentially in the *Encyclopedia, or a systematic dictionary of the sciences, arts, and crafts* (1745-1772) that 'all things must be examined, debated, investigated without exception and without regard for anyone's feelings' and that 'We must ride roughshod over all these ancient puerilities, overturn the barriers that reason never erected', but Keats was not going to use any new 'planet' (or any other discovery) just to rattle a Ptolemaic or medieval paradigm. Just as he was not necessarily all that interested in Hazlitt and Hunt's visions of political revolution, so too he was not really all that interested in the Copernican revolution. More captivatingly, he offers the reader a view *in* to the human mystery (through the lens of poetry), rather than *out* at an alienating constellation of 'realities'. The greatest mystery's real locus, for Keats, is like, though not literally, 'the Pacific' ocean, sparkling and yearning (as humans sparkle and yearn), and teeming with unknown modes of being (as humans teem). 'There will,' said Hunt in an article that praised Keats to the skies, 'be a poetry of the imagination, as long as the first causes of things remain a mystery.' (*Indicator*, August 1820)

By this point in his quest, his pilgrimage to higher realms of soul and spirit (having already that year, 1816, decided not to pursue medicine as a career), the poet found expression for his apprehension just before, and his transformation during, psychic discovery. (At the same time, he found expression for his apprehension about his first real look at high culture.) He was finding himself. He was learning to express emotions from the depths.

Having been given Bonnycastle's *Introduction to Astronomy* in 1811, he would have read about William Herschel's discovery of Uranus 35 years earlier, and he possibly attended Charles Babbage's 1815 'Lectures on Astronomy' at the Royal Institution. Keats did see the point of science. He did not, however, see why, or even how, it could be driven through the irregular aliveness of Psyche (to use the ancient Grecians' term for soul's symbol) without regularising and wasting it. An actual, external, remote entity like Europa, or Uranus, no longer 'swims' 'like a gentle whispering/Of all the secrets of some wondrous thing/That breathes about us' (*Sleep and Poetry*, 29-31) once scientists have fished it out of its celestial provenance and into their own zone of interest. Keats is not interested in looking literally into the bowl of a telescope. He wants to see past the hundred percent bleakness of lumps in space to what they symbolise: 'we look around with prying stare,/Perhaps to see shapes of light, aerial limning,/And catch soft floatings from a faint-heard hymning' (*Sleep and Poetry*, 32-4). In a letter to Haydon, he would discuss 'looking upon the Sun the Moon the stars, the Earth and its contents as materials to form greater things – that is to say ethereal things' (*Letters*, I, 143). This is very different to Herschel's uses of this world (and others), as seen perhaps in how he benefitted from his sister's unflagging devotion to him, or in how his reputation grew still further as his son continued cataloguing well over 500 nebulae and star clusters.

Chapman's verse translation of Homer's *Iliad* helped Keats to get acquainted with a vital, yet neglected, mode of vision at its most powerful: 'Like rich Autumnus' golden lampe, whose brightness men admire,/Past all the other host of Starres, when with his cheerful face,/Fresh washt in lofty Ocean waves, he doth his Skies enchase.' (Book 5) From reading Chapman's Homer, Keats learned to contemplate rather than count (as Homer and Chapman contemplated rather than counted the 'host of Starres'). The comparison of the golden glow of the Greek warrior Diomed's helmet with the glow of the planet Jupiter rising above the sea in autumn is one of the moments in Chapman's Homer that most excited Keats. Clarke, to whom Hunt probably lent a 1616 folio edition of Chapman's translation, remembered that the poet 'sometimes shouted' on hearing certain passages recited during 'a memorable night' (probably during the weekend of 11th to 12th October 1816, in Clerkenwell), after which Keats left Clarke at six o'clock in the morning, and went home with the music of the spheres – and one of the finest works of antiquity – ringing in his head. By ten o'clock in the morning, a postal messenger had delivered Keats's sonnet to Clarke.

Keats's opinion that his beloved Thomas Chatterton's 'medieval' idiom showed Chatterton to be 'the purest writer in the English language' (*Letters*, II, 167) is significant: the first six lines of 'On First Looking into Chapman's Homer' are characterised by antiquated words such as 'bards', 'demesne' and 'fealty', and the speaker has, as he archaically puts it, 'many goodly states and kingdoms seen'. The poem goes on to express something of a purer (and, arguably, more medieval) way of experiencing the presence of the night sky – but in an age of hot air balloons, steam engines and the increasing extent of artificial light in buildings and on streets, contemporary readers were tending to esteem works (and themselves) when they were underpinned by science and utility, and so readers were seeing medievalism in pejorative terms that brought to mind benightedness and *im*purity best sloughed off.

The magical images of the medieval epoch had haunted the human mind luminously and voluminously (Milton's *Paradise Lost* was the last great literary powerhouse of such images) until the decisive cuts of the Enlightenment lancet, and then the mentality of lettered Europe was disinfected from the top down by French intellectualism, through the Industrial Revolution, to the nihilism of the later nineteenth century, right through to the ultra-nihilism of the twentieth century. Our universe is now pitch-black and empty but for the unaccountable mess of stars and statistics. Arthur C. Clarke has told us that, whether we are alone in the universe or not, either possibility is equally terrifying. We might have a special way of being alone, or a special way of being afraid, but as Philip Larkin (laureate of our deprivation) has told us, we are in any case ultimately helpless and the predicament is no different whined at than withstood.

Deep down, some might feel that this sense of our own cosmic insolvency is inadequate as an apprehension of life. Keats's sincerity remains fundamentally animating, and it still has the power to people the vacancy:

> O come! let us haste to the freshening shades,
> The quaintly carv'd seats, and the opening glades;
> Where the faeries are chanting their evening hymns,
> And in the last sun-beam the sylph lightly swims.
>
> – 'Stanzas to Miss Wylie'

The imaginary being once assumed to inhabit the air ('the sylph') is not to be reeled as it 'really' is into the bright, hard light of new, clarity-seeking people. It is not to be pinned as it 'really' is on a cork, its wings outspread. It is not to become, literally, a specimen in a box covered with glass, hung on a wall, and filled with other dead sylphs, as a collection. Keats was one key English writer crucially out of step with the secularisation that would dragoon succeeding generations of men and women through a peculiarly punishing era of psychological hygiene.

The 'real world', if one wants to 'get on' in it, too often puts one in the invidious position of having to be untrue to oneself. While aristocrats such as Byron and Shelley were often seen to have an authority informed by their conviction of having the right to be entirely themselves, cockneys were often thought to be of no consequence because they were 'unacquainted' with anywhere except 'the neighbourhood of London' (as 'Z', with his well-bred brevity, tact, loftiness and malice, evoked the arrogance and ignorance of London's scarcely-travelled, semi-literate little citizens). Keats's brother George probably illustrated a lower-middle class truism – truthfulness is next to joblessness – on having to give up his position at Richard Abbey's counting-house due to a disagreement with Abbey's junior partner, Cadman Hodgkinson (slightly senior to George), whom John hated. It can be perilous, when one has been orphaned and impoverished, to neglect to pay the daily psychic cost involved in parrying or pandering to the moods of a better-connected co-worker.

Nevertheless, the paper on which there may at one time have been a record of the quarrel between George Keats and Cadman Hodgkinson has probably since passed through the intestines of a long-deceased rat, and Keats's separateness from his age can be recognised and celebrated as characteristic of an alternative world-view (whose lineage runs back to Plato) for which the majority of any given generation since the Enlightenment has been clever and keen enough to point out the absence of empirical evidence.

'On First Looking into Chapman's Homer' is replete with mental (rather than merely measurable) realities: four lines from the end of the poem, the narrator is no longer like 'some watcher of the skies', but 'like stout Cortez', the Spanish conquistador who discovered and defeated the Aztecs, and conquered Mexico in 1523. Andrew Motion points out that Keats 'mistakes Balboa ... for Cortez, and so undermines [his] air of learning.' Pointing out, also, that the poet 'succumbs to a moment of awkward translationese ('pure serene') which creates a sense of Keats standing apart from the main event' (Motion, 112), Motion hints that his vantage-point as Keats's biographer is situated somewhere between admiration and vindictiveness. Condescension to Keats has remained commonplace. When Val Hennessy told *Daily Mail* readers that 'Motion possesses a hotline to Keats in heaven', she was soliciting the chattering class sunniness in which sincerity vaporises before getting big enough to bore. And Edmund White, who praised Motion's 'restored' and 'glowing' Keats in the *Observer*, would confess some years later in his freehand memoir,

City Boy (2009), just how craven and untrue to himself he had more than once been as a book reviewer.

Despite the Enlightenment, and Europe's subsequent stress on the importance of reason and the critical reappraisal of existing ideas and institutions, Keats still feels worshipful in the presence of the heavens above. Indeed, he feels worshipful in the presence of anything – from the primary source of light in the whole planetary system to any one of the little lives on earth it makes possible: 'The setting sun will always set me to rights – or if a Sparrow come before my Window I take part in its existence and pick about the Gravel.' (*Letters*, I, 186) He knows his contribution to thought will not involve his resolving, with technologically enhanced eyesight, say, the Milky Way into a 'correct' answer. He knows that the 'problem' cannot be solved because it is not a problem – it is a mystery. But it is not the kind of mystery to be left only to state-funded philosophers. The poet sends his curiosity, his gaze, right into 'Paradise', or 'a dream', or the dark, trying always to remember that when doing so the mind's eye should dilate rather than squint.

Keats felt the weight of the same mystery that burdened the ancient Romans, the ancient Greeks, Dante, Shakespeare, and then Wordsworth and Coleridge, and then Byron and Shelley. He felt the same presence that disturbed them with the joy of elevated thoughts. He sensed, as they did, the same vital flow of connections running both ways between his own soul and the soul of the world. He felt – and made bold to write – the life of his own connection with the mystery. He knew that without lightness he would achieve nothing. Such was the nature of the burden on the poet.

In the Preface to *Foliage*, Hunt said that Shakespeare 'felt the Grecian mythology not as a set of schoolboy common-places which it was thought wrong to give out, but as something which it requires more than mere scholarship to understand – as the elevation of the external world ... to the highest pitch of the graceful, and as embodied essences of all the grand and lovely qualities of nature.' Keats could not read the actual words of Homer or Archimedes, but he recognised and relished what Hunt called 'the deepest taste of antiquity' to be found in plays like *A Winter's Tale* and *The Tempest*. On first looking into Chapman's Homer, Keats found himself on the edge of eureka, and almost dizzy with déjà vu. Like Byron and Shelley, he understood that something deep in his own nature had an appetite for antiquity, the soul of which had been sent through Chapman to greet him. His appetite was fierce. No wonder he shouted.

4

Shelley: Spirit in a Material World

IN 1811, SHELLEY, A FIRST-YEAR UNDERGRADUATE at University College, Oxford, and his friend Thomas Jefferson Hogg, jointly produced the anonymous pamphlet, 'The Necessity of Atheism'. As the title suggests, the publication was deliberately controversial, though the argument is also classical:

> it is urged that man knows that whatever is, must either have had a beginning or existed from all eternity, he also knows that whatever is not eternal must have had a cause. – Where this is applied to the existence of the universe, it is necessary to prove that it was created, until that is clearly demonstrated, we may reasonably suppose that it has endured from all eternity.

In addition to the liberal Enlightenment warmth inspiriting the prose, there is also a little of the teenage rebel's delight in tapping publicly at the fault lines of platitudinous piety: 'In a case where two propositions are diametrically opposite, the mind believes that which is less incomprehensible; it is easier to suppose that the Universe has existed from all eternity, than to conceive a being capable of creating it'. The eighteen-year-old pamphleteer was already known as the author of two Gothic novels: *Zastrozzi* (1810) and *St Irvyne or the Rosicrucian* (1810). The following passage from chapter 15 of *Zastrozzi* reveals Shelley's debt to Matthew Lewis's *The Monk* (1796), including something of a fascination with the overlapping energies of violence and sexual passion:

> 'Die, detested wretch,' exclaimed Mathilda, in a paroxysm of rage, as she violently attempted to bathe the stiletto in the life-blood of her rival; but Julia starting aside, the weapon slightly wounded her neck, and the ensanguined stream stained her alabaster bosom. She fell on the floor, but suddenly starting up, attempted to escape her bloodthirsty persecutor. Nerved anew by this futile attempt to escape her vengeance, the ferocious Mathilda seized Julia's floating hair, and holding her back with fiend-like strength, stabbed her in a thousand places; and, with exulting pleasure, again and again buried the dagger up to the hilt in her body, even after all the remains of life were annihilated. At last the passions of Mathilda, exhausted by their own violence, sank into deadly calm; she threw the dagger violently from her, and contemplated the terrific scene before her with a sullen gaze.

The young writer was already working through his own forbidden desires. He would be keeping only their quintessence by his late twenties. The sense of post-coital enervation suggested by Mathilda's 'sullen gaze' would reappear ten years later, stripped down in 'To a Skylark' to the 'sad satiety' all too familiar to human beings, but unknown to the bird soaring unencumbered by human destructiveness.

The following passage from chapter 10 of *St Irvyne* looks autobiographical (though it is ostensibly Ginotti telling his story to Wolfstein):

> From my earliest youth, before it was quenched by complete satiation, *curiosity*, and a desire of unveiling the latent mysteries of nature, was the passion by which all the other emotions of my

> mind were intellectually organized. This desire first led me to
> cultivate, and with success, the various branches of learning which
> led to the gates of wisdom. I then applied myself to the cultivation
> of philosophy, and the éclat with which I pursued it, exceeded my
> most sanguine expectations. – Natural philosophy ... became the
> peculiar science to which I directed my eager enquiries; thence
> was I led into a train of labyrinthine meditations.

The speaker of Shelley's later poem, *Alastor, or the Spirit of
Solitude* (1815), would suggest what one of these 'eager enquiries'
was: 'I have made my bed/In charnels and on coffins' (*Alastor*,
23-4). One does not have to take this literally to recognise a mind
acquainted with darkness and depths.

Even of his passionate admirers, many have not got beyond
the dramatic impression of the poet, attractive and strange, with
the beating waves or gusting winds uplifting his hair; or as Hogg
once put it, 'like a spirit that had just descended from the sky; like
a demon risen at that moment out of the ground' (Peck, I, 278);
or as Hunt once put it, 'like a spirit that had darted out of its orb
and found itself another planet' (*Lord Byron and his
Contemporaries*, 1828). But how many have felt the power and
sincerity of his poetry? Shelley, known as 'the Eton Atheist' and
'Mad Shelley' (Holmes, 19), was not really known.

He had much to say about what was wrong with society, 'our
state,/This dim vast vale of tears, vacant and desolate' ('Hymn to
Intellectual Beauty', II), and he would have much more to say
about how 'Poets[,] the unacknowledged legislators of the world'
(*A Defence of Poetry*), could put things right if given the chance:
'never joy illumed my brow/Unlinked with hope' ('Hymn to
Intellectual Beauty', VI). 'God help us!' exclaimed Southey in
January 1812, 'the world wants mending, though he [Shelley] did
not set about it exactly in the right way' (Peck, I, 204). This seems

as much to illuminate Southey's character as Shelley's. If the 'right way' meant a reverent submission to authority, then Shelley undoubtedly did 'set about it' in the 'wrong' way.

Shelley's 'passion for reforming the world', as he called it in the Preface to *Prometheus Unbound* (1819), was loathed and rejected by that world: 'But thus much I do not seek to conceal from myself, that I am an outcast from human society; my name is execrated by all who understand its entire import, – by those very beings whose happiness I ardently desire.' (*Letters*, I, 517) Yet he did not give up. Walter Scott gave Shelley some sound advice (unheeded) in May 1811:

> I would ... caution you against an enthusiasm which while it argues an excellent disposition and a feeling heart, requires to be watched and restrained, tho' not repressed. It is apt, if too much indulged, to engender a fastidious contempt for the ordinary business of the world, and gradually unfit us for the exercise of the useful and domestic virtues, which depend greatly on our not exalting our feelings above the temper of well-ordered society. (Peck, I, 38)

These are essentially conservative concepts. Scott saw both Shelley's brilliance of mind and his impatience with the conventional arrangements of British society. But Scott did not positively appreciate the inextricable and explosive nature of the two characteristics. And he does not seem to have been aware of the possibility of the inferiority of his own way of living to Shelley's way: he was implying a rebuke of Shelley for emotionalism, but what he was really objecting to was Shelley's unguarded expression of emotion. Arguably, it is the unguarded expressions that the reader of Shelley should be most grateful for.

The poet was clear about what he was *not* doing. He did not offer 'a reasoned system', and he did not want 'the direct enforcement of reform'. He had in mind something that men of the (commonsense) world tend not to take seriously: 'beautiful idealisms of moral excellence'. He formulated an 'aware[ness] that until the mind can love, and admire, and trust, and hope, and endure, reasoned principles of moral conduct are seeds cast upon the highway of life which the unconscious passenger tramples into dust' (Preface, *Prometheus Unbound*). This is an instance of Shelley's metaphysical precision of thought that impresses few people because they cannot have it reified. He was talking a great deal of sense, but it was mostly to himself.

> Alas! I have nor hope nor health,
>   Nor peace within nor calm around,
> Nor that content surpassing wealth
> The sage in meditation found,
>   And walked with inward glory crowned –
> Nor fame, nor power, nor love, nor leisure.
>   Others I see whom these surround –
>   Smiling they live, and call life pleasure;
> To me that cup has been dealt in another measure.
>   – 'Stanzas Written in Dejection Near Naples' iii

This tall, pale young gentleman, with his stooping shoulders, inky cloak and cosmic melancholy, might come across at first as rather settled in his loneliness and lunacy, in this respect even a bit like Wordsworth's 'Mad Mother':

> ... they say that I am mad,
> But nay, my heart is far too glad;
> And I am happy when I sing
> Full many a sad and doleful thing ...

But 'Mad' Shelley would prove, as a rule, stark raving sane. His vision is more radiant and essential than the cleverness and power of memory so busily exhibited by uninspired people. It represents what *is*, and is always present, including feeling and emotion. The poet includes the whole cosmos, the phenomenal as well as the noumenal. He declares the presence of the unknown, and celebrates it:

> Let every seed that falls
> In silent eloquence unfold its store
> Of argument; infinity within,
> Infinity without, belie creation;
> The exterminable spirit it contains
> Is Nature's only God ...
>
> — *Queen Mab*, VII, 19-24

The unknown is anathema to most people, especially educated or professional people, who can become indignant at the mildest inference that the exertions that got them where they are today were not necessarily best applied:

> ... but human pride
> Is skilful to invent most serious names
> To hide its ignorance.
>
> — *Queen Mab*, VII, 24-6

The majority of readers want merely to be indulged in their own comfort zones, and many poets (John Betjeman at his most popular might come to mind) have provided them with the requisite literature. Many readers tend to feel chagrined by the presence of unfamiliar colours and urgent voices. Shelley saw such easily piqued complacency as a sort of Bastille to be stormed by the radical energies of real life and truth.

Look at the apparently churchy and predictable statement of public grief in the following passage from Shelley's *An Address to the People on the Death of the Princess Charlotte* (1817), the first ten sentences of which appear to deliver a ready rush of journalistic sympathy for the recently deceased Princess Charlotte.

Mourn then, People of England. Clothe yourselves in solemn black. Let the bells be tolled. Think of mortality and change. Shroud yourselves in solitude and the gloom of sacred sorrow. Spare no symbol of universal grief. Weep – mourn – lament. Fill the great City – fill the boundless fields with lamentation and the echo of groans. A beautiful Princess is dead: she who should have been the Queen of her beloved nation and whose posterity should have ruled it forever ... She was amiable and would have become wise, but she was young, and in the flower of youth the despoiler came. LIBERTY is dead.

The last short sentence is a shock. There is something in it of the guerrilla ambush, the news of which is bound to elicit strong feelings. The writer can attract a conventional mourner of Princess Charlotte unwittingly down into the ghastly purlieus of republican politics before revealing his true colours. With the fierce release of 'LIBERTY' at just the point where one would have expected something familiar and sanctimonious, Shelley has declared a republic of words in which royalty and sentimentality have suddenly evaporated. The poet now announces what has really happened to liberty. For most well-fed and well-mannered subjects of the Crown, liberty is not a person to have strong feelings about, and it would be almost incomprehensibly hateful of anyone to write more feelingly about an abstract noun than about poor Princess Charlotte. And yet her death just happened to coincide with the public hanging and quartering of three Pentrich Revolution leaders. Seizing the canting royalist mood of the moment – and including consideration of the government skulduggery leading to the deaths of Jeremiah Brandreth, Isaac Ludlam and William Turner (Holmes, 384-6) – Shelley uses the momentum of journalistic melodrama and catches false consciousness on the hop – 'LIBERTY is dead.' He then pursues the logic of his argument to its extravagantly revolutionary conclusion:

> If One has died who was like her that should have ruled over this
> land, like Liberty, young, innocent, and lovely, know that the power
> through which that one perished was God, and that it was a private
> grief. But *man* has murdered Liberty ... Let us follow the corpse of
> British Liberty slowly and reverentially to its tomb; and if some
> glorious Phantom should appear and make its throne of broken
> swords and sceptres and royal crowns trampled in the dust, let us
> say that the Spirit of Liberty has arisen from its grave and left all
> that was gross and mortal there, and kneel down and worship it as
> our Queen. (Holmes, 388)

There was, however, a problem. Shelley's publisher, Charles Ollier,
was scared of getting into trouble with the authorities and therefore
printed only a limited edition of the pamphlet. The poet did not
have the contemporary political impact on a large reading public
that he should have had. This would not be the last missed
opportunity.

Writers who would make friends and influence people tend
not to express themselves so incorrigibly. Publishers and readers
prefer on the whole to handle and absorb more congenial
sentiments. Hence generations of British schoolchildren have
learned to recite Wordsworth's 'Daffodils', and have remained
unaware of the tortured political uncertainties from which
Wordsworth produced the 'Residence in France' section of *The
Prelude* like a painful pearl.

Shelley's insights and passions are inextricable, and therefore
they can come across as 'mad' when really they are elemental.
They can imply that if Revolution comes not as naturally as the
leaves to a tree it better not come at all. Many of these passionate
insights – or insightful passions – have lain in dust and handwriting
for over a hundred years. For example:

> the spring rebels not against
> winter but it succeeds it –

the dawn rebels not
against night but it
disperses it – (Wroe, 265).

Here was the poet hidden in the light of thought. Publishers often found Shelley's writing too dangerously subversive, or else just too obscure. In terms of publications, sales, and acclaim, he was not particularly successful in his day. Even in a comparatively encouraging contemporary review of his work that he *did* get published, the poet's lack of chemistry with his nation's readers does not go unmentioned:

> Mr Shelley can never become a popular poet. He does not sufficiently link himself with man; he is too visionary for the intellect of the generality of his readers, and is ever immersed in the clouds of religions and meta-physical speculations. His opinions are but skeletons, and he does not sufficiently embody them to render them intelligible.
>
> – 'On the Philosophy and Poetry of Shelley',
> *Gold's London Magazine*, 1821

By the time he wrote his 10,000-word essay, *A Defence of Poetry* (1821), he had formulated and refined what he was about as a poet (though the world, of course, would continue to be just as foolish and wicked as it had been on the poet's arrival into it):

> All the authors of revolutions in opinion are not only necessarily poets as they are inventors, nor even as their words unveil the permanent analogy of things by images which participate in the light of truth; but as their periods are harmonious and rhythmical, and contain in themselves the elements of verse; being the echo of the eternal music.

This is particularly appropriate to Shelley's visionary poetry: the poet discovered, or rediscovered, 'the hidden beauty of the world'

(*A Defence of Poetry*), or, as he had his chorus of spirits define their provenance in Act IV of *Prometheus Unbound*,

> the mind
> Of humankind ...
>
> that deep abyss
> Of wonder and bliss,
> Whose caverns are crystal palaces (93-101).

Most people ignore the presence of essential reality when it is intangible. And people tend to shy away from sharing spiritual recognitions that call forth the sort of words (such as 'holy' or 'soul') that Enlightenment thinking and materialism have alleged misguided. Shelley's use of the word 'spirits' – like his use of the word 'atheist' – is part of the rough magic of his estranged mode of eloquence. 'The Atheist', he wrote in *A Refutation of Deism* (1814),

> is a monster among men ... He dreads no judge but his own conscience, he fears no hell but the loss of his self-esteem. He is not to be restrained by punishments, for death is divested of its terror, and whatever enters into his heart to conceive, that he will not scruple to execute ...

Many eminent critics, including Matthew Arnold, W.H. Auden and Marilyn Butler, have not found particularly compelling in Shelley (or in anyone) the central issue of 'thought-wingèd Liberty' ('Lines Written Among the Euganean Hills', 207). Instead, at their most sympathetic – or rather their least unsympathetic – they have, for example, understood that the poet conceived a fresh means of political struggle. The passive resistance to tyranny in 'The Masque of Anarchy' (1819) would show Gandhi a way for the people of India to emancipate themselves from British colonial rule:

'And if then the tyrants dare,
Let them ride among you there,
Slash, and stab, and maim, and hew;
What they like, that let them do.

'With folded arms and steady eyes,
And little fear, and less surprise,
Look upon them as they slay,
Till their rage has died away.

'Then they will return with shame
To the place from which they came;
And the blood thus shed will speak
In hot blushes on their cheek.

The *King James Bible* already contained similar wisdom: 'If thine enemy be hungry, give him bread to eat; and if he be thirsty, give him water to drink' (*Proverbs*: 25, v21). 'But I say unto you, Love your enemies, bless them that curse you, do good to them that hate you, and pray for them which despitefully use you, and persecute you' (*St Matthew*: 5, v44). 'Therefore if thine enemy hunger, feed him; if he thirst, give him drink: for in so doing thou shalt heap coals of fire on his head' (*Romans*: 12, v20.) In some of the freer modern translations of the *Bible*, 'thou shalt heap coals of fire on his head' becomes 'you will make them burn with shame'. At any rate, Shelley had an aptitude for sifting ancient texts and revitalising wise spiritual guidance. He was no atheist. He just detested the practice of organised religion, particularly the Christianity of his contemporaries.

Some critics have celebrated Shelley's 'street-protest' songs as his best achievements. Others have derided them as the dispensable vapourings of a 'Riviera socialist' who, in his own words, 'lay asleep in Italy' ('The Masque of Anarchy') at the time of the atrocity in

Manchester known as the Peterloo Massacre (1819). Implicit in both these views is the assumption that politics and political 'realities' form the level from which all writers, including visionary poets, must take all their bearings.

Visionary poetry is not restricted to the poet's personal concerns or the politics of his day. Shelley himself, however, in 1811, in the vainglory of youth and in the grip of a violent desire to dispense with cultural prohibitions, affixed the inflammatory title, 'The Necessity of Atheism', to what was really a rather mild (and prentice) philosophical argument. He had to put it in the windows of the Oxford bookshops himself because no one would publish it. He sent copies to the bishops and the heads of the colleges. As a result of his early drive for notoriety, the poet ended up misleading the majority of his contemporaries, and posterity, about what he really is. So did Keats. So too did Byron.

5

Introducing the Byronic Hero

'I KNOW NOUGHT. NOTHING I DENY,/Admit, reject, contemn,' says Byron in *Don Juan* (XIV, iii), effectively speaking as an agnostic (though the word 'agnostic' would not exist until later in the nineteenth century). Until he learns more about what life (and death) means (if it means anything), he must provisionally accept that life is just a squalid prison house from which there is no escape except out into the Nothing (for all we know) of death. Anyone seeming to deny that this life is unsolved and inescapably unsolvable – such as Keats, whom Byron accused of 'drivelling idiotism' and 'mental masturbation', or Wordsworth, whose poetry Byron called 'unintelligible', or Coleridge, whom Byron called upon to 'explain his Explanation' of metaphysics – must be delusional: 'we die, you know – /and then – /What then? – I do not know, no more do you – ' (*Don Juan*, I, cxxxiii).

There is more than just one kind of Byronic hero. One kind finds expression in the narrator of *Childe Harold's Pilgrimage*:

> But my soul wanders; I demand it back
> To meditate amongst decay, and stand
> A ruin amidst ruins ...
>
> *– Childe Harold*, IV, xxv

The narrator of this poem is the Hamlet figure, around whose soul sorrow has contracted, pressurizing him into poetry. This incarnation of Byron is young, pure, noble and beautiful, and he is shut away from cheerful light and wholesome air, obliged to contemplate his own sinking under a load which he can neither support nor resolve to abandon:

> Existence may be borne, and the deep root
> Of life and sufferance make its firm abode
> In bare and desolated bosoms ...
>
> *– Childe Harold*, IV, xxi

Caught up in, and insulated by, his general sense of his own apathy and fatalism, he nevertheless tells his reader that his life is a sort of chamber in which he is subjected to ever more ingenious tortures:

> But ever and anon of griefs subdued
> There comes a token like a Scorpion's sting,
> Scarce seen, but with fresh bitterness imbued ...
>
> *– Childe Harold*, IV, xxiii

Like Hamlet in his tangle of feelings about 'the thousand natural shocks' that make up a life, Byron's soliloquist is an advanced young sensualist who has already learned that pleasure is nothing if it is not pain refined, and vice versa.

> ... it may be a sound –
> A tone of music – summer's eve – or spring –
> A flower – the wind – the Ocean – which shall wound,
> Striking the electric chain wherewith we are darkly bound
>
> *– Childe Harold*, IV, xxiii

Another kind of Byronic hero finds expression in satire. The speaker takes the measure of the elegant and hypocritical society around him, and demolishes it. In the following example he explodes, almost in passing, the idea that there could really be such a thing as a happily married couple:

> Don José and the Donna Inez led
> For some time an unhappy sort of life,
> Wishing each other, not divorced, but dead;
> They lived respectably as man and wife,
> Their conduct was exceedingly well-bred,
> And gave no outward signs of inward strife,
> Until at length the smother'd fire broke out,
> And put the business past all kind of doubt.
>
> – *Don Juan*, I, xxvi

Compared with the gentle spirit of knowing better that informs Jane Austen's ironic conclusions about couples being 'married happily ever after', Byron's wisdom is inclined to offend and equipped to fight.

The dark and bright heroic natures in Byron's works do often intermingle. Amusing, and almost as if bathed in Mediterranean daylight, as *Don Juan* is, the poem's roots are lost in the same darkness that nourishes the poet's moodier meditations such as 'Darkness' and *Childe Harold's Pilgrimage*:

> Ecclesiastes said, 'that all is vanity' –
> Most modern preachers say the same, or show it
> By their examples of true Christianity:
> In short, all know, or very soon may know it;
> And in this scene of all-confessed inanity,
> By Saint, by Sage, by Preacher, and by Poet,
> Must I restrain me, through the fear of strife,
> From holding up the nothingness of Life?
>
> – *Don Juan*, VII, vi

The darkness in Byron (in us all) cannot be fathomed. But it can be acknowledged, and this can be liberating. For example, Manfred in Byron's play, *Manfred*, says

> My pang shall find a voice. From my youth upwards
> My Spirit walked not with the souls of men,
> Nor looked upon the earth with human eyes;
> The thirst of their ambition was not mine,
> The aim of their existence was not mine;
> My joys – my griefs – my passions – and my powers,
> Made me a stranger; though I wore the form,
> I had no sympathy with breathing flesh ... (II, ii, 50-57).

The loneliness and pain in the individual man have been sent up into mental space as a starry constellation that may be looked at and learned from. That is to say, they have been written down as poetry. In the mirror that the poet holds up to human nature, it can be seen almost letter for letter that others' lives spell out our evils. It is as if 'some Columbus of the moral seas' has shown 'mankind their soul's antipodes.' (*Don Juan*, XV, ci)

Perhaps it was the apparent ease with which Byron could produce canto after electrifying canto that most annoyed those writers who could not. Tom Paulin has identified something about Hazlitt that goes some way to explaining Hazlitt's dislike of Byron:

> Hazlitt's sense of inferiority as a prose-writer emerges in his lecture 'On Poetry in General', where he speaks of the 'jerks, the breaks, the inequalities, and harshness of prose', which destroy the flow of poetic imagination, as 'a jolting road or stumbling horse disturbs the reverie of an absent man'. He is saying that there is something gauche, thrawn, lumpish, dissonant – even downright annoying – about prose ... prose and plodding [may be] linked ... (Paulin, 92).

In Paulin's view, Hazlitt is labouring to contain the bitterness of the second-rate writer: even if he succeeds in becoming the best prose writer of his time, Hazlitt will never be one of the poets.

Shelley heard Byron recite Canto V of *Don Juan* in 1821, including the following lines:

> The wind swept down the Euxine, and the wave
> Broke foaming o'er the blue Symplegades;
> 'T is a grand sight from off 'the Giant's Grave'
> To watch the progress of those rolling seas
> Between the Bosphorus, as they lash and lave
> Europe and Asia ...

Shelley wrote to tell his wife Mary about the experience. The letter reveals a Shelley who seems to have felt almost as if he had been caught up in a fierce storm, so buffeted was he by Byron's imagination:

> It [*Don Juan*] sets him not above but far above all the poets of the day: every word has the stamp of immortality. – I despair of rivalling Lord Byron, as well I may: and there is no other with whom it is worth contending. This canto is in style, but totally, & sustained with incredible ease and power ... there is not a word which the most rigid assertor of the dignity of human nature could desire to be cancelled ...

> – *Letters*, II, 198

Shelley himself had composed 'Ode to the West Wind' in the stormy woods above Florence, in 1819:

> O Wild West Wind, thou breath of Autumn's being,
> Thou, from whose unseen presence the leaves dead
> Are driven, like ghosts from an enchanter fleeing,
>
> Yellow, and black, and pale, and hectic red,
> Pestilence-stricken multitudes ...
>
> Black rain, and fire, and hail, will burst ...

But there was one further element that gave Byron's poetry additional force. It was an element that Shelley envied. It was humour:

> ... the loud tempests raise
> The waters, and repentance for past sinning
> In all, who o'er the great deep take their ways:
> They vow to amend their lives, and yet they don't;
> Because if drowned, they can't—if spared, they won't.
>
> – *Don Juan*, V, vi

The last two lines above show how Byron could give readers an absurd and instant sense of themselves as little more than divine dummies spring-loaded with the seven deadly urges. It was not in Shelley's repertoire to illuminate human nature with such lightning-flashes of humour. He did try though. In *Peter Bell the Third* (1819), for instance, he managed more of an odd than a funny sort of funny on the subject of Wordsworth ('Peter'):

> But from the first 'twas Peter's drift
> To be a kind of moral eunuch,
> He touched the hem of Nature's shift,
> Felt faint – and never dared uplift
> The closest, all-concealing tunic.
>
> – *Peter Bell the Third*, Part the Fourth, xi

In the live-evil mirror of Byron's versifying a more immediate and hilarious Wordsworth might have been seen conflicted by curiosity and embarrassment about country matters.

Shelley was, first and foremost, a self-professed improver of mankind. Though he could often be tenderly sympathetic, Byron was not interested in being any such improver. The lack of agenda in Byron left him freer than Shelley to hammer out all the mordant quirks and accidents, which formed the fantail of sparks around his un-political anvil:

She snatched it, and refused another morsel,
Saying he had gorged enough to make a horse ill.

— *Don Juan*, II, clix

Shelley tried to generate some of his poetry in the same smithy as Byron — yet without himself becoming engulfed by Byron's 'full Hell/Within' ('Julian and Maddalo', 351-2). In 'The Witch of Atlas' (1820), another of Shelley's attempts to reach Byron's wide audience, there is an absence of fun the more conspicuous for Shelley's attempt to invoke it:

The king would dress an ape up in his crown
And robes, and seat him on his glorious seat,
And on the right hand of the sunlike throne
Would place a gaudy mock-bird to repeat
The chatterings of the monkey. — Every one
Of the prone courtiers crawled to kiss the feet
Of their great Emperor when the morning came;
And kissed — alas, how many kiss the same!

— 'The Witch of Atlas', LXXXIV

The shadow of seriousness on the subject of how wrong it is to have a royal family in the first place falls too heavily for Byronic fun and frivolity to shine.

Byron produced poetry at tremendous speed. He began to compose *The Corsair: A Tale* on 16 October 1813; and having written 200 lines a day he completed the first draft by 27 October 1813. The poem was published on 1 February 1814, and sold 10,000 copies on that day. It was reprinted five times in the first month and six times more by the end of the next month. The velocity is extraordinary. Byron achieved verbally something akin to what Napoleon Bonaparte achieved militarily. When Hazlitt called Byron's spirit 'fiery, impatient, wayward, indefatigable', he could just as easily have been describing the spirit of his — and

Byron's – greatest hero, Napoleon. And when Hazlitt said that 'Lord Byron's verse glows like a flame, consuming everything in its way', he could just as easily have been describing Napoleon's battle campaign. (Just substitute the name Napoleon for Byron, and the word 'army' for 'verse'.) Napoleon gathered together a force of professional fighters and arrogantly dominated a France bleary-eyed with post-revolutionary exhaustion; so (in the realm of poetry), Byron would assert the supremacy of his own individual will in a depleted England. He wrote to Lady Melbourne in September 1813:

> 'Tis said – *Indifference* marks the present time
> Then hear the reason – though 'tis told in rhyme –
> A King who *can't* – a Prince of Wales who *don't* –
> Patriots who *shan't* – Ministers who *won't* –
> What matters who are *in* or *out* of place
> The *Mad* – the *Bad* – the *Useless* or the *Base*?

Much later, Byron would still be showing, with undulled alacrity, English society back to itself:

> Society is now one polished horde,
> Formed of two mighty tribes, the *Bores* and *Bored*.
> > – *Don Juan*, XIII, xcv

His stylistic looseness seems (as he meant it to seem) symptomatic of the defiant intelligence bent on leaping intuitively rather than analysing exhaustively: 'poetry is in itself passion, and does not systematize. It assails, but does not argue; it may be wrong, but it does not assume pretensions to Optimism.' (*Letters and Journals*, V, 582) The looseness allowed for Byron's startling deployment of enjambment –

> Bob Southey! You're a poet – Poet laureate,
> And representative of all the race;

> Although 'tis true that you turn'd out a Tory at
> Last ...
>
> *– Don Juan*, Dedication, i –

and wholly unexpected rhymes:

> But – Oh! ye lords of ladies intellectual,
> Inform us truly have they not hen-peck'd you all?
>
> *– Don Juan*, I, xxii

There is cussedness in the poet's apparent lack of attention to detail. One of the narrative voices of *Don Juan* appears to be a foreigner claiming to know 'some words of Spanish, Turk, and Greek,/Italian not at all, having no teachers'. The 'foreign' voice continues, and the reader is to understand (satirically) that the newcomer to learned England has no need of the English language as used by Shakespeare and Milton:

> Much English I cannot pretend to speak,
> Learning that language chiefly from its preachers,
> Barrow, South, Tillotson, whom every week
> I study, also Blair – the highest reachers
> Of eloquence in piety and prose –
> I hate your poets, so read none of those.
>
> *– Don Juan*, II, clxv

Byron has no problem in writing, from his position in exile, as a foreigner in order to offend those English readers who aspire to live their lives in accordance with the p/reachings of Barrow, South and Tillotson. While Shelley, at his best (and least 'Byronic') applied his words and phrases with a sense of sacred care, Byron disrespectfully splashed, sloshed, spilled and swilled his emotional responses to the world that he felt had rejected him. He would occasionally express remorse about the way he wrote. His confession to Thomas Moore (later his biographer) that it had only taken him ten days to deliver *The Corsair* ('it proves my own want of judgement in publishing, and the public's in reading things, which cannot have stamina for permanent attention') suggests a poet concerned that his work lacks something (to be found in Shelley's work, perhaps) that is more lasting.

Shelley, for whom (in *A Defence of Poetry*) true poets were 'compelled to serve the power which is seated in the throne of their own soul', confided his belief in a letter to Peacock in July 1816 that Byron was 'a slave to the vilest and most vulgar prejudices'. Hazlitt, also, called Byron a 'pamperer of the public's prejudices'. In light of those views, it seems that Byron was not as interested as Shelley in using his imagination as 'The great instrument of moral good'; nor did he seem as interested as Shelley in 'defeat[ing] the curse which binds us to be subjected to the accident of surrounding impressions' (*A Defence of Poetry*). The verbal by-blow (such as the rhyming of 'morsel' with 'horse ill' or 'intellectual' with 'hen-peck'd you all') was Byron's stock-in-trade.

In *Don Juan* the narrator is the figure who raises readers up and knocks them down. The narrator is always interfering, like Laurence Sterne's Tristram Shandy:

> But then the fact's a fact – and 'tis the part
> Of a true poet to escape from fiction
> Whene'er he can; for there is little art
> In leaving verse more free from the restriction
> *– Don Juan*, VIII, lxxxvi

The narrative is never straightforward, and it is always at an oblique angle to the main subject. It is a modern reading experience to not know where one is as a reader, and to experience the ready confusion between author and subject. In the following example, there is some philosophical speculation about what thought actually is, but that enquiry is soon shoved aside by something more assertive, and readable:

> I won't describe, – that is, if I can help
> Description; and I won't reflect, – that is,
> If I can stave off thought, which – as a whelp
> Clings to its teat – sticks to me through the abyss
> Of this cold labyrinth; or as the kelp
> Holds by the rock; or as a lover's kiss
> Drains its first draught of lips: – but, as I said,
> I *won't* philosophize, and *will* be read.
>
> – *Don Juan*, X, xxviii

The poet's ostentatious avowal of base sentiments, irreverently intermeshed with hiccups of high seriousness, often made him perplexing for readers more interested in seeing guidelines to the good life than in seeing someone laughing at its impossibility.

Byron said things that marked him out as a 'bad' man, but he knew how he wanted to market himself. He would not aspire to perfect his readers. In the 1820s, the cantos of *Don Juan* were pouring out of him like cataracts of negatives and nay saying: he '*won't* philosophize', and when he '*will*' do anything, he might just amuse and offend Christians with tales of adultery or cannibalism. As a satirist, he could hit society hard with straight reflections of its appalling self:

> Without, or with, offence to friends or foes,
> I sketch your world exactly as it goes.
>
> – *Don Juan*, VIII, lxxxix

Like Samuel Johnson's in *The Vanity of Human Wishes*, Byron's voice is extremely serious but, importantly, the high seriousness is never toppled by the low humour with which it necessarily coexists. The fibre of the vision is much too tough and tensile to be undone by the humorous twists. In fact, the *jeu d'esprit* illuminates the revisited human appetites, desires and fears all the more brightly. In the following stanza, the shipwrecked and famished Don Juan is nursed back to health by Zoe, whose illiteracy has not stopped her from getting to know, through the spoken word alone (as put so breezily in parenthesis), how best to help a starving man:

> But Zoe ...
> Knew (by tradition, for she ne'er had read)
> That famished people must be slowly nurst,
> And fed by spoonfuls, else they always burst.
>
> – *Don Juan*, II, clviii

Another character, Haidée, teaches Don Juan the natives' language 'by dint of fingers and of eyes,/And words repeated after her', and there is a directness about this passing on of knowledge which is – the exiled poet implies – more *alive* than the white, sepulchral English educator at work:

> Thus Juan learned his *alpha beta* better
> From Haidée's glance than any graven letter.
>
> – *Don Juan*, II, clxiii

Just as Johnson had, 'with extensive view/Survey[ed] mankind', and found again and again that 'rarely reason guides' human beings' decision-making processes in matters great or small, so Byron, having traced humans' 'path[s].. through perplexing ways', can confront canting morality and say that it is a 'pity ... that/ Pleasure's a sin, and sometimes Sin's a pleasure' (*Don Juan*, I, cxxxiii). He can get right under the skin of society and lay bare the interchangeable dynamics of its hypocrisy. Like Johnson, Byron includes the panorama of humanity in his vision, and he also has the motivation to reflect upon the symptoms of Britons' connective disease. There could not be a more serious theme. Paradoxically, there could not be more potential for comedy.

In everyday matters he allowed himself to live badly – not just badly to others, but badly to himself. With regard to his eating habits, he was

> Caught in a vicious circle of indulgence and abstinence [and] he would devour a heavy meal, generally of vegetables and fish, only to be visited by ... hideous nightmares that left him sweating and shaken – wild dreams in which the dead returned to pursue – or open his eyes to the agonies of a bilious headache. It is not surprising that his liver was often recalcitrant, that he suffered from fits of spleen and depression ... (Quennell, 164).

One reason for all the inwardly and outwardly directed badness was that he considered it a matter of the utmost urgency 'to feel that we exist – even through pain.' (*Letters and Journals*, III, 109) The monotony of always eating one's dinner in the correct manner or always treating everyone politely through thick and thin can become, frankly, intolerable. Life – *feeling* life – is too short for such joyless games: 'When one subtracts from life infancy (which is vegetation), sleep, eating, and swilling – buttoning and unbuttoning – how much remains of downright existence? The summer of a dormouse.' (Quennell, 164) The poet defined his preference for sensation over monotony in his *Detached Thoughts* (October 1821-May 1822): 'I have a notion that Gamblers are as happy as most people, being always *excited* ... every turn of the card, and cast of the dice, keeps the Gamester alive'. Hence, he allowed risky glimpses of his sexual predilections into his letters. He wrote to Henry Drury in June 1809, projecting an essay on 'Sodomy simplified or Paederasty proved to be praiseworthy from ancient authors and modern practice.'

He looked his own demons square in their faces. Knowing that such demons were contained, concealed or discarded by pious and obedient sons and daughters of the English church, he knew instead that acknowledgment and ownership of them were essential before exorcism. As in any conflict, and however unpalatable the idea, one must at some point open up a dialogue with the enemy, especially if one's worst enemy is oneself.

He did think that it would be best to 'unteach Mankind the lust to shine or rule' (*Childe Harold's Pilgrimage*, III, xliii), but he did not want that thought to become part of a sect or system that he would have to stand over for the rest of his life: he just thought it, and uttered it, before moving on to the next thing. Like an agile, restless child on a climbing frame, he had fun amongst words, and his poetry often communicates his sheer joy in the activity. Here, lyrical hyperbole accommodates the restless self-importance of Juan's mother:

> His mother was a learnéd lady, famed
> For every branch of every science known –
> In every Christian language ever named,
> With virtues equalled by her wit alone:
> She made the cleverest people quite ashamed,
> And even the good with inward envy groan,
> Finding themselves so very much exceeded,
> In their own way, by all the things that she did.
>
> *– Don Juan*, I, x

Here, suggestive understatement is in synch with the sexual chemistry between Julia and Juan:

> Yet Julia's very coldness still was kind,
> And tremulously gentle her small hand
> Withdrew itself from his, but left behind
> A little pressure, thrilling, and so bland
> And slight, so very sight, that to the mind
> 'T was but a doubt; but ne'er magician's wand

Wrought change with all Armida's fairy art
Like what this light touch left on Juan's heart.

– *Don Juan*, I, lxxi

Although it may be possible to postulate a formal classification of Byron's poetry, any schematising attempts invariably simplify the complex and subtle interweaving of moods and techniques. A single passage of a few lines may move from a moment of intense lyricism to a passage of sharp analysis or deflating irony, but Byron's imagination created a context and a psychology for all the modulations. The results were saleable. Readers caught sight of their own secret selves in the toils of life's pleasures and pains.

He became a bad husband on the day of his marriage. 'I got a wife and a cold on the same day, but have got rid of the last pretty speedily', he told Lady Melbourne in January 1815. In December 1815, when his wife Annabella was giving birth to Augusta Ada, the poet was shooting his pistols in the room below. He may have been jealous of the new arrival: the presence of a new life, trailing clouds of glory and filling nappies, would no doubt have had its effect on any enthusiasm remaining in Annabella for her husband, who was himself an only child. But Byron was frequently violent before as well as after the birth of his daughter. He often smashed his own prized possessions (though biographers Phyllis Grosskurth and Fiona McCarthy reassure us that he never touched his wife). That violence was the less beguiling manifestation of the passion informing the poetry. He cut his swathe through books, experiences and people, subordinating them all to his requirements as a creative writer. His mind was strong enough to master it all, to assimilate and incorporate it with the flow of his thinking, and so to make it fit in with the unity of his insight, which, though huge, was always growing. In the process, his own thinking always dominated and was never drowned by others' thinking. Langley Moore has discussed the difference between Lord and Lady Byron on their separation 'after a year of lacerating incompatibility':

> In the end, Lady Byron proved the more grievously hurt. He had resilience, she almost none. He was self-critical and, in acknowledging 'the nightmare of my own delinquencies', could in some measure purge them. She was self-admiring, and contemplated with ever renewed amazement the transcendent injustice of her ill-usage, feeling more and more virtuous, more and more wronged, as the years went by. He was able to distil from his experiences new materials, new ideas about life ... (Langley Moore, 216).

One thing that Byron learned to do as a writer was to preserve the fluidity of his thinking and feeling without trying to proclaim 'unity' or justification:

> '*Que sais-je?*' [*what do I know?*] was the motto of Montaigne,
> As also of the first academicians:
> That all is dubious which man may attain,
> Was one of their most favourite positions.
> There's no such thing as certainty, that's plain
> As any of Mortality's conditions;
> So little do we know what we'er about in
> This world, I doubt if doubt itself be doubting.
>
> – *Don Juan*, IX, xvii

Some people suppose that the energy that drives the Byronic heroism of a Childe Harold or a Don Juan is generated by the existence of a real, cankering, secret of the author – Byron's 'central iniquity', as the later poet, Francis Thompson, would put it in his essay, *Shelley* (1889). In light of the biographical evidence, such a view is hard to resist. It seems that on 17 May 1824, Byron's friends took action to protect his posthumous reputation. They burned his memoirs (which may have contained explicit, well-informed references to incest and sodomy) in the grate of John Murray's Albemarle Street drawing room.

This was the first era in English history in which there were so many daily newspapers. Celebrity, in the modern sense, became possible. Byron was a very well-known figure. Inevitably, when he wrote a poem about some figure with a strange dark secret, people would wonder what the secret was. They would speculate that it was something to do with Byron's marriage, and rumours spread quickly that he was having an affair with his half-sister, Augusta Leigh, whilst practically on his honeymoon with Annabella. Regency society was scandalised, and in this way Byron's work and his life became bound up together in the popular mind. But sodomy, unlike incest, was an offence beyond the pale, and still punishable in England by death. Byron had to leave England in 1816. He would never return. He became even more sharply defined as the outsider, with the pariah's privilege of frank expression:

> The consequence is, being of no party,
> I shall offend all parties: – never mind!
> My words, at least, are more sincere and hearty
>
> – *Don Juan*, IX, xxvi

6

Keats's *Endymion* Embattled

HAVING GLIMPSED VISIONARY TRUTH WITH THE 14 lines of 'On First Looking into Chapman's Homer', Keats wanted to prolong the vision in an epic poem. He wanted to 'make 4000 Lines of one bare circumstance and fill them with Poetry' (*Letters*, I, 170). He knew at heart, however, that at that point in his development he would not produce a work with the uniformity of impression that distinguishes, say, Milton's *Paradise Lost* (in which the sensual, the sexual, the spiritual and the political become, somehow, the synergism of a single, epic insight from the other side of time), because he knew he could 'only write in scraps & patches' (*Letters*, I, 206).

Endymion did present the metropolitan wits with plenty of easy targets for criticism. In inscribing the poem to the memory of Chatterton – the boy poet of 'low' origins who faked 'medieval' poems, and after discovery killed himself – Keats was all but asking for trouble. In the poem itself, there are, as Shelley told Keats in a letter dated 27 July 1820, 'treasures ... though poured forth with indistinct profusion. This, people in general will not endure'. Here is an example of the kind of half-alchemised imagery that Shelley thought 'people' would 'not endure':

> ... Love's madness he had known:
> Often with more than tortured lion's groan
> Moanings had burst from him; but now that rage
> Had pass'd away: no longer did he wage
> A rough-voic'd war against the dooming stars ...
> The lyre of his soul Æolian tun'd
> Forgot all violence, and but commun'd
> With melancholy thought: O he had swoon'd
> Drunken from pleasure's nipple ...
>
> – *Endymion*, II, 860-9

Even that great essayist, opium-eater and appreciator of poetic dreamscapes, Thomas De Quincey, so hugely impressed by Keats's later poetry, referred to *Endymion* as 'the very midsummer madness of affectation.' (De Quincey, 307) Motion has been struck by the number of times in *Endymion* that the hero 'confuses sexual longing with the need to be mothered', the number of times love is described 'as a nourishing drink', and the amount of time the hero spends 'gazing at women's breasts' (Motion, 42). It is taking Keats rather a long time to outgrow this particular fascination. In 'Hadst thou liv'd in days of old' (1817), he keeps returning to 'those beauties, scarce discern'd,/Kept with such sweet privacy,/That they seldom meet the eye' and 'the silver sheen/Of thy broider'd floating vest/Cov'ring half thine ivory breast .../Keeping secret what is fair.' And still, in the passage from *Endymion* above, the hero appears to simultaneously whimper like a tormented lion and quaff something medicinal from the teat of an abstract noun.

There is something cluttered and incomplete about much of *Endymion*. There is a want of humility and even simplicity in the writing. Who does he think he is? The following, from a letter to Bailey, shows what he thinks he is: 'Men of Genius are great as certain ethereal Chemicals operating on the Mass of neutral intellect – b[ut] they have not any individuality, any determined Character.' In the same letter, he shows what he does not think he is: 'I would call the top and head of those who have a proper self Men of Power.' (*Letters*, I, 184) He is not interested in being a Man of Power. And he is not interested enough in developing in himself the quick, corrupt, sophisticated intelligence more likely to be found in a journalist or an academic. The journalistic or academic kind of intelligence is an enemy of imaginative fluency, and it would only inhibit the poet's expression by making it seem reckless. 'In Endymion, I leaped headlong into the Sea, and thereby have become better acquainted with the Soundings, the quicksands, & the rocks, than if I had stayed upon the green shore, and piped a silly pipe, and took tea & comfortable advice. – I was never afraid of failure; for I would sooner fail than not be among the greatest.' (*Letters*, I, 374)

Endymion was Keats's first long poem, and he wanted it to be 'a regular stepping of the Imagination towards a Truth.' (*Letters*, I, 218) He wanted to prove to his friends, the public, and himself that he could retell classical myth in a sustained and independent way. But there was a problem, and it seemed a very big one at the time. He had no Greek. At this point in his career, Keats was demonstrably as indebted to Hunt's *The Story of Rimini* (1816) as he was to the writers of antiquity:

> For a warm eve, and gentle rains at night,
> Have left a sparkling welcome for the light,
> And there's a crystal clearness all about;
> The leaves are sharp, the distant hills look out;
> A balmy briskness comes upon the breeze;

And smoke goes dancing from the cottage trees;
And when you listen, you may hear a coil
Of bubbling springs about the grassy soil ...
                                    – *The Story of Rimini*, I

In his sonnet, 'On Leigh Hunt's Poem 'The Story of Rimini'',
Keats again venerates Hunt's 'region of his own' and his 'bower
for his spirit' in a way that suggests Keats aspires to having *his*
own 'region' and *his* own 'bower'. At the time of writing and
publishing *Endymion*, Keats seemed to hope that readers would
make the most of his fits and starts, and make out the contours of
a maturity (and even a Miltonic consistency) not yet properly
realised: 'The imagination of a boy is healthy, and the mature
imagination of a man is healthy; but there is a space of life between,
in which the soul is in ferment, the character undecided, the way
of life uncertain, the ambition thick-sighted: thence proceeds
mawkishness, and all the thousand bitters which those men I speak
of must necessarily taste in going over the following pages.'
(Preface, *Endymion*) In traversing the 'ferment' between boyhood
and manhood, the poet (argues the poet) is forced to leave the
excrescences that he fears will rob, for many readers, the scattered
jewels of their shine.

Perhaps the teenager writing *Sleep and Poetry* and *Endymion*
– divided from, and coveting, the rank of the classically educated
– was conscious of a vulgarity (not just an immaturity) about his
life and work. He seems to have worried that it was already too
late for the deficit of sophistication to be made good. In many of
his utterances he seems to share more in common with Scott's
Edward Waverley (so sensible of his own want of finish) than
with Cervantes's Don Quixote (so flawlessly deluded):

There were a few other youths of better education, and a more
liberal character; but from their society ... our hero was in some

degree excluded ... The idea of having committed the slightest
solecism in politeness, whether real or imaginary, was agony to
him; for perhaps even guilt itself does not impose upon some minds
so keen a sense of shame and remorse, as a modest, sensitive and
inexperienced youth feels from the consciousness of having
neglected etiquette, or excited ridicule ...

– *Waverley*, Chapter 4

Keats's self-image wavered. On one day (for example, 14 October
1818) he could be convinced that he would be among the English
poets after his death. On another day, in a different mood, he felt
sure that his own name would merely be writ in water. He often
worried that anything he could ever write would have something
inadequate and even insulting about it to readers who knew better.
The worry is like a watermark that will always be seen when the
paper on which Keats's apologia is printed is held up to the light:

This may be speaking too presumptuously, and may deserve a
punishment: but no feeling man will be forward to inflict it: he
will leave me alone, with the conviction that there is not a fiercer
hell than the failure in a great object. This is not written with the
least atom of purpose to forestall criticisms of course, but from
the desire I have to conciliate men who are competent to look,
and who do look with a zealous eye, to the honour of English
literature.

– Preface, *Endymion*

Byron had first introduced himself to the British public via his
preface to *Hours of Idleness* (1807). The effortless arrogance of
Byron's entreaty not to be indulged in reviews on account of his
nobility turned reviewers against him. Now Keats was emerging
as a more comical target. How could the scalp-hunters of the
book-reviewing world not be roused by the leakage of lower middle
class humility? The Preface to *Endymion* does rather look like the
author's attempt to unburden himself with appeals to the kindness

of strangers. It is also imbued with his love of the light in which he knows he will stand condemned: 'I hope I have not in too late a day touched the beautiful mythology of Greece, and dulled its brightness: for I wish to try once more, before I bid it farewell.'

For poetry lovers, the best passages of *Endymion* illustrate the longevity, rather than the frailty, of poetic exaltation:

> ... Nor do we merely feel these essences
> For one short hour; no, even as the trees
> That whisper round a temple become soon
> Dear as the temple's self, so does the moon,
> The passion poesy, glories infinite,
> Haunt us till they become a cheering light
> Unto our souls ...
>
> – *Endymion,* I, 25-31

The fusion in imagination of trees and temple brings what Hunt called 'the deepest taste of antiquity'. Furthermore, for the poet, 'these essences' do not merely shine 'Unto our souls', but they are, more vitally, 'bound to us so fast,/That, whether there be shine, or gloom o'ercast,/They always must be with us, or we die.' (*Endymion,* I, 31-3) In other words, the world in which one thinks and feels has been put there by the power of poetry. And once it has been put there, it cannot be taken away:

> A thing of beauty is a joy for ever:
> Its loveliness increases; it will never
> Pass into nothingness; but still will keep
> A bower quiet for us, and a sleep
> Full of sweet dreams ...
>
> – *Endymion,* I, 1-5

In order to produce such pearls, the young poet takes life to heart (or lets himself be taken to life's heart), in an intensity of 'self-indulgence' and 'narcissism' easily spotted by those trained to weed unguarded emotions out of themselves, that they may mount and melt in the upper air of bourgeois indifference. The hack reviewers were obviously more technically proficient than Keats when it came to the ancient Greek language, but this brought them no awareness, at all, of the poet's communion with ancient Greek ways of apprehending real experience.

For pedants, *Endymion* is replete with verbal and conceptual problems. Sometimes, for example, the poet's forced impostures in reaching for the word that rhymes, and the higgledy-piggledy syllable-count, can look a bit temporary – as if they'll have to do for now:

> I clung about her waist, nor ceas'd to pass
> Fleet as an arrow through unfathom'd brine,
> Until there shone a fabric crystalline,
> Ribb'd and inlaid with coral, pebble, and pearl.
>
> – *Endymion*, III, 626-9

Keats had already made clear – be it remembered – his desire for readers to tolerate (if not endorse) any shabbiness about the appearance of the poem:

> What manner I mean, will be quite clear to the reader, who must soon perceive ... every error denoting a feverish attempt, rather than a deed accomplished. The two first books, and indeed the two last, I feel sensible are not of such completion as to warrant their passing the press; nor should they if I thought a year's castigation would do them any good; – it will not: the foundations are too sandy. It is just that this youngster should die away: a sad thought for me, if I had not some hope that while it is dwindling I may be plotting, and fitting myself for verses fit to live.
>
> – Preface, *Endymion*

Shelley did recognise the poem as a harbinger of 'the greatest things' from Keats. However, in the meantime, Keats had to make his way despised. The Tory politician John Wilson Croker and John Gibson Lockhart – the 'Z' of the *Blackwood's* series of articles, 'The Cockney School of Poetry' – denounced *Endymion* with predictable relish. Here is an excerpt from Croker's anonymous review in the September 1818 *Quarterly*:

> This author is a copyist of Mr Hunt, but he is more unintelligible, almost as rugged, twice as diffuse, and ten times more tiresome and absurd than his prototype, who, though he impudently presumed to seat himself in the chair of criticism, and to measure his own poetry by his own standard, yet generally had a meaning. But Mr Keats had advanced no dogmas which he was bound to support by examples; his nonsense therefore is quite gratuitous ...
> – *Keats: Narrative Poetry*, 43

For Croker, Keats is the deep and meaningless Cockney romantic – the all-dreaming, non-thinking imitator of the egregious King of the Cockneys, Hunt.

The thunderhead of judgement seemed slower to gather in Lockhart's *Blackwood's* review (August 1818). Lockhart surveyed Britain's cultural decline in general, and then introduced Keats as a mere symptom of that decline:

> Of all the manias of this mad age, the most incurable, as well as the most common, seems to be no other than the *Metromanie*. The just celebrity of Robert Burns and Miss Baillie has had the melancholy effect of turning the heads of we know not how many farm-servants and unmarried ladies; our very footmen compose tragedies, and there is scarcely a superannuated governess in the island that does not leave a roll of lyrics behind her in her band-box.
> – *Keats: Narrative Poetry*, 41

For Lockhart, Keats (who had become eligible to practise as an apothecary, physician and surgeon in July 1816) was of little higher origin than a farm-servant or a footman, stomping through the thoughts of finer sensibilities heavily and unseeingly. Having drolly contemplated the new cultural confusion in which any Tom, Dick or Harry could get into print, Lockhart alerted readers to the embarrassing sight of yet another new poetaster ('Mr John') fancying himself not only not incontinent but winged with the poetic impulse:

> His friends, we understand, destined him to the career of medicine, and he was bound apprentice some years ago to a worthy apothecary in town. But all has been undone by a sudden attack of the malady to which we have alluded. Whether Mr John has been sent home with a diuretic or composing draught to some patient far gone in the poetical mania, we have not heard. This much is certain, that he has caught the infection, and that thoroughly.
>
> – *Keats: Narrative Poetry*, 41

Finally, after breaking into mock earnestness and appearing to deliver a home-truth personally to the talented (though, it had to be affirmed, barbarian and bold) young man, Lockhart ushered him to the outskirts of high culture: 'It is a better and a wiser thing to be a starved apothecary than a starved poet; so back to the shop Mr John, back to the 'plasters, pills, ointment boxes', &c ... ' (*Keats: Narrative Poetry*, 41).

In 1820, a year before Keats's death, an unsigned review in the *London Magazine* said that Keats's 'knowledge of Greek and Mythology seem[ed] to mystify him on every occasion'. Keats had no university education at all, and for his harshest critics he was guilty of something unforgivably plebeian: though he was 'without Greek', he still had the effrontery 'to talk about the gods'. In short, he was just another Londoner with pretensions (and an inexcusably reform-minded track record).

Francis Jeffrey appeared to some extent to keep his attitude to Keats aloof and chilly:

> He deals too much with shadowy and incomprehensible beings, and is too constantly rapt into an extramundane Elysium, to command a lasting interest with ordinary mortals, and must employ the agency of more varied and coarser emotions, if he wishes to take rank with the enduring poets of this or of former generations.

What could better flatter the complacency of ignorance than a magazine review expressing concern about a new young writer's inability to condescend to 'coarser emotions'? Jeffrey delivered vintage Augustan sentiment to British readers both great and good, the maintenance of whose collective self-image – righteous and very intelligent, but battered by the rising vulgarity – entailed their reading their favourite weeklies as a sort of self-medication whilst their country and culture went to the dogs.

For Keats's most damaging critics, he simply had not had the direct means of mental culture that could have corrected and matured his ideas. All he seemed to his critics to be able to do was salivate over lip-smacking use of the English language. 'There is a cool pleasure,' he wrote as a marginal note on *Paradise Lost* (I, 321), 'in the very sound of the word vale. The English word is of the happiest chance ... It is a sort of Delphic Abstraction – a beautiful thing made more beautiful by being reflected and put in a mist.' (Barnard, 519)

Keats had read in Gilbert Burnet's *History of My Own Times* that *Paradise Lost* was 'the beautifullest and perfectest poem that ever was writ'. But (felt the critics) in the process of learning the real language of Homer, Keats's ideas could have become more independent of words, with the result of his paying keener attention to the weight and worth of words, and their assembly and organisation. He could have learned how to make them fixed and fluid with superior accuracy, and so he could have become more properly skilled not only at expressing essential thoughts, but at preserving them as well. Furthermore, he could have learned to feel the right level of respect for the English language, and thus been protected from any attempt to adapt it in an irresponsible or uninformed way. He would then, surely, not have had the temerity to declare that he 'look[ed] upon fine Phrases like a Lover.' (*Letters*, II, 139) There was the general feeling in the literary establishment of Keats's time that if even one classically uneducated writer could publish a piece of work called *Endymion* and remain unscathed, then the profession of serious author might be brought into justifiable disrepute. Keats's – like Shelley's, though for different reasons – was a voice not understood.

And yet, even as the hostility came to a head, Keats himself could be reflective and sublime – even shamanic – in his indifference to ideas about him in the heads of others:

> Praise or blame has but a momentary effect on the man whose love of beauty in the abstract makes him a severe critic on his own Works. My own domestic criticism has given me pain without comparison beyond what Blackwood or the Quarterly could possibly inflict. [A]nd also when I feel I am right, no external praise can give me such a glow as my own solitary reperception & ratification of what is fine ... [*Endymion*] is as good as I had power to make it – by myself.
>
> – *Letters*, I, 374

Keats's ownership of his latest product is passionately expressed here, despite its being despised so emphatically by the critics: 'Had I been nervous about its being a perfect piece, & with that view asked advice, & trembled over every page, it would not have been written; for it is not in my nature to fumble – I will write independently.' (*Letters*, I, 374)

His 'limitations' and 'want of tact' were not the only things about him to excite negative or begrudging comments. He was assumed by some commentators to lack character. Even Hazlitt, notable elsewhere for his fondness for Keats, said 'All he wanted was manly strength and fortitude.' ('On Effeminacy of Character', *Table Talk*, 1822) Keats's 'lack' was supposed to go hand in hand with his 'sugary' style of poetry. Thomas Carlyle, who in *Sartor Resartus* (1840) paid honour to the 'strong, just man' as against the apathetic, corrupted masses, said that 'Keats wanted a world of treacle!' The poet's Victorian readers included a great many women. (Women were not classically educated.) They did take pleasure in Keats's poems as exquisite – but, importantly, temporary – flights from mundane life. But the Victorian readership by and large preferred their male poets to have masculine strength and fortitude (which is why Wordsworth's popularity increased as it did during his later years, and still more after his death in 1850). Matthew Arnold's recognition of what is good about *Endymion* is, if anything, discreet, whereas his grieving over the waste from which he feels condemned to pick what is worthwhile is more plainly in view: he wrote to Sidney Colvin on 26 June 1887, 'What is good in *Endymion* is not, to my mind, so good as you say, and the poem as a whole I could wish to have been suppressed and lost. I really resent the space it occupies in the volumes of Keats's poetry.' (Lucas, 193)

Later, the twentieth-century critics tended to agree that Keats's promise was greater than his achievement. The sheer quantity of *Endymion* seems to have obliged even admirers of the poet's shorter and greater works (such as the great odes) to include everything in their evaluation of the poet's overall achievement, instead of taking delight in the quintessence he left behind. In *The Use of Poetry and the Use of Criticism* (1933), T.S. Eliot said that Keats's views on poetry as expressed in his letters show that his critical acuity was superior to the poetry he wrote. This was faint praise indeed from one poet to another. Eliot was not the only influential figure to advise modern readers not to waste too much time with Keats's poetry. William Empson, F.R. Leavis, I.A. Richards and others were busy razing everything to the discursive level – a level at which, say, Keats's belief in 'nothing but of the holiness of the Heart's affections and the truth of Imagination' (*Letters*, I, 184) would look like a crank's proclamation without a trace of seriousness to interest the modern passer-by; something to be tidied away in the box of 'outgrown' modes of thought and discourse marked 'Romantic'.

7

Shelley: Perennial Wisdom
and Political Exile

W ITH MATURITY, WHICH DEVELOPED IN HIM as
rapidly as it did in Keats, Shelley would not write on behalf
of any theory, or with deference to any fad or fashion of
contemporary thought. He would write from within the tradition
of philosophy, or wisdom, known as perennial. The perennial
wisdom flows through all ages, often out of sight, and sometimes
emerging to revitalise humanity:

> ... one majestic River,
> The breath and blood of distant lands, forever
> Rolls its loud waters to the ocean waves,
> Breathes its swift vapors to the circling air.
>
> – 'Mont Blanc', IV, 123-6

It is difficult to convert into discursive language 'The everlasting
universe of things' ('Mont Blanc', I, 1) without evaporating the
invaluable unknown out of it. Its flow through the ages has been
a special source of inspiration to visionary writers (such as
Shakespeare), yet it has been overlooked by most educators.
Coleridge caught it briefly but spectacularly in 'Kubla Khan' (1797)

– but of course one is to understand that that was just a dream, and just a fragment of a dream at that.

The perennial wisdom is almost completely unknown to the modern mind conditioned by modern education. And yet the following view of the fugitive nature of ultimate reality, expressed by Thomas Taylor the Platonist (the first English translator of the entire works of Plato, and of whose works all the major English Romantic poets were aware), is as applicable in the twenty-first century as it was when first written:

> ... in short, to pursue matter through its infinite divisions, and wander in its dark labyrinths, is the employment of the philosophy in vogue. But surely the energies of intellect are more worthy of our concern than the operations of sense ... Where ... is the microscope which can discern what is smallest in nature? Where is the telescope that can see at what point in the universe wisdom first began? Since, then, there is no portion of matter which may not be the subject of experiments without end, let us betake ourselves to the regions of mind, where all things are bounded in intellectual measure; where everything is permanent and beautiful, eternal and divine.
>
>   – from Taylor's Introduction
>   to Plotinus's 'Essay On the Beautiful'

Shelley never forget about such 'regions of mind' whose universal nature he could intuitively comprehend, the quality of whose being he could strongly feel, and with which he could sustain a vital relationship. He would not think the priceless, timeless gift away in exchange for the 'philosophy in vogue':

>   ... Thou mayst behold
> How cities, on which Empire sleeps enthroned,
> Bow their towered crests to mutability.
>
>   – *Hellas*, 844-6

He could not – and would not – bear the omission of the essential. He could hardly bear how other people insisted on the omission:

> Facts are not what we want to know in poetry, in history, in the lives of individual men, in satire, or panegyric. They are the mere divisions, the arbitrary points on which we hang, and to which we refer those delicate and evanescent hues of mind, which language delights and instructs us in precise proportion as it expresses.
>
> – *Letters*, II, 277

For Shelley, the essential remains present regardless of the materialization of air balloons, underground safety lamps or steam engines. The essential is intangible. There is no factual evidence to prove the location, or even the existence, of beauty, for example. For Shelley, the essential

> Floats though unseen among us, – visiting
> This various world with as inconstant wing
> As summer winds that creep from flower to flower;
> Like moonbeams that behind some piny mountain shower ...
> – 'Hymn to Intellectual Beauty', I

The idea of interpreting infinitely multifaceted and multidimensional life with the gimcrack terminology of 'this wrong world' ('Letter to Maria Gisborne', 160) is abhorrent to a poet determined to include the 'forgotten dream' (*Hellas*, 842) and 'the uncreated deep' (*Hellas*, 858) in his contemplations. Shelley pursues the essence of the very mystery that is left out of most other poetry:

> It visits with inconstant glance
> Each human heart and countenance;
> Like hues and harmonies of evening,
> Like clouds in starlight widely spread,
> Like memory of music fled,

> Like aught that for its grace may be
> Dear, and yet dearer for its mystery.
>
>   – 'Hymn to Intellectual Beauty', I

His emotions, interests and prejudices are present as he selects, relates and sifts. He is working in a field, the human mystery, in which human emotions, interests and prejudices are pervasively relevant; a field moreover in which experiment is impossible. To most people he appears to play a strange, or even ludicrous, game. All his efforts relate to the single question whose very unanswerable nature (if the poet is not considered beneath contempt for contemplating it) elicits mirth more than wonder: 'What is life?' ('Essay On Life', 1819) When the poet is perceived as continuing to amuse himself with the pursuit of something that cannot be pursued, he is unlikely to gain the admiration of people with no wish to think about what is beyond their five senses. He has no words with which to make people believe they will receive from him something he cannot give:

> Thoughts and feelings arise, with or without our will, and we employ words to express them. We are born, and our birth is unremembered, and our infancy remembered but in fragments; we live on, and in living we lose the apprehension of life. How vain it is to think that we can penetrate the mystery of our being!
>
>   – 'Essay on Life'

His most haunting works have about them the deep dissatisfaction of a poet who can find respite in nothing that is actually available to him. 'I am one of those whom nothing will fully satisfy' (*Letters*, II, 153), he told Hunt in 1819. On the one hand he is the part of us that knows that from beneath the surface of everyday life, the rhythms of an ontological pressure can override all our gnat-whining. On the other hand, there are moments when the poet can represent, in pellucid beads of compassion, the predicament of we who whine:

> We look before and after,
>   And pine for what is not;
> Our sincerest laughter
> With some pain is fraught;
> Our sweetest songs are those that tell of saddest thought.
>   – 'To A Skylark', 86-90

As a seeker after truth, Shelley will continue to devote his life to a pursuit that to many people looks silly. The best treatment that such a writer can expect from his contemporaries is to be left alone, so that he can live and work 'hidden/In the light of thought'.

The perennial philosophy is the only philosophy that is said to be inborn in human beings, expressing the natural structure of the human mind: 'the metaphysics that recognizes a divine Reality substantial to the world of things and lives and minds', as Aldous Huxley has put it in *The Perennial Philosophy* (1946). This explains its constant periodic reappearances:

> Poised by the flood, e'en on the height thou holdest,
> Thou mayst now learn how the full tide of power
> Ebbs to its depths.
>   – *Hellas*, 847-9

Its influence is evident in ancient civilizations such as China and Egypt, which remained highly cultured for thousands of years. The superior dialecticians of these countries contemplated the fundamental problems that concern all human beings including moral obligation and the significance of life and death. The great perpetuator of this philosophy, or way of seeing things, Plato, preserved and transmitted it in western culture. Shelley, who revered Plato, did the same.

The universal wisdom has been an occult or hidden source of inspiration to poets, mystics and prophetic writers for many centuries. The physician, traveller and astronomer, James Lind, introduced Shelley to Plato's *Phaedrus* and the *Symposium* during Shelley's last two years at Eton. At this time Plato was considered too subversive to be taught officially in schools or universities. It is very significant that the eccentric and radical Lind took on the eccentric and radical young Shelley, and helped to instil in him a lifelong Platonic orientation.

Lind's protégé would soon, at university, get busy asserting how *politically* different he was from those around him, and from those who had brought him up. At University College Oxford in 1811, before authoring the many sustained expressions of neo-Platonism that would identify him, for good or ill, as a being of another element, Shelley certainly did attract the attention of contemporaries of material consequence. One of them, the Reverend J. Walker, a Fellow of New College, entered the Oxford booksellers Munday and Slatter just minutes after 'The Necessity of Atheism' had gone on sale there (in March 1811). Walker immediately saw to it that all copies but one were burnt in the back kitchen. It is possible that another Shelley pamphlet, the *Poetical Essay on the Existing State of Things* (1811), received similar treatment there and then. Curiously, this pamphlet, though known about, was actually missing until 2006. H.R. Woudhuysen's article in the *Times Literary Supplement* (14 July 2006), 'A Shelley Pamphlet Come to Light', has offered some new insights concerning the political controversy around Shelley: the pamphlet was written in support of Peter Finnerty, the radical Irish journalist and supporter of the United Irishmen who was then serving an eighteen-month sentence in Lincoln Gaol for libel. In the Preface to the *Poetical*

Essay, Shelley calls for 'a total reform in the licentiousness, luxury, depravity, prejudice, which involve society' by 'gradual, yet decided intellectual exertions'. But Shelley's more outspoken lines on the subject of Lord Castlereagh (whom Finnerty accused of trying to silence him), and his views about colonial India and the monarchy surely made Shelley's expulsion from Oxford inevitable.

Shelley's father, Sir Timothy Shelley, was deeply upset about his son's behaviour and expulsion, but he would not be the last person to suffer as the poet evolved. It was in the poet's highly strung and exceptional nature to be at odds with institutions, and he knew how to wield language in a way that would make those he despised either hit back at him or run for cover. The 'Clientism, patronage and borough-mongering' (Wroe, 17-18) which ran in the aristocratic Shelley family was already among the poet's unhappily formative thought-patterns as he set about criticising the lacework of privilege known as society:

> Commerce has set the mark of selfishness,
> The signet of its all-enslaving power,
> Upon a shining ore, and called it gold;
> Before whose image bow the vulgar great,
> The vainly rich, the miserable proud,
> The mob of peasants, nobles, priests and kings ...
> – *Queen Mab*, V, 53-60

The Shelleys were connected to the Duke of Norfolk, the great local landowner. Shelley's grandfather, Sir Bysshe, had been the first baronet, and Shelley's father, Sir Timothy, inherited the title when Sir Bysshe died in 1815. Sir Timothy was an inoffensive man, an MP for Shoreham, and a moderate Tory. But the poet, 'tameless, and swift, and proud' as he was, would not simply complete his education at his father's old college and then go into

politics mildly and inoffensively like his father. He would say in a
letter to his father that

> *Obedience* is in my opinion a word which should have no existence
> – you regard it as necessary. –
>
> Yes, you can command it. The institutions of society have made
> you, tho' liable to be misled by passion and prejudice like others,
> the *Head of the family* ...
>
> – *Letters*, I, 115

He could become frantically impatient with the limitations he felt
other people imposing upon him:

> Thou knowest ... that ... among the haunts of humankind,
> Hard-featured men, or with proud, angry looks,
> Or cold, staid gait, or false and hollow smiles,
> Or the dull sneer of self-loved ignorance,
> Or other such foul masks, with which ill thoughts
> Hide that fair being whom we spirits call man ...
>
> – *Prometheus Unbound*, III, iv

To live and work with the wearers of such 'foul masks' entails an
unavoidable abundance of unacknowledged self-sacrifices. Merely
turning a blind eye (or the other cheek) to swaggering mediocrity
seemed to the poet to close vistas, and therefore to kill poetry:

> thy forgotten dream;
> A dream itself, yet less, perhaps, than that
> Thou call'st reality.
>
> – *Hellas*, 843-5

He was prepared to forfeit a craven security in order to win back
the wonder of life. He recognised in the Greek gods (whose stories
he read for himself in the original Greek) the numinous principle
which seemed to him absent from his country's prevailing religion.
He absorbed the stories with the same impassioned delight as he

handled chemistry sets and microscopes. His annoyance after an Oxford lecture on mineralogy, for example, was plain when he said that the lecturer talked 'About stones! – stones, stones, stones; – nothing but stones! – and so drily. It was wonderfully tiresome.' (Peck, I, 72-3) He witnessed placeman mediocrity preaching at its ease from within its inherited systems, and with its imposing facts (including facts about stones) – for Shelley, 'not what we want to know' (*Letters*, II, 277) – and he knew that such complacency is incompatible with spiritual attainment: 'The source of poetry is native and involuntary but requires severe labour in its development.' (Medwin, 347) Keats, too, would write about the prolonged intensity of the labour involved in 'Soul-making'.

In 'Julian and Maddalo' (1818), Julian (based on Shelley himself) argues with Maddalo (based on Byron) about the concept of human freedom:

> It is our will
> That thus enchains us to permitted ill.
> We might be otherwise; we might be all
> We dream of happy, high, majestical.
> Where is the love, beauty and truth we seek,
> But in our mind? and if we were not weak,
> Should we be less in deed than in desire?
>
> – 'Julian and Maddalo', 170-6

The contrast between what we actually are and how much better we could be is expressed without inhibition. Such brightness and directness are characteristic of youth yet to be corrupted. A conventional initiation into the mysteries of compromise, hypocrisy and so on, out of which one is supposed to emerge as a sociable and serviceable adult, was eschewed by the poet. He would keep himself bright, direct and uncompromised as a writer. He was profoundly restless in a university – and, indeed, in a country

– where, whichever way he looked, he saw conscious oppression, unconscious oppression, and the tyranny of the unimaginative.

Shelley's liberalism can flow and erupt in his poetry, but in his actual life he could appear less liberal, and the contradiction has made an easy target of him for some critics. In 1818-19, the experience of being in Naples was ruined for him by the 'deformity & degradation' of its inhabitants (*Letters*, II, 488). Nonetheless, to call him misanthropic is merely to understand him incompletely. His eagerness to re-examine the premises upon which civilization exists is a world away from the cynicism, dandyism and pessimism of later Romantic writing. In his prose poem, 'One O'Clock in the Morning' (1862), Charles Baudelaire would define his need to lock himself alone in his room away from the 'Horrible life! Horrible city!', and he would tell of his compulsion to 'produce a few lines which will prove ... I am not the lowliest of men, that I am not inferior to those I despise!' Shelley, too, despised people, but his deepest concern was not the polishing to a perfect shine of an individual brand of contempt for humanity. His lifelong interest in healing, somehow, the underlying causes of what he found himself despising is what makes him interesting. In the following passage from the Preface to *The Revolt of Islam* the poet understands how the general attitude of post-Revolutionary pessimism has become increasingly attractive to so many readers:

> The revulsion occasioned by the atrocities of the demagogues and the reestablishment of successive tyrannies in France was terrible, and felt in the remotest corner of the civilized world ... Thus, many of the most ardent and tender-hearted of the worshippers of public good have been morally ruined by what a partial glimpse of the events they deplored appeared to show as the melancholy desolation of all their cherished hopes.

Mary Wollstonecraft had sagely expressed concern during the early phase of the French Revolution: 'if the aristocracy of birth is levelled with the ground, only to make room for that of riches ... the morals of the people will not be much improved by the change, or the government rendered less venal.' (Peck, II, 46) So it appears that Shelley and the mother-in-law he never met were essentially in agreement here. In all systems of strict convention, hypocrisy is never far behind.

> Hence gloom and misanthropy have become the characteristics of the age in which we live, the solace of a disappointment that unconsciously finds relief only in the wilful exaggeration of its own despair. This influence has tainted the literature of the age with the hopelessness of the minds from which it flows.
>
> – Preface, *The Revolt of Islam*

(Or, to borrow the words of W.B. Yeats in 'The Gyres', 'Conduct and work grow coarse, and coarse the soul'.) This ability to see into the malaise of the age is as far from journalistic exaggeration as it is from the ostentatiously unemotional nature of academic analysis. Journalists and their readers are symbiotically prejudiced, and academics argue (often while claiming not to) that institutions of Terror are/are not excusable. Shelley opposed such 'talk/Which makes the heart deny the *yes* it breathes' (*Prometheus Unbound*, III, iv, 149-50). Suffering Oxford University, which was 'insipid to me, uncongenial with my habits of thinking' (*Letters*, I, 227), only goaded him into unfolding his beautiful, terrible wings all the wider: 'I am accustomed to speak my opinion unreservedly ... language is given us to express ideas – he who fetters it is a BIGOT and a TYRANT' (*Letters*, I, 147). Shelley, like Byron, hated feeling fettered. So he beat his wings hard.

8

Byron Before the Madness,
Badness and Dangerousness

HAVING ARGUED IN 1807 THAT WORDSWORTH'S 'force and expression [wa]s that of a genuine poet, feeling as he wr[ote]' (*Letters and Journals*, I, 341), Byron would later that same year offer a harder point of view:

> Oh! how I hate the nerveless, frigid song,
> The ceaseless echo of the rhyming throng,
> Whose labour'd lines, in chilling numbers flow,
> To paint a pang the author ne'er can know!
> — 'Answer to Some Elegant Verses'

It did not help the young poet that his egotism ('I seek not glory from the senseless crowd') in the above poem contradicted what he said in the Preface to *Hours of Idleness*: 'I should be loth to ... triumph in honours granted solely to a title.' Lord Henry Brougham, who reviewed Byron's book with what Jerome McGann has called 'delightfully urbane acidity' (McGann, 4), sarcastically thanked his lordship for his concern.

But Byron thought it was Francis Jeffrey, not Brougham, who was the reviewer of *Hours of Idleness*. The poet wanted revenge, so he wrote *English Bards and Scotch Reviewers,* which was a petulant clearing of the throat indeed by the up and coming poet who would go on to produce *Childe Harold's Pilgrimage* and *Don Juan*:

> Behold! in various throngs the scribbling crew,
> For notice eager, pass in long review:
> Each spurs his jaded Pegasus apace,
> And Rhyme and Blank maintain an equal race;
> Sonnets on sonnets crowd and ode on ode;
> And Tales of Terror jostle on the road;
> Immeasurable measures move along;
> For simpering Folly loves a varied song ...
>> – *English Bards and Scotch Reviewers,* 143-150

Bright is the adolescence in all those adjectives. The new boy on the block has set about proving himself badass by egging the front doors and windows of some eminent fogeys. Wordsworth is described as 'simple' (237); Coleridge 'brays' and is a 'Laureate of the long-eared kind' (264); and Southey has 'chaunt[ed] too often and too long' (225). Then Byron wrongly identifies Francis Jeffrey (the near-name-sake of the Judge, George Jeffreys, who officiated at the trial of Algernon Sydney) as the most obnoxious reviewer in the universe:

> Health to immortal JEFFREY! once, in name,
> England could boast a judge almost the same;
> In soul so like, so merciful, yet just,
> Some think that Satan has resigned his trust,
> And given the Spirit to the world again,
> To sentence Letters, as he sentenced men.
>> – *English Bards and Scotch Reviewers,* 438-445

The poem was published anonymously in March 1809. The poet was very cautious about putting his name to a second edition. He had quickly become embarrassed about the poem and wished to cancel many things in it, but he then realised that the manly course would be to just stand over it. It would not, in truth, have been particularly worrying for a writer to be attacked in *English Bards*, partly because the poem was obviously the result of immaturity and paranoia. Like young Byron the vampire, young Byron the satirist was more fledgling than biting. He had yet to grow his sharp teeth, and he had yet to determine his dark halo.

Of the many poets that Byron targeted in *English Bards and Scotch Reviewers*, only Wordsworth could not forgive him. It was as if Byron's contemporaries knew and at some level sympathised with the promising writer's hunger for recognition. Speaking daggers but using none, Byron spins out a sense of his own harmlessness that has an affinity with Hamlet's:

> The time hath been, when no harsh sound would fall
> From lips that now may seem imbued with gall;
> Nor fools nor follies tempt me to despise
> The meanest thing that crawled beneath my eyes:
> But now, so callous grown, so changed since youth,
> I've learned to think, and sternly speak the truth;
> Learned to deride the critic's starch decree,
> And break him on the wheel he meant for me ...
> – *English Bards and Scotch Reviewers*, 1053-1060

Byron's allusion to Pope's 'Epistle to Dr Arbuthnot' ('Satire or Sense, alas! can *Sporus* feel?/Who breaks a butterfly upon a wheel?') suggests Byron's self-recognition on looking into the work of another writer.

When he asked his nominal guardian, the Earl of Carlisle, to present him in the House of Lords, Carlisle replied unhelpfully, directing the poet vaguely in the direction of the appropriate paperwork. Byron retaliated by erasing the complementary lines he had written about Carlisle, and inserting the following:

> No Muse will cheer, with renovating smile,
> The paralytic puling of CARLISLE.
> The puny schoolboy and his early lay
> Men pardon, if his follies pass away;
> But who forgives the Senior's ceaseless verse,
> Whose hairs grow hoary as his rhymes grow worse?
> – *English Bards and Scotch Reviewers*, 725-730

Having alluded to Carlisle's nervous disorder ('paralytic puling'), Byron sarcastically summarised Carlisle's accomplishments:

> What heterogeneous honours deck the Peer!
> Lord, rhymester, petit-maître, pamphleteer!
> – *English Bards and Scotch Reviewers*, 731-732

Byron would shortly feel embarrassed about this, and he would say, in 1816, that Carlisle's 'provocation was not sufficient to justify such acerbity.' This could well have been more of a case of the poet's remorse about style than any scruples about having hurt someone's feelings: in *English Bards*, he had failed as a satirist because he picked up missiles too indiscriminately and flung them too formulaically. By the time he came to write *Don Juan*, he had honed his satire like a precision mechanism. Like the operator of a state of the art guillotine, the author of *Don Juan* would heave and release his gleaming versification with more detachment, more efficiency, and more of a sense of occasion and spectacle than he had achieved in his earlier works. But that would be in the future. For the time being, in *Childe Harold*, the sheer wealth and vigour of Byron's sense of the things that happen to him resembles Hamlet's in that the variety and the lack of an exact type of causal logic for every detail are part of the point.

9

Keats's Madwoman
and the Pot Plant

Arnold would express disappointment with the overall effect of Keats's 'Isabella; or, the Pot of Basil', despite its isolated aesthetic assets:

> The poem of Isabella, then, is a perfect treasure-house of graceful and felicitous words and images: almost in every stanza there occurs one of those vivid and picturesque turns of expression, by which the object is made to flash upon the eye of the mind, and which thrill the reader with a sudden delight ... But the action, the story?
> – *Keats: Narrative Poems*, 54

This judgment, of the Professor of Poetry at Oxford (1857-62), would be inwardly digested on a widespread basis.

Keats did not want the poem, which he based on Boccaccio's *Decameron* (IV, v), to be published. In her essay, 'The Material Sublime: Keats and *Isabella*' (1974), Louise Z. Smith (not to be confused with the other Z) has resisted the general negativity about the poem, but she has still felt the need to call it 'the wallflower among Keats's narratives.' Richard Woodhouse would tell John Taylor that Keats 'could not bear ['Isabella'] now [some 18 months

after writing it]. It appeared to him mawkish.' (*Letters*, II, 162)
Keats himself would write to Woodhouse:

> I will give you a few reasons why I shall persist in not publishing
> The Pot of Basil – It is too smokeable ... There is too much
> inexperience of live [life], and simplicity of knowledge in it ... There
> are very few would look to the reality. I intend to use more finesse
> with the Public. It is possible to write fine things which cannot be
> laugh'd at in any way. Isabella is what I should call were I a reviewer
> 'A weak-sided Poem' with an amusing sober-sadness about it.
>
> – *Letters*, II, 174

Keats was worried that wits about town reviewing 'Isabella' might
recognise his lack of experience – including his lack of sexual
experience – and scribble with amusement at his expense (or
smoke him, as Keats, borrowing the term from Restoration
comedy, put it). He was right to worry, given that (to give just
one instance) he had referred to Isabella's breasts in the poem as
'Those dainties made to still an infant's cries'.

Keats's poem does convey his distaste for the world of
commerce: ' ... many a weary hand did swelt/In torched mines
and noisy factories ... ' ('Isabella', XIV). At the beginning of the
poem, the humble Lorenzo's two deceitful and ruthless employers
do not know that their sister, Isabella, is Lorenzo's lover. The
brothers' plan has always been 'to coax her by degrees/To some
high noble and his olive trees.' ('Isabella', XXI) When the
treacherous brothers – 'these money-bags', or 'ledger-men' – find
out that Isabella and Lorenzo have been secretly attached, they
plan to murder Lorenzo:

>   ... they fix'd upon a surest way
> To make the youngster for his crime atone;
> And at the last, these men of cruel clay
> Cut Mercy with a sharp knife to the bone;

> For they resolved in some forest dim
> To kill Lorenzo, and there bury him.
>
> – 'Isabella', XXII

One can see the young poet's continuing struggle to work his various resources into a credible unity. (Can 'Mercy' in any convincing sense be 'Cut ... with a sharp knife to the bone'?) A little later, Keats allows the reader to witness Lorenzo being led 'Into a forest quiet for the slaughter', but the poet decides to leave it – for the time being – to the reader's imagination exactly how the slaughter happens, saying only: 'There was Lorenzo slain and buried in,/There in that forest did his great love cease ... ' ('Isabella', XXVIII).

Just as some of Wordsworth's narrative poems can follow with empathy the feelings of a woman left destitute (as in 'The Mad Mother'), so Keats documents Isabella's psychological deterioration since hearing of the loss of her lover:

> She weeps alone for pleasures not to be;
> Sorely she wept until the night came on,
> And then, instead of love, O Misery!
> She brooded o'er the luxury alone:
> His image in the dusk she seem'd to see,
> And to the silence made a gentle moan,
> Spreading her perfect arms upon the air,
> And on her couch low murmuring 'Where? O where?'
>
> – 'Isabella', XXX

Isabella also echoes the desolation of Wordsworth's Martha Ray in 'The Thorn' ('O Misery!'). Just as we could sympathise with the jilted, impoverished and grief-stricken Martha (who went mad and possibly killed her own baby), so too we could sympathise with Isabella (who will sever the head from her murdered lover's corpse, bring it home and keep it secretly in the soil of a pot-plant).

Claude L. Finney's *Evolution of Keats* (1936) and Bernard Blackstone's *The Consecrated Urn: An Interpretation of Keats in Terms of Growth and Form* (1959) have both placed 'Isabella' in the context of Keats's peculiarly rapid progress as a poet. Still experimenting with different tones and techniques, Keats can show a Wordsworthian understanding of the unhappy Isabella in one stanza, and then generate the Gothic phosphorescence of her vision (in which she learns the true circumstances surrounding her lover's disappearance) in the next:

> [Dead Lorenzo's] eyes, though wild, were still all dewy bright
> With love, and kept all phantom fear aloof
> From the poor girl by magic of their light,
> The while it did unthread the horrid woof
> Of the late darken'd time, – the murderous spite
> Of pride and avarice, – the dark pine roof
> In the forest, – and the sodden turfed dell,
> Where, without any word, from stabs he fell.
>
> – 'Isabella', XXXVII

The reader learns about the manner of Lorenzo's death only now (in the thirty-seventh stanza) with Isabella, and through the ghostly messenger, 'the pale shadow' ('Isabella', XXXVI).

The poet retains the element of compassion for Isabella, even as she, helped by 'that aged Dame' ('Isabella', XLIV), severs Lorenzo's head from the rest of his body and takes it home with her:

> In anxious secrecy they took it home,
> And then the prize was all for Isabel:
> She calm'd its wild hair with a golden comb,
> And all around each eye's sepulchral cell
> Pointed each fringed lash; the smeared loam
> With tears, as chilly as a dripping well,

> She drench'd away: – and still she comb'd, and kept
> Sighing all day – and still she kiss'd, and wept.
>
> – 'Isabella', LI

For John Whale, no wonder Keats – whose poetic sophistication would continue to increase exponentially – became more anxious about the poem's reception:

> Faced with such pathological detail [as in the stanza above] many readers will immediately consign this part of the poem to the category ludicrous. There's something deeply unsettling about Isabella's activity here, and not simply because it strains the credibility of a forensically informed imagination. It is, for one thing, horribly reminiscent of a girl's grooming of her doll, right down to the straightening of the eye-lashes. (Whale, 63)

Now in his twenties, and nearing his full potential, but still with some lingering adolescence to be burnt off as he continued to transform himself, Keats would often find himself ashamed of last year's – or even last month's – effort. It could be suggested, however, that Whale's appreciation of the poem has been reductively forensic (and even misleadingly finicky). In Boccaccio's *Decameron*, Lorenzo's body had been untouched by decay and putrefaction. It has taken the apprentice surgeon Keats to introduce a perishable Lorenzo. Keats's Isabella will eventually be left with no material Lorenzo – just a lover's memories and intense grief (not actually there, materially, to be measured by her money-bags brothers, but real all the same).

The exhumation of Lorenzo is Isabella's soul's desperate attempt to connect again with her cruelly dispatched lover. Keats knows that expressions of soul are misrepresented in this world. And the soul is too often reduced to feeding on what it does not really hunger for. The brothers misrepresented Lorenzo (lying that he went on sudden business for them abroad and simply failed to return) and deprived Isabella of that which she most needed (namely, the love of Lorenzo), but she – in touch with her own soul – got to know better. Whale seems to imagine Keats's Isabella to be like a serial killer with a corpse. But Keats's psychological acuity is like Shakespeare's in that it can make an old story newly haunting, and it makes crime scene investigations uncalled for. Does Hamlet's fascination with the late Yorick's skull consign the graveside scene in *Hamlet* to 'the category ludicrous'? The dead human head, like the ruins of Tintern Abbey, may be touched by presences for which there is no empirical evidence – all we have is the impression of Hamlet's fondness for Yorick who had carried him on his back a thousand times, and who had set the table on a roar with his flashes of merriment. All we have is Isabella's obvious and inextinguishable love for her chop-falling (remember, not yet chop-fallen) Lorenzo. How abhorred in the imagination it is. One's gorge rises at it. One's need for further support in open court is self-evidently superfluous. The spirit of love for Isabella that animated Lorenzo's head before he was murdered would have been what the poor woman desperately wanted to recapture. Now, in the absolute zero of his absence, caressing the part of his corpse that once bore the impress of his face is the closest she can get back to their warm relationship.

In July 1820, Charles Lamb had the geniality and generosity to pick out the brilliance of 'Isabella' rather than linger over the poem's deficiencies:

> Two Florentines, merchants, discovering that their sister Isabella has placed her affections upon Lorenzo, a young factor in their employ, when they had hopes of procuring for her a noble match, decoy Lorenzo, under pretence of a ride, into a wood, where they suddenly stab and bury him. The anticipation of the assassination is wonderfully conceived in one epithet, in the narration of the ride –

So the two brothers, and their *murder'd* man,
Rode past fair Florence, to where Arno's stream
Gurgles –

                              – *Keats: Narrative Poems*, 52

For Louise Smith, 'Isabella' is Keats's 'last poetic failure'. In writing it, it is as if Keats was self-administering homeopathic allusions to Greek myth, continuing to set himself up for higher and higher poetic pollen counts:

Moan hither, all ye syllables of woe,
From the deep throat of sad Melpomene!
Through bronzed lyre in tragic order go,
And touch the strings into a mystery;
Sound mournfully upon the winds and low;
For simple Isabel is soon to be
Among the dead: She withers, like a palm
Cut by an Indian for its juicy balm.

                              – 'Isabella', LVI

'Moan hither ... ' might be hard to take very seriously. Keats anticipated contemporary reviewers' reactions to the poem: 'it ... might do very well after one's death – but not while one is alive. There are very few would look to the reality.' (*Letters*, II, 174) Arnold would be singeing in his opinion of how the poem compared with the work it tried to emulate: 'Let the reader, after he has finished the poem ... turn to the same story in the Decameron [of Boccaccio]: he will then feel how pregnant and interesting the same action has become in the hands of a great artist, who above all things delineates his object; who subordinates expression to that which it is designed to express ... ' (*Keats: Narrative Poems*, 54).

At any rate, the young poet completed the story. The brothers 'watch'd in vain;/For seldom did she go to chapel-shrift,/And seldom felt she any hunger-pain ... ' ('Isabella', LIX). Curious as to the reason for Isabella's self-neglect, they steal the basil-pot, and find that 'The thing was vile with green and livid spot,/And yet they knew it was Lorenzo's face ... ' ('Isabella', LX). They flee, taking with them the basil pot from their sister. Isabella is left with nothing, and has nothing to look forward to: 'And so she pined, and so she died forlorn' ('Isabella', LXIII). Now, at the age of twenty-three, Keats himself had less than three years left to live, but he was becoming sublimely attuned to the most important (least material) exigencies of existence, and the 'innumerable compositions and decompositions which take place between the intellect and its thousand materials before it arrives at that trembling delicate and snail-horn perception of Beauty.' (*Letters*, I, 265)

10

Shelley's Unseen Power
and Some Critics' Attitudes

RICHARD HOLMES'S INFLUENTIAL BIOGRAPHY HAS identified as unsatisfactory, and unwoven, the impression of Shelley the 'angel' believed in by generations of 'Shelley lovers'. Sir Stephen Spender has called Holmes's *Shelley: The Pursuit* (1974) 'The best biography of Shelley ever written', and Spender has celebrated a long-awaited coming of common sense to Shelley, and Romantic, studies:

> The great emphasis that Mr Holmes lays on Shelley's politics, philosophy and social activities corrects the usual view of an extraordinarily idealized, ethereal, spiritualized kind of poetry combined with an extraordinarily incoherent life ... He has taken the Shelley story out of the realm of myth and made it far more convincing and significant.

But to whom has Holmes made the poet 'far more convincing and significant'? Presumably, the mid-1970s readership to whose collective materialism Holmes and Spender were keenly and capably attuned. One Shelley lover unmentioned in Holmes's biography is the poet Francis Thompson. Thompson had a kind

116

of lucidity and an ardour for the divine in line with Shelley's before him, and Shakespeare's before Shelley, and Plato's before Shakespeare: 'When we become conscious in dreaming that we dream, the dream is on the point of breaking; when we become conscious in living that we live, the ill dream is but just beginning.' (Thompson, 29)

Holmes says that 'Shelley was at no point completely converted to Platonism' (Holmes, 432). Shelley himself told Peacock in 1820 that 'Plato and Calderón have been my gods' (*Letters*, II, 245). 'I read the Greek dramatists & Plato forever' (*Letters*, II, 364), he told John Gisborne in October 1821. As Holmes says, Shelley was 'critical and comparative' and he 'selected, disregarded and explored as he went' (Holmes, 432), but the poet himself has put the issue of his spiritual orientation in a nutshell: 'I had rather err with Plato than be right with Horace.' (*Letters*, II, 75) It can be seen that Shelley's inheritance from the perennial wisdom facilitated his mystical vantage-point over the death of Keats (and over his own death perhaps):

> Peace, peace! he is not dead, he doth not sleep –
> He hath awakened from the dream of life –
> 'Tis we, who, lost in stormy visions keep
> With phantoms an unprofitable strife,
> And in mad trance strike with our spirit's knife
> Invulnerable nothings. *We* decay
> Like corpses in a charnel; fear and grief
> Convulse us and consume us day by day,
> And cold hopes swarm like worms within our living clay.
> – *Adonais*, XXXIX

And the specifically Platonic lustre of the following lines is incontrovertible:

> The One remains, the many change and pass;
> Heaven's light forever shines, Earth's shadows fly;
> Life, like a dome of many-colored glass,
> Stains the white radiance of Eternity,
> Until Death tramples it to fragments. – Die,
> If thou wouldst be with that which thou dost seek!
> Follow where all is fled! – Rome's azure sky,
> Flowers, ruins, statues, music, words, are weak
> The glory they transfuse with fitting truth to speak.
>
> – *Adonais*, LII

Though it contains no direct evidence of his awareness of the *philosophia perennis*, or Plato's transmission of it as an actual source for Shelley, Francis Thompson's personal enthusiasm for Shelley's work is infectious. Thompson appreciates the poet's ability, and need, to skip the sort of petty details that lure most other writers into the run of the mill. (Shakespeare was uninterested in the casualty figures of the Battle of Bosworth when he wrote *Richard III*, and it is unlikely that Hamlet counted his thousand natural shocks.)

Shelley's assertion that 'Nought may endure but Mutability' is, again, in agreement with the Platonic conception of the eternal unchanging forms:

> We are as clouds that veil the midnight moon;
> How restlessly they speed, and gleam, and quiver,
> Streaking the darkness radiantly! – yet soon
> Night closes round, and they are lost forever
>
> – 'Mutability'

The world of experience is illusory. Anyone with the time and inclination to still the blether of the conscious mind knows this. The conscious mind churns thoughts associated with money, pleasure, luxury, sex, and so on. Underneath all this are present the incomparably more sublime and meaningful archetypes (such as truth, justice and beauty), which have no figure, colour, magnitude or number – in fact no separate distinctive traits at all. Yet their power, eternal, invincible and undeniable, can take possession of hearts and minds.

As early as June 1811, Shelley was already offering people advice with regard to how to think about life and death. 'You have read Locke,' he told Elizabeth Hitchener, '– you are convinced that there are no innate ideas, & that you do not always think when asleep. Yet, let me enquire in these moments of intellectual suspension, do you suppose that the soul is annihilated[?]' (*Letters*, I, 116). Warming to the theme in this letter, Shelley shows an engagement with Philosophy which, though immersive, has not clogged the arterial flow of his poetic vision:

> You cannot suppose [that the soul is annihilated during sleep], knowing the infallibility of the rule, '*From nothing, nothing can come, to nothing nothing can return*' – as by this rule it could not be annihilated, or if annihilated could not be capable of resuscitation. This brings me to the point. Those around the lifeless corpse are perfectly aware that *it* thinks not: at least they are aware that when scattered thro' all the changes which matter undergoes it cannot then *think*. You have witnessed *one* suspension of intellect in dreamless sleep – you witness another in Death.
>
> – *Letters*, I, 116

By 1815, he was expressing his view of the interactivity between individual human beings and divinity:

> We live and move and think; but we are not the creators of our own origin and existence. We are not the arbiters of every motion of our own complicated nature; we are not the masters of our own imaginations and moods of mental being. There is a Power by which we are surrounded, like the atmosphere in which some motionless lyre is suspended, which visits with its breath our silent chords at will.
>
> – 'Essay on Christianity'

By 1816, he was contemplating the spectacle of Mont Blanc in the Vale of Chamouni and finding himself responsive to the great mountain's 'voice ... to repeal/Large codes of fraud and woe' ('Mont Blanc', III, 81). For the poet, the mountain's presence somehow makes the impostures of Christianity even clearer to him. The energy in the flux of phenomena gushes exhaustlessly from an ancient source, or as Byron would call it, 'the controlless core':

> The everlasting universe of things
> Flows through the mind, and rolls its rapid waves,
> Now dark, now glittering, now reflecting gloom,
> Now lending splendor, where from secret springs
> The source of human thought its tribute brings
> Of waters, – with a sound but half its own,
> Such a feeble brook will oft assume
> In the wild woods, among the mountains lone,
> Where waterfalls around it leap forever,
> Where woods and winds contend, and a vast river
> Over its rocks ceaselessly bursts and raves.
>
> – 'Mont Blanc', I, 1-11

Shelley was keen to conceptualise the fundamental energy of the 'everlasting universe', whether it was driving the clouds in the sky or vivifying the waters and woods below, in the perennial master-context:

> ... this Whole
> Of suns, and worlds, and men, and beasts, and flowers,
> With all the silent or tempestuous workings
> By which they have been, are, or cease to be,
> Is but a vision; all that it inherits
> Are motes of a sick eye, bubbles, and dreams;
> Thought is its cradle and its grave, nor less
> The future and the past are idle shadows

Of thought's eternal flight – they have no being;
Nought is but that which feels itself to be.

– *Hellas*, 776-85

It is perhaps reasonable now to reintroduce the point that Byron had little of Shelley's enthusiasm for Plato, as the following stanza from Canto I of *Don Juan* shows:

O Plato! Plato! you have paved the way,
    With your confounded fantasies, to more
Immoral conduct by the fancied sway
    Your system feigns o'er the controlless core
Of human hearts, than all the long array
    Of poets and romancers: – You're a bore,
A charlatan, a coxcomb – and have been,
At best, no better than a go-between.

– *Don Juan*, I, cxvi

The outburst is free of real malice, though, and it also contains an acceptance of Plato's achievement as a 'go-between' or an intermediary between the 'core/Of human hearts' and the intellects at the tips of the finest poets' (including Shelley's) senses.

In the early nineteenth century, Platonism had found its way far enough into popular English reading habits (if not into mainstream education) to become interesting to satirists. 'Mr Mystic', in Peacock's novel *Melincourt* (1817), was based on Thomas Taylor. Byron had a unique knack of mirroring to the bourgeois reading public the metastases of any of its latest pretensions. But Byron knew that Shelley too was unique and utterly free from pretension. Byron knew that although most Greek-less, self-professed Plato-enthusiasts probably found (even translations of) the *Phaedrus* and the *Symposium* hard work (or even just plain boring), Plato was a continually vitalising presence for Shelley.

On reading chapter 3 of Mary Shelley's *Frankenstein* (1818), one recognises in the brilliant and fiery young Victor Frankenstein something of the poet Shelley, or a Thomas Taylor, or a Blake commencing his 'Mental Fight' against dispiriting compromise, hypocrisy and authoritarian impositions. A Frankenstein, a Taylor, a Blake or a Shelley will not cease until he has built 'Jerusalem' or self-destructed in the effort:

> 'The ancient teachers of this science,' said he [the conventional university lecturer employed to dispense the received wisdom of the day], 'promised impossibilities and performed nothing. The modern masters promise very little; they know that metals cannot be transmuted, and that the elixir of life is a chimera'.

Shelley's learning, like Frankenstein's, belongs to the older European (pre-Enlightenment) civilization whose cognoscenti were less anxious to dismiss, say, human hope, with its non-measurable beauty and force, as a non-existent 'chimera'. On listening to the professor's encomium on the newly authoritative figures of modern science, Frankenstein feels stirring in himself an impulse to oppose their Academy, even though the struggle will probably end in his own personal ruin:

> Such were the professor's words – rather let me say such were the words of fate, enounced to destroy me. As he went on, I felt as if my soul were grappling with a palpable enemy ... So much has been done, exclaimed the soul of Frankenstein – more, far more, will I achieve ... I will pioneer a new way, explore unknown powers, and unfold to the world the deepest mysteries of creation.
>
> – *Frankenstein*, chapter 3

Mary Shelley's Frankenstein is based on her husband, who wrote his Dedication of *The Revolt of Islam* to her in 1817:

And from that hour did I with earnest thought
Heap knowledge from forbidden mines of lore;
Yet nothing that my tyrants knew or taught
I cared to learn ...

– 'To Mary', V

It was from ancient wisdom dismissed so frequently by his contemporaries that Shelley, like Frankenstein, drew boldness and power, and with this wisdom the poet said things of fundamental importance to humanity. He had no interest in the personal destruction of aristocrats, nor indeed in continuing to be an aristocrat himself. Instead, he wanted to get people to think about the direction of human energy and whether it may not be better directed:

> I am not an aristocrat, or any *crat* at all but vehemently long for the time when man may *dare* to live in accordance with *Nature* & Reason, in consequence with Virtue – to which I firmly believe that Religion, its establishments, Polity & its establishments, are the formidable tho' destructible barriers.

– *Letters*, I, 116-17

It is worth pausing to consider the scale of Shelley's ambition as a poet. He cared about humanity, he believed it could be better than it is, and he cared about producing work that would redound to humanity. These are cares that later poets have tended not to have.

Marilyn Butler's contention that Shelley was an 'atheist' (Butler, 3) can be unhelpful. Even the intellectual vantage point reached by Shelley in his late teens throws in the shade much of the 'down to earth' terminology of twentieth-century Romantic studies: '*Atheism* appears a terrific monster at a distance; *dare* to examine it, look at its companions, it loses half its terrors ... ' (*Letters*, I, 116). Francis Thompson, who knew and loved Shelley's work with a poet's osmosis of understanding, wished to help continue the transmission of the mystical vision:

> The universe is his box of toys. He dabbles his fingers in the day-fall. He is gold-dusty with tumbling amidst the stars. He makes bright mischief with the moon. The meteors muzzle their noses in his hand. He teases into growling the kennelled thunder, and laughs at the shaking of its fiery chain. He dances in and out of the gates of heaven: its floor is littered with his broken fancies. He runs wild over the fields of ether. He chases the rolling world. (Thompson, 45-6)

Anyone who has delighted in the 'Ode to the West Wind' – 'Drive my dead thoughts over the universe/Like withered leaves to quicken a new birth!' (V) – may feel a fitness about Thompson's stratospheric rapport with the lyric poet at work. But throughout the essay Thompson's Catholic principles keep him disconnected from Shelley's Platonic source of power. Better a faded rocket, though, than never a burst of light.

Readers bored by more terrestrial restrictions may find unexpected afflatus in some of the more earthbound accounts of Shelley. Hogg, who knew Shelley personally at Oxford (though he had little time for poetry), enumerated the contents of Shelley's university rooms, apparently leaving the pleasure of 'tumbling amidst the stars' with the poet to others:

> Books, boots, papers, shoes, philosophical instruments, clothes, pistols, linen, crockery, ammunition, and phials innumerable, with money, stockings, prints, crucibles, bags, and boxes, were scattered on the floor and in every place. – The table, and especially the carpet, were already stained with large spots of various hues, which frequently proclaimed the agency of fire. An electrical machine, and an air pump, the galvanic trough, a solar microscope, and large glass jars and receivers, were conspicuous amidst the mass of matter. Upon the table by his side were some books lying open, several letters, a bundle of new pens ... (Peck, I, 68).

From Hogg's account, the reader may get a sense of the velocity and voluminosity of Shelley's sense of wonder. This would remind one of young Frankenstein's almost frenzied dedication to 'unfold to the world the deepest mysteries of creation.' It may be the case that Hogg, writing his *Life of Percy Bysshe Shelley* in 1858, is remembering his friend through the prism of *Frankenstein* and some fragments of Mary Shelley's projected life of Shelley:

> He [Shelley] proceeded, with much eagerness and enthusiasm, to show me [Hogg] the various instruments, especially the electrical apparatus: turning round the handle very rapidly, so that the fierce, crackling sparks flew forth; and presently standing upon the stool with glass feet, he begged me to work the machine until he was filled with the fluid, so that his long, wild locks bristled and stood on end. Afterwards he charged a powerful battery of several large jars; labouring with vast energy, and discoursing with increasing vehemence of the marvellous powers of electricity, of thunder and lightning; describing an electrical kite that he had made at home, and projecting another and an enormous one, or rather a combination of many kites, that would draw down from the sky an immense volume of electricity, the whole ammunition of a mighty thunderstorm: and this being directed to some point would produce the most stupendous results. (Peck, I, 68-9)

The material details for Shelley (as for Plato, and Shakespeare) were in reality the shades of, or the symbols for, what is most important, and most real. Until he could reveal to a readership what existence really is (and it really is *not* the product of the Christian God to whom, as *Genesis* has it, it all seemed like a good idea at the time), he would be obliged to be labelled an 'atheist', which he was not, as his 'Hymn to Intellectual Beauty' (for example) shows:

> I vowed that I would dedicate my powers
> To thee and thine – have I not kept the vow?

> With beating heart and streaming eyes, even now
> I call the phantoms of a thousand hours
> Each from his voiceless grave ...
> They know that never joy illumed my brow
> Unlinked with hope that thou wouldst free
> This world from its dark slavery, –
> That thou, O awful Loveliness,
> Wouldst give whate'er these words cannot express.
>   – 'Hymn to Intellectual Beauty', VI

Marilyn Butler, whose book, *Romantics, Rebels & Reactionaries* (1981), 'would influence thinking about the Romantics for years to come' (*Byron Journal*), has laconically rehearsed a general impression of Shelley along the lines of Arnold's, Holmes's and Spender's accounts of the poet:

> Shelley has not been the same man in our century since posterity in his own transformed him into Ariel: beautiful, ethereal, with the waves washing or the wind blowing through his hair.
>
> From the start, the notion of the poet as rebel was a generous one. Along with the flamboyant Byronic model it could accommodate something more manageable, the sensitive individual who rejected worldliness, and even, literally, this vulgar material world for a better.

Butler's dryness implies the acceptance of rigorous standards, submission to ascertainable facts, and the aspiration of historiography towards the status of an exact science – as if Shelley had not heard harmonious madness in the Skylark, and as if he had not authored *A Defence of Poetry, Prometheus Unbound* and 'Hymn to Intellectual Beauty': 'Readers who were religious idealists – and there were many of these in the 1830s and 1840s – soon found it possible to forget the inconvenient Shelleyan atheism in this congenial otherworldliness.' (Butler, 3) Butler has not been alone in Romantic studies in taking issue with art in general, calling it 'an unsocial, unspecific, timeless zone ... set up by post-Romantic intellectuals as a tax haven where there is nothing to pay'. Is this a complaint about the general arrangement of western industrial civilization, in which the poor academics and politicians and football stars literally have to pay their taxes? An academic's salary and three square meals a day will concentrate his or her mind on matters in which the poets had no interest, such as testing disciplinary boundaries, jumping canonical fences and *inversion* in general. One might wonder why Homer, or Shakespeare, didn't just realise at the time that poetry is really only an adjunct of Cultural Studies, or perhaps Psychology or Peace and Conflict Studies. Homer and Shakespeare lived before the birth of that Swedish exponent of explosive, fundable change, Alfred Nobel. So too did Byron, Keats and Shelley, though by the time these three were writing, the Social Sciences were already well-advanced, and busily overturning barriers that Reason had never erected in the first place.

Like Keats's 'Negative capability', Shelley's 'harmonious madness' might not look immediately useful to a busy school inspector, a professional biographer, or a proudly tax-paying university professor. Yet the Platonic concept is right at the heart of Shelley. It is deeper than the sanity and commonsense with which educators have tended to promote a mentality somewhat mechanised in its approach to everything from warfare to love poetry. Writing to Peacock in August 1818, Shelley would commend specifically 'a wonderful passage ... in [Plato's] *Phaedrus* ... in praise of poetic madness, and in definition of what poetry is, and how a man becomes a poet.' (*Letters*, II, 29) The passage Shelley has in mind is Socrates' speech:

> There are several kinds of divine madness. That which proceeds from the Muses taking possession of a tender and unoccupied soul,

awakening, and bacchically inspiring it towards songs and other
poetry, adorning myriads of ancient deeds, instructs succeeding
generations; but he who, without this madness from the Muses,
approaches the poetical gates, having persuaded himself that by
art alone he may become sufficiently a poet, will find in the end
his own imperfections, and see the poetry of his cold prudence
vanish into nothingness before the light of that which has sprung
from divine insanity. (*Letters*, II, 29)

Shelley effectively describes how he himself has coped as a
marginalized figure:

Every man who lives in this age and desires to write poetry, ought,
as a preservative against the false and narrow systems of criticism
which every poetical empiric vents, to impress himself with this
sentence [quoted above from *Phaedrus*]

– *Letters*, II, 29-30

And so Shelley's consciousness of his possessing (or being
possessed by) an exulted imagination as intense as, and
corresponding to, the finest of antiquity had driven him to write
Queen Mab (1813), and would drive him through to *The Triumph
of Life* (1822).

He is uncompromising in his belief that we can and should
be better than we are, according to our birthright as human
beings:

Man is of soul and body, formed for deeds
Of high resolve; on fancy's boldest wing
To soar unwearied ...

– *Queen Mab*, IV, 154-6

There are echoes in this of Hamlet, lingering over an ideal even as
he is aware at some level that the outward events of life are carrying
him towards madness (of the pathological, non-harmonious
variety), maturity, mediocrity, middle-age, or some other dreary

burial-place where high hopes are so often put to rest: 'What a piece of work is a man, how noble in reason, how infinite in faculties, in form and moving how express and admirable, in action how like an angel, in apprehension how like a god: the beauty of the world, the paragon of animals!' (*Hamlet*, II, ii) Man (for Shakespeare 'this quintessence of dust') is, for Shelley, all too often

> formed [by corrupt society] for abjectness and woe,
> To grovel on the dunghill of his fears,
> To shrink at every sound, to quench the flame
> Of natural love in sensualism ...
>
> – *Queen Mab*, IV, 159-62

Shelley retains and renews his disgust for a society that actually creates, preserves and rewards professional weaklings:

> Then grave and hoary-headed hypocrites,
> Without a hope, a passion or a love,
> Who through a life of luxury and lies
> Have crept by flattery to the seats of power,
> Support the system whence their honours flow.
>
> – *Queen Mab*, IV, 203-7

Many people are, of course, proficient at bottling any finer feelings, and undertaking ambitious, practical careers based on material, quantifiable results or rewards: 'Falsehood demands but gold to pay the pangs/Of outraged conscience' (*Queen Mab*, V, 197-8). Such people make up a substantial proportion of the labour force on whose votes the political parties depend for their existence and power:

> ... manhood tamely does
> His bidding, bribed by short-lived joys to lend
> Force to the weakness of his trembling arm.
>
> – *Queen Mab*, IV, 224-6

Manipulative politics is all about having people face away from, and never towards, their own needs. Only in the inner space of imagination can symbolism hold sway over the syllogisms devised by tyrants to make us work for them, and end up wanting to be owned by them. It's not as if Orwell has since taken readers beyond Shelley's innocent imaginings.

11

Childe Byron's Pilgrimage

BYRON USED THE TRADITIONAL SPENSERIAN stanza, which he said he picked up from the Scottish poet, James Beattie. Here is a sample from Beattie's *The Minstrel; or, The Progress of Genius*, Book I (1771):

> In truth he was a strange and wayward wight,
> Fond of each gentle and each dreadful scene.
> In darkness and in storm he found delight:
> Nor less, than when on ocean-wave serene
> The southern sun diffused his dazzling sheen.
> Even sad vicissitude amused his soul:
> And if a sight would sometimes intervene,
> And down his cheek a tear of pity roll,
> A sigh, a tear so sweet, he wished not to control.

Here is a sample from Byron's *Childe Harold's Pilgrimage*, Canto III:

> Self-exiled Harold wanders forth again,
> With naught of Hope left – but with less of gloom;
> The very knowledge that he lived in vain,

> That all was over on this side the tomb,
> Had made Despair a smilingness assume,
> Which, though 'twere wild, – as on the plundered wreck
> When mariners would madly meet their doom
> With draughts intemperate on the sinking deck, –
> Did yet inspire a cheer, which he forbore to check.
>
> – *Childe Harold*, III, xvi

Childe Harold's Pilgrimage, though influenced by much of the same melancholy in Wordsworth's poetry, was originally intended by Byron to be full of humour. But it is not very humorous. The style seems not to allow the poet to do what he is really naturally good at. *Don Juan* would later allow him to give full vent to his force as a poet. The achievement of *Childe Harold* is that it gives the sense of travelogue (in which everything ordinary is made to seem extraordinary), and the sense of melancholy:

> There is a very life in our despair,
> Vitality of poison, – a quick root
> Which feeds these deadly branches; for it were
> As nothing did we die; but Life will suit
> Itself to Sorrow's most detested fruit,
> Like to the apples on the Dead Sea's shore,
> All ashes to the taste ...
>
> – *Childe Harold*, III, xxxiv

Duncan Wu's view of Byron's 'obsession with Wordsworth' (Wu, 179) offers a good way of appreciating Byron's ambivalence. For all his professions of opposition to Wordsworth's 'simple' poetry, Byron spent much time immersed in it:

> I live not in myself, but I become
> Portion of that around me; and to me
> High mountains are a feeling, but the hum
> Of human cities torture ...
>
> – *Child Harold*, III, lxxii

One thinks of Wordsworth's 'Lines composed a few miles above Tintern Abbey, on revisiting the banks of the Wye' (1798), in which the colours and the forms of Cumbria's mountainous scenery were recalled by Wordsworth as 'An appetite', whereas he had since found the city 'joyless' and 'unprofitable'.

Byron adds to this the feeling in the reader that the protagonist is interesting and mysterious. When the narrator of *Childe Harold's Pilgrimage* asks 'What deep wounds ever closed without a scar?' (III, lxxxiv) the reader is intrigued by the autobiographical possibilities. After all, a few stanzas earlier, Byron mentioned the first confessional autobiographer (in the modern sense), Jean-Jacques Rousseau,

> The apostle of Affliction, he who threw
> Enchantment over Passion, and from Woe
> Wrung overwhelming eloquence ...
> ... yet he knew
> How to make Madness beautiful ...

– Childe Harold, III, lxxvii

The reader will of course wonder exactly what 'Madness' Byron has made beautiful, and may look in the newspapers for a plainer view. His friend, John Cam Hobhouse, wrote in his dairy: 'the great success of *Childe Harold* is due chiefly to Byron's having dared to give utterance to certain feelings which every one must have encouraged in the melancholy and therefore morbid hours of his existence'. In his dedication to Canto IV, Byron confesses to the reader for the first time that 'there will be found less of the pilgrim than in any of the preceding, and ... little slightly, if at all, separated from the author speaking in his own person. The fact is, that I had become weary of drawing a line which every one seemed determined not to perceive.' So, at Canto IV Byron forfeits the disguise, insouciantly claiming that he prefers to let his readers make of his work – and of him – what they will.

Byron can make readers understand him at once. To read the beginning of Canto IV of *Childe Harold's Pilgrimage* is to view, as it were, the theatre of one's mind being lit up to its lavish potential:

> I stood in Venice, on the 'Bridge of Sighs':
> A palace and a prison on each hand:
> I saw from out the wave her structures rise
> As from the stroke of the Enchanter's wand ...
>
> – *Childe Harold*, IV, i

Byron's imagination unites a diction so well ordered that it lulls the senses, like a transfixing melody. So ingenious, so masterly is the poet's choice of words that none could with justice be robbed of its right to be there. One feels that the poet has opened up a wide perspective that sets one dreaming of its meaning, at once precise and manifold.

But his power to conjure this picture and feeling becomes powerless in the mind of an unresponsive reader. The critic Samuel Rogers (who was also one of the most popular poets of the time) used the above lines as an illustration of Byron's 'carelessness':

> There is a great deal of incorrect and hasty writing in Byron's works; but it is overlooked in this age of hasty readers. For instance,
>
> > I stood in Venice, on the Bridge of Sighs,
> > A palace and a prison *on each hand.*
>
> He meant to say, that on one hand was a palace, on the other a prison ...
>
> – *Recollections of the Table Talk of Samuel Rogers*, 244

In any moments when he experienced the anxieties of the nervous practitioner of poetry, Byron himself would have agreed with Rogers's view (as he did, privately, with Thomas Moore when, having published *The Corsair*, he worried about his 'own want of judgement'). But Byron was nevertheless driven to write the way he did, feeling in his heart that there was something *else* in his writing, something more original, significant and rigorous than the mere readability and textual thinness perceived by unkind critics. With regard to his striving against all doubtings, Lord Byron was as iron in his resolve as cockney Keats. Rogers – like many first-class lovers of the English language (arguably pedants in many cases) – feels something or other painful on reading the beginning of *Childe Harold*, Canto IV, and he feels offended. He professes his concern with the business of words meaning what they mean, and not meaning something else. His point is, if you really understand the English language, Byron's sentence about the palace and the prison is not saying what Byron thinks it is saying, and the sad thing (for Rogers) is that it means to many readers what the writer erroneously thinks it means. (Byron, classically educated, is made out to have a pair of hands unsafe like any little cockney chancer's.) Rogers is foreshadowing the reservations of some of the Victorian critics about Byron's writing. In a letter of 21 September 1869, George Eliot would call Byron 'the most *vulgar-minded* genius that ever produced a great effect in literature' (*George Eliot Letters*, ed. Gordon S. Haight, 1954-5, V, 57). Later still, T.S. Eliot would say that 'The bulk of Byron's verse is distressing in proportion to its quality ... We have come to expect poetry to be something very concentrated, something distilled; but if Byron had distilled his verse, there would have been nothing whatever left.' (*On Poetry and Poets*, 1937) This lack of responsiveness to what is best in Byron has been transmitted so resoundingly (virtually up to this day) that even Rupert

Christiansen has said 'It is no use considering Byron now as a serious poet.' (Christiansen, 198) One thinks of Pope's insight:

> Whoever thinks a faultless piece to see,
> Thinks what ne'er was, nor is, nor e'er shall be ...
> Applause, in spite of trivial faults, is due ...
> Most critics, fond of some subservient art,
> Still make the Whole depend upon a Part ...
>
>   – *An Essay on Criticism*, II

When we read for ourselves the opening lines of *Childe Harold*, Canto IV, we do (of course) know what Byron means to mean. We accept, as elegant symmetry, the presentation in poetry of the palace and the prison. Charmed at the prospect of the poet's continuing to share with us his imaginative riches, we are no more interested in correcting shaky grammar than we are in correcting crumbling Venice.

The poet has read his Gibbon (*The History of the Decline and Fall of the Roman Empire*) –

> The Suabian sued, and now the Austrian reigns –
> An Emperor tramples where an Emperor knelt;
> Kingdoms are shrunk to provinces, and chains
> Clank over sceptred cities ...
>
>   – *Childe Harold*, IV, xii –

and so can exercise a grasp of European history that is extremely persuasive in alliance with his whip-smart elegising. The effect is 'dishevelled', like the re-emergence of a resistance fighter from the smoke and rubble after his latest shootout with the Establishment. Hence, the consistently 'faulty' poetry of the 'flawed angel' (as Grosskurth has called Byron), with, as Walter Scott noticed, its 'solecisms' and 'singularities' (*Quarterly Review*, XIX, 1818); or, as Swinburne would call them, the 'blundering, floundering, lumbering and stumbling stanzas'. One would think the poetry really wasn't up to much.

Influentially, Thomas Carlyle wrote his indictment of Byron's dissatisfaction in *Sartor Resartus* (1833-34), his spiritual autobiography:

> I asked myself: What is this that, ever since earliest years, thou hast been fretting and fuming, and lamenting and self-tormenting, on account of? Say it in a word: it is not because thou art not HAPPY? Because the THOU (sweet gentleman) is not sufficiently honoured, nourished, soft-bedded, and lovingly cared-for? Foolish soul! A little while ago thou hadst no right to *be* at all. What if thou wert born and predestined not to be Happy, but to be Unhappy! Art thou nothing other than a Vulture, then, that fliest through the Universe seeking after somewhat to *eat*; and shrieking dolefully because carrion enough is not given thee? Close thy *Byron*; open thy *Goethe*.

The above passage is surely a record of Carlyle attacking something in himself that Byron's poetry had actually enabled him to identify. Carlyle seems to have seen in Byron's work the too vivid apparition of his own naked sorrows, and wants to flee to the work of Goethe who, although he had invented the suicidal Romantic outsider in his novella, *Die Leiden des Jungen Werthers* (1774), refused afterwards to indulge again the negative emotions that made the writing of that book necessary. Joylessly continuing to exist somehow came to seem preferable to having fun with language and seeing what it can do. Even though Byron has simultaneously very funny and very serious things to say, critics equipped typically to discuss literary theories have tended to have limited (if any) enthusiasm for the individual stylistic exuberance. It seems that the more space taken up in a book or article admiring the poet's artistry, the less space will be left in which to gather the subject up into a hashtagable category.

Byron's poetry's power and refinement still gives off new savours, and new intoxications:

> But unto us she [Venice] hath a spell beyond
> Her name in story, and her long array
> Of mighty shadows, whose dim forms despond
> Above the Dogeless city's vanished sway;
> Ours is a trophy which will not decay
> With the Rialto; Shylock and the Moor,
> And Pierre, can not be swept or worn away –
> The keystones of the Arch! though all were o'er,
> For us repeopled were the solitary shore.
>
> – *Childe Harold*, IV, iv

> ... by these Spirits supplied,
> First exiles, then replaces what we hate;
> Watering the heart whose early flowers have died,
> And with a fresher growth, replenishing the void.
>
> – *Childe Harold*, IV, v

The above lines speak to the reader directly about what Venice means to Byron – and to the reader, who has been made complicit in the poet's sense of wonder (at the shared riches in the mental commonwealth).

Contemporary readers were attuned to Byron's poetry in the same sort of way that devotees of pop and rock music would be attuned to their heroes' utterances. (In the 1960s, dissenting musicologists would not reverse many enthusiasts' passion for the songs of Lennon and McCartney.) There is the feeling in reading Byron's work that one will not have to retrace too many steps taken in pursuit of misunderstood metaphors. All is bright and clear to view – the sights of Venice, and the narrator's vivid sense of that city's history, are dropped into the reader's mind, which seems somehow to share with the poet the higher faculty of an electric aptitude for seizing analogies and passing over like lightning from one topic to another:

> A thousand Years their cloudy wings expand
> Around me, and a dying Glory smiles
> O'er the far times, when many a subject land
> Looked to the winged Lion's marble piles,
> Where Venice sate in state, throned on her hundred isles!
>
> – *Childe Harold*, IV, i

Shelley's poetry is more difficult to understand, and it is no surprise that at the time Shelley's works sold poorly in comparison. Francis Thompson has explained that Shelley 'stood ... at the very junction-lines of the visible and invisible, and could shift the points as he willed', and that 'He could express as he listed the material and the immaterial in terms of each other.' But Shelley's reader has to work to attune himself to the poet's use of imagery, and to adapt himself to the poet's world. In the Preface to *Prometheus Unbound* (1820), Shelley does recognise the difficulty: 'The imagery which I have employed will be found, in many instances, to have been drawn from the operations of the human mind, or from those external actions by which they are expressed. This is unusual in modern poetry, although Dante and Shakespeare are full of instances of the same kind.' In Shelley's vision, imagery and symbolism are closely akin. Throughout his work, the same caves, islands, journeys, moonlight, and starlight recur. They are all associated with the acquisition of wisdom, but the poet does not explain the pattern.

There was no system of poetry, or philosophy, with which readers had to be *au fait* before they could consider themselves able to read Byron. *Childe Harold* can be read, or rather consumed, as passively as an undemanding novel. 'He simply discovered that he could do it, do it fast ... and that people bought the results.'

(Christiansen, 198) He did concede in one stanza of *Childe Harold* that 'The Beings of the Mind are not of clay', and that,

> Essentially immortal, they create
> And multiply in us a brighter ray
> And more beloved existence: that which Fate
> Prohibits to dull life in this our state
> Of mortal bondage ...
>
> — *Childe Harold*, IV, v

But in the next stanza he asserted the even greater luminosity of facts: 'Yet there are things whose strong reality/Outshines our fairy-land' (*Childe Harold*, IV, vi). When he describes 'meek Dian's crest' 'Float[ing] through the azure air – an island of the blest!', he feels the need to include a footnote asserting the veracity of the image: 'The above description may seem fantastical or exaggerated to those who have never seen an Oriental or an Italian sky; yet it is ... literal'. Byron is often keen to maintain his hold on the actual, so in this instance he asserts that he has actually seen what he describes. In that case, how are we to feel when, two stanzas later, he conveys the sense of transition from day to night by describing the various stages of the death of a dolphin?

> ... a paler Shadow strews
> Its mantle o'er the mountains; parting Day
> Dies like the Dolphin, whom each pang imbues
> With a new colour as it gasps away –
> The last still loveliest, till – 'tis gone – and all is gray.
>
> — *Childe Harold*, IV, xxix

Did the poet once stand idly by and watch the final struggle of a washed up dolphin? And, for that matter, did he once watch a horse dying too?

And there lay the steed with his nostril all wide,
But through it there rolled not the breath of his pride;
And the foam of his gasping lay white on the turf,
And cold as the spray of the rock-beating surf.
                    – 'The Destruction of Sennacherib', IV

Such images are intriguing and unsettling.

Unhampered by the exigencies of maintaining a pious reputation, Byron traces the roots of his flourishing moral ambivalences down into the personal darkness that nourishes them. He says, in one stanza, that 'alone ... man with his God must strive' (*Childe Harold*, IV, xxxiii), but in the next stanza he balances his overall view of the heavenly and hellish sources of human creativity:

Or, it may be, with Demons, who impair
The strength of better thoughts, and seek their prey
In melancholy bosoms – such as were
Of moody texture from their earliest day,
And loved to dwell in darkness and dismay,
Deeming themselves predestined to a doom
Which is not of the pangs that pass away;
Making the Sun like blood, the Earth a tomb
The tomb a hell – and Hell itself a murkier gloom.
                    – *Childe Harold*, IV, xxxiv

The Byronic vision was easily translatable, so the poet had a European audience. (The radiance of many Shelleyan metaphors would be dulled in translation.) The common reader could quickly comprehend Byron's poetry, so not only was there a huge difference between Byron's and Keats's readerships; there was also a huge difference between Byron's and (the aristocratic) Shelley's readerships.

In *Nightmare Abbey* Peacock satirised Byron ('Mr Cypress') as the bad husband:

Mr Cypress. – Sir, I have quarrelled with my wife; and a man who has quarrelled with his wife is absolved from all duty to his country. I have written an ode to tell the people as much, and they may take it as they list.

Peacock also satirised Byron as one of England's most prolific encouragers of despair and negativity:

Mr Cypress. – I have no hope for myself or for others. Our life is a false nature; it is not in the harmony of things; it is an all-blasting upas, whose root is earth, and whose leaves are the skies which rain their poison-dews upon mankind. We wither from our youth; we gasp with unslaked thirst for unattainable good; lured from the first to the last by phantoms – love, fame, ambition, avarice – all idle, and all ill – one meteor of many names, that vanishes in the smoke of death.

– Nightmare Abbey, XI

In the above passages, Mr Cypress is about to leave England (as Byron actually did in 1816). Compare the passage with these stanzas from Byron himself:

We wither from our youth, we gasp away –
Sick – sick; unfound the boon – unslaked the thirst,
Though to the last, in verge of our decay,
Some phantom lures, such as we sought at first –
But all too late,– so are we doubly curst.
Love, Fame, Ambition, Avarice – 'tis the same,
Each idle – and all ill – and none the worst –
For all are meteors with a different name,
And Death the sable smoke where vanishes the flame.

– Childe Harold, IV, cxxiv

Our life is a false nature – 'tis not in
The harmony of things, – this hard decree,
This uneradicable taint of Sin,
This boundless upas, this all-blasting tree,

Whose root is Earth – whose leaves and branches be
The skies which rain their plagues on men like dew –
Disease, death, bondage – all the woes we see,
And worse, the woes we see not – which throb through
The immedicable soul, with heart-aches ever new.

> – *Childe Harold*, IV, cxxvi

In Peacock's prose the madness is just madness, and it may be contemplated (like the poet's badness and the dangerousness) safely and with sane amusement by educated and self-esteeming readers. In Byron's verse, however, life has not been lifted out of its unknowable context in which everything is mysteriously connected to everything else. In Byron, the soul is what it is in life: 'immedicable'. In Byron, the core of human hearts is what it is in life: control-less. In Byron, systems of thought are dismissed as boring or false, and at best no better than go-betweens. In Byron, the sincerest laughter with some pain is fraught, and the sweetest songs are those that tell of saddest thought. The madness that flows from Byron's lips is harmonious, as is the madness that flows from Shelley's, and Keats's. The reader should listen then.

12

Keats Reads *King Lear*

WRITING 'ON SITTING DOWN TO READ King Lear Once Again' in January 1818 (before 'Isabella'), Keats signals a marked intensification of the poet's golden raptness that initially took hold of him on first looking into Chapman's Homer. He tells 'Golden-tongued Romance' to take her 'serene lute' away because the sound, however lovely, does not really represent the actual struggles of life. So why invoke her in the first place?

> O Golden-tongued Romance, with serene lute!
>> Fair plumed Syren, Queen of far-away!
>> Leave melodizing on this wintry day,
> Shut up thine olden pages, and be mute:
> Adieu!

This formal dismissal of a key part of one's being has something of the drama of George Herbert's spiritual discontent – and his momentary desire to tear himself away from it – at the beginning of 'The Collar':

> I struck the board, and cry'd, 'No more.

> I will abroad!
> What? shall I ever sigh and pine?
> My lines and life are free; free as the road,
> Loose as the wind, as large as store.'

Like Herbert, one might try to achieve independence, or at least the feeling of independence, by some sort of declaration (followed by some decisive behaviour, or even some emotional violence, to make good that declaration). One is tempted continually to lock oneself up within a new system in order to live there in peace with the world and oneself. Such a peace, however, would only be temporary, and would grant one merely a different kind of damnation which would compel one to renege perpetually. To remain independent it would always be necessary to be devising a new structure, and the exertion entailed would be an exacting penalty. By the end of 'The Collar', having vented some of the pent up frustration of his unrewarded piety, Herbert will again be ready to return to his 'board' and his God. By the end of *King Lear*, having sloughed off his burdensome kingship, and having then felt how sharper than serpents' teeth people can be when no longer officially obliged to respect him, Lear will see again – though, alas, too late – the love he has always shared with Cordelia. Shakespeare knows that Lear's scheme for a new system to cushion him in his dotage is like any ageing person's attempt (in, say, converting to Buddhism) to get rid of the tiresome pileup of baggage (guilt about love not given, time torn off unused, etc.) that seems to constitute too much of his soul. At the time the gesture of good riddance can feel liberating and lightening, but the actual accomplishment of it will lead to misery and madness, because spontaneous, unexpected upshots of life's general vitality – or indeed its relentless entropy – will spill and swell, sooner or later, with a force ruinous to even the most fiercely turreted resolutions. Anyone who has struggled to keep a New Year's resolution knows how fluently temptation can speak the language of rectitude, and with what puritanical airs wantonness will subvert the best intentions. If one attempts to move or extend any of the values informing one's current entrenchment, one will always straggle behind the uncontrollable energy of life, and yet one will never really want to stop pursuing multiform, multicoloured, mysterious beauty as it moves outside one's limits on its own limitless terms. Cordelia's death was so shocking to Dr Johnson that he could not bear to reread *King Lear* for years. But what Shakespeare had taught could not be unlearned, regardless of how long it took any reader, Johnson included, to steel himself for another wintry blast of the essential truth that is unwelcome in the false paradise of most literary culture.

Sentenced interminably to the mortification of a new transition, one might take a radically different decision: to avoid the unpleasantness of philosophical apostasies, one might proudly resign oneself to diffidence, and become more at ease with dreaming, and feeling, rather than attempting again in vain to think things through thoroughly – that is, one might look for sanctuary in unimpeachable naivety. Such a (vain) yearning for simplicity can be found in Anna Laetitia Waring's hymn, 'Father, I know that all my life' (1850):

> I would not have the restless will
>   That hurries to and fro
> Searching for some great things to do
>   Or secret thing to know
> I would be treated as a child
>   And guided where to go.
>
> – *Hymns and Meditations*

This is how many people think they would settle and put their scruples to rest. But they cannot. Many know only too well that ambition in many individuals is often accompanied by the capacity to hate or hurt members of their own families. There are Gonerils and Regans everywhere. And people tend to know – as Blake did when he wrote 'Jerusalem' – that if one does not have one's own system, one will be enslaved by someone else's. Even a so-called Fool can tell a king why a snail has a house: 'Why, to put's head in; not to give it away to his daughters, and leave his horns without a case.' (*King Lear*, I, 5, 26) Ignorance, or wilful ignorance, of what Keats called 'the agonies, the strife/Of human hearts' (*Sleep and Poetry*, 124-5) will not save you from your own agonies, and the fierily restless mind (let alone any central force beneath that), as Byron knows, will not be 'snuffed out' by a skin-deep system of sanity or commonsense. By rereading *King Lear*, and thence involving himself in the 'fierce dispute/Betwixt damnation and impassion'd clay', Keats is being, in a sense, ceremonial, and offering himself up to the 'Begetters of our deep eternal theme'. Strangely, he is taking a break from revising his problematically Romantic *Endymion* when he is interrupted, so to speak, by an urgent messenger (the author of *King Lear*) arrived as if out of the dark, and he is freshened and darkened, and will think and write differently. The delivery from the dark includes Lear's terrible words: 'my poor fool is hanged!' (*King Lear*, V, 3, 305) The inescapable meaning of these words is that it is Cordelia, not the 'Fool', who has been hanged. Why does Shakespeare have Lear refer to his most loving, but now tragically dead, daughter as a fool? It may be something to do with the dementia, or lexical loosening, as one slips into the dark (Lear dies just 16 lines later). Or, as Edgar puts it almost at the very end of the play, 'The weight of this sad time we must obey;/Speak what we feel, not what we ought to say.' (*King Lear*,V, 3, 323-4)

Keats feels that in too much of *Endymion* he has been saying what he thought he ought to say. He himself, at his worst, has been speaking from behind his (not always convincing) mask of poetic decorum. *King Lear* teaches him that he cannot really escape the most terrible energies of life simply by dilating the sphere of Romance and disappearing into it. Lear's request to his imaginary apothecary for civet to sweeten his state of mind (*King Lear* IV, 6,129) is made by a desperate man on the run from bitter clarity. In his earlier poem, 'Fill for me a Brimming Bowl', Keats had already begun to shine some light on what he himself was running from, but he was still (like most people) habitually tempted to relieve himself of the pressures of present anxieties with his ad hoc asceticism. He well knew that his improvised approach was not relevant enough to the complexity of the challenges, and he knew that it would simply, and therefore only temporarily, *seem* to be his shield against life's thousand shocks. The ache for female company, for example, was to Keats, in certain moods, such a distressingly enslaving sensation that it brought about in him the equally tumescent urge to rid himself of it entirely, as Odysseus had himself tied to his ship's mast in order to stop himself from abandoning the ship in pursuit of the sirens at the sound of their ravishing voices:

> Fill for me a brimming bowl
> And let me in it drown my soul:
> But put therein some drug, designed
> To banish Woman from my mind:
> For I want not the stream inspiring
> That heats the sense with lewd desiring;
> But I want as deep a draught
> As e'er from Lethe's waves was quaft ...
>
>   – 'Fill for me a Brimming Bowl', 1-9

In one mood, having impetuously wanted to burn off the sexual impulse once and for all, there is now, in another mood, a part of Keats that wants to burn *Endymion*. He wants rid of it because he recognises it as something that he really should have left behind long ago if he is to become the sort of poet he most wants to be. But as Motion points out, 'He had invested too much in it, too publicly, and he had been advanced money he could not afford to return. He gritted his teeth and pressed on ... ' (Motion, 223).

The writing of *Endymion* brought Keats to a fascinating point in his poetic development, like the draughty and uncomfortable predicament of a new life half in and half out of the womb. Or, to put it another way, he was inspirited by new hopes, yet he was still situated amidst the smouldering ruins of former hopes. His desire for purification and transcendence was violent. On being touched by the sparks from *King Lear*, Keats knew what must become of his own build-up of literary brushwood – and he longed to be 'cooked', or transmuted, in the very flames raised so magically by the bard of Avon (and shirked so instinctively by the moralist and lexicographer from Lichfield). If it was through Chapman that the first glow of lasting consequence got into Keats's work, it was through Shakespeare that the powerful refining flame with which he would ultimately transform himself was now issuing.

13

Incendiary Shelley

*T*HE REVOLT OF ISLAM, 1818 (ORIGINALLY *Laon and Cythna*, 1817), would have nothing to do with Islam but much to do with 'kindling within the bosoms of my readers a virtuous enthusiasm for ... liberty and justice,' as Shelley says in the poem's Preface. His skylark 'never wert' a bird – indeed, 'What thou [the skylark] art we know not' – but it has about it the attributes of a bearer of news just arrived into the temporal world as an emissary of the great mystery. Shelley's bird, like Keats's, is located on a frontier between outward impressions and inward legibility. Only in the rarefied air of such a frontier is the poet enabled to raise the flame that will weld the waking and the dreaming mind; and so it is with something of the skylark's harmonious madness that the poet sings of what he has seen in the heart of a very human need. Having seen it he feels even more strongly the need to be at a distance from the ideological dialectic of materialism:

> 'The iron rod of penury still compels
> Her wretched slave to bow the knee to wealth,

And poison, with unprofitable toil,
A life too void of solace to confirm
The very chains that bind him to his doom ...

– *Queen Mab*, V, 127-31

His hatred of the machismo that causes war is justly and solidly present, both in the main text of *Queen Mab* itself and in his own notes to the poem. In the notes, war's wrongness seems all the more far-reachingly wrong in the context of the great mystery of the cosmos:

That which appears only like a thin and silvery cloud streaking the heaven is in effect composed of innumerable clusters of suns, each shining with its own light and illuminating numbers of planets that revolve around them. Millions and millions of suns are ranged around us, all attended by innumerable worlds ...

To employ murder as a means of justice is an idea which a man of an enlightened mind will not dwell upon with pleasure. To march forth in rank and file, and all the pomp of streamers and trumpets, for the purpose of shooting at our fellowmen ... to inflict upon them all the variety of wound and anguish; to leave them weltering in their blood; to wander over the field of desolation, and count the number of the dying and the dead, – are employments which in thesis we may maintain to be necessary, but which no good man will contemplate with gratulation and delight.

To this day, such powerful views are habitually regarded as 'simplistic' by producers and consumers of media in warlike nations. *Queen Mab* has been babbled into being as poetry that any competent reactionary could write off as political baby talk:

'War is the statesman's game, the priest's delight,
The lawyer's jest, the hired assassin's trade,
And to those royal murderers whose mean thrones
Are bought by crimes of treachery and gore,
The bread they eat, the staff on which they lean.

– *Queen Mab*, IV, 168-72

One decidedly competent reactionary critic, Paul Johnson, has said that from Shelley's teens, his

> approach to politics was coloured both by his taste for secret societies and by the conspiracy theory of history preached by the Abbé [Barruel, author of *Memoirs Illustrating the History of Jacobitism* (1797-98), which had put the blame for society's ills at the feet of the Illuminati, the Masons, the Rosicrucians and the Jews] and his kind. He could never shake it off, and it effectively prevented him from understanding British politics or the motives and policies of men like Liverpool and Castlereagh, whom he saw merely as embodied evil. (Johnson, 32)

Johnson makes the arresting point that 'some of Shelley's acquaintances [including Peacock] never saw his politics as anything more than a literary joke, a mere projection into real life of Gothic romance.' But Johnson has absorbed from Holmes's 'superb' (Johnson, ix) biography the insights of pathology, and remained impervious to Shelley's Platonism. Johnson has learned from Holmes that Shelley's fantasies sometimes 'came near to hallucinations' (Holmes, 113), and that

> The outlet for his [Shelley's] own tension, found in the tendency to terrorize his feminine companions, has been noted from his earliest childhood. The themes of ghosts and hauntings were endemic to his poetry, providing a powerful source of private imagery, which reflected his alienation from the society around him. Moreover, the imaginative investigation of these abnormal states in himself and in others, conducted almost in the spirit of the psychologist, had a permanent fascination for him ... (Holmes, 114).

The fact that Plato is not mentioned once in Johnson's essay is an excellent little illustration of the ubiquity of Psychology and Psychiatry, and the dearth of Philosophy and Poetry, in twentieth-century literary studies. Already diminished by the time the

Romantics were writing (or why would they have written with such vehemence?), philosophy and poetry have since been diminished even more, to the point that

> Like a star of Heaven
>   In the broad daylight
> Th[ey] ar[e] unseen
>
> – 'To A Skylark', 18-20

The visionary poet can remain attuned to the least possibility of the miraculous, even amidst the general lack of interest in such a frequency. For him, the skylark is only *temporarily* out of sight until it comes down again near enough for him to see it. The 'star of Heaven' is only *temporarily* undetectable by his eye until the paradoxically illuminating fall of night. The real riches in poetry can only be *temporarily* obscured by daylight priorities, such as a general commitment to utility, or a general concern about propriety, or Oxbridge left-ism, or whatever other mode of discourse happens to be mushrooming in the space between the poets and the world that should be listening to them.

'Circumstances meant so little to him,' as Arthur Symons has said, 'that he was unconscious of the cruelty of change of sentiment, and thus of the extent of his cruelty to women. He aimed at moral perfection, but was really of a perfect aesthetic selfishness.' (Peck, I, 371) Undoubtedly, Shelley the man was driven by the urges that stir any male with such remorseless triviality. The suicide in 1816 of his first wife, Harriet Shelley (née Westbrook) and his marriage that December to Mary Wollstonecraft Godwin suggest that Shelley's sorrow as a widower was not as strong enough to kill off his sexual desire. However, one thing might be of prevailing importance to those readers who don't need visionary poets to be nice people: Shelley was motivated in his writing by what is finest and noblest in humanity. 'Our most imperial and stupendous qualities,' he says,

> – those on which the majesty and power of humanity is erected – are, relatively to the inferior portion of its mechanism, active and imperial; but they are the passive slaves of some higher and more omnipotent Power. This Power is God; and those who have seen God have, in the period of their purer and more perfect nature, been harmonized by their own will to so exquisite a consentaneity of power as to give forth divinest melody, when the breath of universal being sweeps over their frame.
>
> – 'Essay on Christianity'

Protesting that Shelley 'has never had fair play', a reviewer in the *Paris Monthly Review* claimed that 'His pen, when it was directed against his revilers, seemed to be guided by the hand of Love, and acrimonious expressions rarely fell from his lips.' The point is a fair one, in that Shelley's love of Athenian democracy does, with maturity, outshine his hatred of the corruption of contemporary British life:

> But Greece and her foundations are
> Built below the tide of war,
> Based on the crystàlline sea
> Of thought and its eternity;
> Her citizens, imperial spirits,
> Rule the present from the past;
> On all this world of men inherits
> Their seal is set.
>
> – *Hellas*, 696-703

The idea expressed in the lines above, from *Hellas* (1821), is that the premise of a superior civilization is like an eternal rock 'below' the shallower flux and reflux of conflict. It should not be very surprising, then, that by the time he wrote *Hellas*, Shelley had moved away from Britain – bounded as she was by her choppy seas and governed as she was by her churchmanly falsifiers of experience – to the brightness of the Mediterranean. 'I now understand,' he told Peacock in January 1819,

> why the Greeks were such great Poets, & above all I can account, it seems to me, for the harmony the unity the perfection the uniform excellence of all their works of art. They lived in a perpetual commerce with external nature and nourished themselves upon the spirit of its forms. Their theatres were all open to the mountains & the sky.
>
> – *Letters*, II, 74

He found clarity in his isolation which, after all, brought him intimacy with places he hallowed more than Britain:

> Their [the ancient Greeks'] temples were mostly upaithric [in the open air]; & the flying clouds the stars or the deep sky were seen above. O, but for that series of wretched wars which terminated in the Roman conquest of the world, but for the Christian religion which put a finishing stroke to the ancient system; but for those changes which conducted Athens to its ruin, to what an eminence might not humanity have arrived!
>
> – *Letters*, II, 74-5

There is the suggestion in this letter that as a result of his mind-expanding reading and travel, Shelley has discovered a possible cause of the British narrowness and tyranny he detests so much: it is the remote yet inevitable outcome of roofs having been put over theatres and places of worship. This looks like mere whimsy on Shelley's part. His belief seems to be that roofs on certain buildings block 'the deep sky' and other manifestations of divinity from people's notice, and therefore from their habits of thinking. (Again, Byron was more streetwise and witty than Shelley when it came to smuggling seriousness through his fellow-countrymen's customs checks.) Shelley is one of those thinkers out of whose stockpile of allegedly silly sayings one could compile an anthology, for the chain book stores, with their outlets in thousands of glittering malls. These allegedly silly sayings, however, have their roots and contexts, serious investigations of which tend not to be found in anthologies. The idiosyncrasy, fascination, and naivety of Shelley's suggestion about roofs is characteristic of his life's work in setting up an alternative world-view and way of life. In his essay, *A Vindication of Natural Diet* (1812), he claimed that if Parisians in the early 1790s had been vegetarians, there would have been no Terror. If this idea too is, in the end, part of a grandiloquent fantasy, it also has a tincture of humanity, and even of the tragic sense that must go together with the Romantic ideal. Is s/he not a hardhearted and ignorant reader who will dismiss the idea without wandering with it, musing upon it, reflecting from it, bringing home to it, prophesying upon it, and dreaming upon it?

Away from Britain, Shelley finds more mental space and strength to be who he really is, and express what he really thinks. 'I think I have an accession of strength since my residence in Italy,' (*Letters*, II, 153) he told Hunt in November 1819. The parallel worlds – Britishness and Shelley's alternative – could not have inhabited the same space and time on speaking terms. The following extract is from an anonymous attack on *The Revolt of Islam* in the *Quarterly* (April 1819), at the time the most popular and influential review in Britain:

> Mr Shelley would abrogate our laws – this would put an end to felonies and misdemenours at a blow; he would abolish the rights of property, of course there could thenceforward be no violation of them ... he would overthrow the constitution, and then we should have no expensive court, no pensions or sinecures ... no army or navy; he would pull down our churches, level our Establishment,

and burn our bibles ... marriage he cannot endure, and there would at once be a stop put to the lamented increase of adulterous connections amongst us, whilst repealing the cannon of heaven against incest, he would add to the purity and heighten the ardour of those feelings with which brother and sister now regard each other; finally, as the basis of the whole scheme, he would have us renounce our belief in our religion ... (Holmes, 544).

The *Quarterly* consistently and authoritatively expressed the British reactionary spirit, and John Taylor Coleridge (the author of the review) saw it as his duty to recognise evil and fight it with deadly seriousness (rather than allow readers to think Shelley's badness and madness were honourable enough to be dissolved in merely urbane acidity):

Like the Egyptian of old, the wheels of his chariot are broken, the path of mighty waters closes in upon him behind, and a still deepening ocean is before him: – for a short time are seen his impotent struggles against a resistless power, his blasphemous execrations are heard, his despair but poorly assumes the tone of triumph and defiance, and he calls ineffectually to others to follow him to the same ruin – finally, he sinks 'like lead' to the bottom, and is forgotten. So it is now in part, so shortly will it be entirely with Mr Shelley. (Holmes, 544-5)

The hint of Shelley as an albatross around the neck of a nation that will slough him off ('like lead') into the sea looks remarkably prescient.

Southey would link Shelley with Byron as part of the so-called Satanic school of poets:

Men of diseased hearts and depraved imaginations, who, forming a system of opinions to suit their own unhappy course of conduct, have rebelled against the holiest ordinances of human society, and hating that revealed religion which, with all their efforts and bravadoes, they are unable entirely to disbelieve, labour to make others as miserable as themselves, by infecting men with a moral virus that eats into the soul! The school which they have set up may properly be called the Satanic school ...

— Preface, *A Vision of Judgement*

It seems that Shelley's 'atheism' hung around him like a dreadful aura, and as the brittle and pernickety reading-public flipped through its weekly papers, it would learn to despise, fear or simply ignore the poet. Mrs Elizabeth Grant's account of Shelley at Eton and Oxford has the reasonableness (or the mechanical incredulity) instilled in people by conventional educators:

> The ringleader in every species of mischief within our grave walls was Mr Shelley, afterwards so celebrated, though I should think to the end half-crazy. He began his career by every kind of wild prank at Eton, and when kindly remonstrated with by his tutor, repaid the well-meant private admonition by spilling an acid over the carpet of the gentleman's study, a new purchase, which he thus completely destroyed. He did no deed so mischievous at University, but he was very insubordinate, always infringing some rule, the breaking of which he knew could not be overlooked. He was slovenly in his dress, and when spoken to about these and other irregularities, he was in the habit of making such extraordinary gestures, expressive of his humility under reproof, as to overset first the gravity, and then the temper, of the lecturing tutor. Of course these scenes reached unpleasant lengths, and when he proceeded so far as to paste up atheistical squibs on the chapel doors, it was considered necessary to expel him ... (Peck, I, 107).

Mrs Grant's account says very little about what Shelley thought or wrote.

In his essay. 'On Paradox and Commonplace', Hazlitt wished to show how immature (if not dangerous) Shelley was:

> It would seem that [Shelley] wanted not so much to convince or inform, as to shock the public by the tenor of his productions, but

I suspect he is more intent upon startling himself with his electrical experiments in morals and philosophy; and though they may scorch other people, they are to him harmless amusements, the coruscations of an Aurora Borealis, that play around the head, but do not reach the heart! Still I could wish he would put a stop to the incessant, alarming whirl of his Voltaic battery.

– Table Talk: Essays on Men and Manners, 1822

Despite all the attacks from the left, right and centre, the poet continued producing 'hymns unbidden'.

On 8 July 1822, he would meet death (seemingly foretold by J.T. Coleridge in the *Quarterly* three years earlier) by drowning in his sailboat, the *Don Juan* (named after Byron's poem), during a storm off the Bay of Leghorn. Oddly, it looks as if he himself had also anticipated the event in his poem, *Alastor:*

> The boat fled on, – the boiling torrent drove, –
> The crags closed round with black and jaggèd arms,
> The shattered mountain overhung the sea,
> And faster still, beyond all human speed,
> Suspended on the sweep of the smooth wave,
> The little boat was driven. A cavern there
> Yawned, and amid its slant and winding depths
> Ingulfed the rushing sea. The boat fled on
> With unrelaxing speed. – 'Vision and Love!'
> The Poet cried aloud, 'I have beheld
> The path of thy departure. Sleep and death
> Shall not divide us long!'

– Alastor, 358-69

According to Edward Trelawny, Shelley – curious and restless as he was – effectively ransacked heaps of books in pursuit of life's meaning, 'his eyes glistening with an energy as fierce as that of the most sordid gold-digger who works at a rock of quartz, crushing his way through all impediments, no grain of the pure ore escaping his eager scrutiny.' (Peck, I, 77) Perhaps the impatience culminated, in the end, in a sort of clumsy experiment – a question that Shelley put to Nature, trying to force her to 'render up the tale/Of what we are.' (*Alastor*, 28-9) Shelley's final experiment – if that is what it was – involved the destruction of the very consciousness putting the question and awaiting the answer. Again, this puts one in mind of Hamlet, who is prepared to follow, and speak with, the ghost 'though hell itself should gape/ And bid me hold my peace.' (*Hamlet*, I, ii) And again, it puts one in mind of Frankenstein, determined 'to procrastinate all that related to my feelings of affection until the great object, which swallowed up every habit of my nature, should be completed.' Or (to recognise an equivalent to Shelley in the literature of antiquity he knew so well) it puts one in mind of Sophocles's Oedipus who, determined to find out his fate, pursued his enquiry, even when he knew that something appalling awaited him in the answer. Shelley did not give way to the Jocasta in the heart that the rest of us give way to. How fitting, then, that Shelley is said to have had a copy of Sophocles in his pocket when he died. (Wu, 179)

Yes, he did attack, say, in *Queen Mab*, 'the slavish priest [who]/ Sets no great value on his hireling faith' (*Queen Mab*, V, 198-9). Yes, he did produce some discardable polemics on the subject of organised religion: 'How ludicrous the priest's dogmatic roar!' (*Queen Mab*, VI, 64). But even during the hangover occasioned by the surfeit of Gothic fiction, his ability to lay bare the perniciousness of the opinion-mongers of his day is sobering, and uplifting:

> The weight of his [the priest's] exterminating curse
> How light! and his affected charity,
> To suit the pressure of the changing times,
> What palpable deceit!
>
> – *Queen Mab*, VI, 65-8

The dispenser of the 'exterminating curse', affecting 'charity', is

'the priest' in Shelley's era, but it could just as easily be a hireling
reviewer, journalist or politician of any era since.

Shelley's life was short, but he finessed his spiritual orientation
at such a rate that by his late twenties he was 'defeat[ing] the
curse which binds us to be subjected to the accident of surrounding
impressions'. He most valued the supernal elevation with which
Platonic writers such as Dante and Shakespeare could see
humanity's animal instincts at work *and* the divine context in
which humanity has its place. Privileged by the parallax, he saw
things differently from his critics:

> Thou [Heaven] art but the mind's first chamber,
> Round which its young fancies clamber,
>   Like weak insects in a cave,
> Lighted up by stalactites;
>   But the portal of the grave,
> Where a world of new delights
>   Will make thy best glories seem
>   But a dim and noonday gleam
>   From the shadow of a dream!
>
> – 'Ode to Heaven' (1819)

The charge of otherworldliness has been levelled at the poet,
but it is this world that the reader can revisit and reconsider
through his writings because he (like Byron and Keats in their
own ways) actually dared to share his different view of this world.
Since that fateful time at Oxford when he lit a blue touch paper,
he rapidly matured past the conflagration, and wrote a Revolution
not as doctrine but 'In the depths of the dawn' (*Prometheus
Unbound*, IV, 4). With poetic sensitivity like heliotropism, he
releases the sensation of a new beginning to the roots of posterity.
He liberates readers with the feeling of hope, and with the further
feeling that it is right to hope. Through Shelley, one learns of a
sunrise that has to be believed to be seen.

14

Byron Orientalising

Stick to the East; – the oracle, Staël, told me it was the only poetical policy. The North, South and West, have all been exhausted; but from the East, we have nothing but Southey's unsaleables ... the public are orientalising. (Christiansen, 195)

BYRON TOOK MADAME DE STAËL'S ADVICE. *The Giaour: A Fragment of a Turkish Tale* (1813) was his first Oriental tale, and it was even more popular than *Childe Harold.* It is a long narrative poem that, as Byron stated in the Advertisement, was presented in 'disjointed fragments'. His memories of his travels were importunate in him. They needed to be articulated. Byron told Thomas Moore in 1821 that 'if I don't write to empty my mind, I go mad ... I feel it as a torture, which I must get rid of, but never as a pleasure' (*Letters and Journals*, VIII, 55). Caroline Franklin notes that 'The first MS draft had been 406 lines and the first published edition 685, but by the seventh the poem had swelled to 1334 lines.' (Franklin, 51) Byron told Murray that *The Giaour* was 'a snake of a poem' and said that it had been 'lengthening its rattles every month' (*Letters and Journals*, III, 100). One might think of the poet, turbaned, charming the ever-lengthening 'snake' from its basket, white minarets and mosque glittering in the background; or one might think of the poet in agony, in the throes of delivering something unaccountably long and reptilian.

Byron claimed that poetry 'won't come when called'. Such a claim suggests that poetry is a form of life, and that it does its own thing with or without the poet's leave: it will spread its wings (or lengthen its rattles) in a frightening way, or it will remain curled in the basket indefinitely, so that one would come to believe that it is not there at all. And still, Byron feels that it *is* there, and he feels that there is no frustration quite the equal of intuiting a coherence that refuses to emerge into the full daylight of objectifying comprehension. Byron's view on the subject of the poet's relationship to the muse has been influential: 'I have thought over most of my subjects for years before writing a line ... You might as well ask me to describe an earth-quake whilst the ground was trembling under my feet.' (Edward John Trelawny, *Records of Shelley, Byron and the Author*, 221) Coleridge would preface 'Kubla Khan' with the claim that the images of the poem 'rose up before him as *things* ... without any sensation or consciousness of effort.' How interesting it is, then, that Coleridge published 'Kubla Khan' in 1816 – that is, three years after the publication of *The Giaour* – with Byron's encouragement, and through Byron's publisher.

The story of *The Giaour* is based on a real event from Byron's travels in Turkey. He is supposed to have rescued at gunpoint a Turkish woman sewn up in a sack and about to be drowned by the Turks for adultery. Fiona MacCarthy does not let it escape her notice that there are two versions of the story. In the other version, the woman was already dead in the sack. (MacCarthy,

132) At any rate, the story of *The Giaour* involves the adventure of Leila, a female slave who is freed from the harem of the Turkish warrior, Hassan, by her lover, a young Venetian known as the Giaour. Recaptured, Leila is thrown into the sea for infidelity. She is avenged by her lover.

The multiplicity of different narrative viewpoints in *The Giaour* has perplexed and divided academics. The poet's method seems messy. Did he mean to leave a problematic piece of work (in the same way that James Joyce would knowingly leave *Finnegans Wake*), or was it beyond (or beneath) him to make the necessary corrections and revisions? Franklin sees something playful in Byron's approach:

> Some critics have assumed this method of composition to be the slipshod practice of a dilettante, too lazy to ensure coherence and unity. But it was rather that the poet was aiming at a daring experiment in abandoning his original straightforward plot. He was testing readers' reactions in assessing how far he could go in breaking down narrative into evocative fragments narrated from differing points of view for the reader to piece together. (Franklin, 51)

It may well be the case that the poet was experimenting with increasingly wanton narrative dislocation. Or it may be that he was 'too lazy to ensure coherence and unity.' (A reader might, after all, see the lacunae in Shelley's notebook poetry as evidence of the poet's laziness.)

The Giaour is like a box from which, when opened, Arabia breathes:

> And if at times a transient breeze
> Break the blue crystal of the seas,
> Or sweep one blossom from the trees,
> How welcome is each gentle air
> That wakes and wafts the odours there!
>
> – *The Giaour*, 16-20

The melancholic Byron appeals to an audience amongst which there are many women. He appeals to anyone, in fact, with a penchant for sensual reading experiences:

> And grateful yields that smiling sky
> Her fairest hue and fragrant sigh.
> And many a summer flower is there,
> And many a shade that Love might share,
> And many a grotto, meant for rest,
> That holds the pirate for a guest;
> Whose bark in sheltering cove below
> Lurks for the passing peaceful prow,
> 'Till the gay mariner's guitar
> Is heard, and seen the Evening Star;
> Then stealing with the muffled oar,
> Far shaded by the rocky shore ...
>
> – *The Giaour*, 32-43

Byron's Giaour moves through the exotic scenery:

> Why looks he o'er the olive wood?
> The Crescent glimmers on the hill,
> The Mosque's high lamps are quivering still ...
>
> – *The Giaour*, 221-223

Giaour is an Arabic term of contempt and reproach used in the Ottoman Empire for non-Muslims, especially Christians. Byron's Giaour is a citizen of no country, a believer in no god, and a servant of no king. In other words, the Giaour is Byron in a parallel dimension. The exotic scenery is not necessarily the Giaour's provenance, but it is certainly Hassan's:

> 'Twas sweet of yore to see it [the stream] play
> And chase the sultriness of day,
> As springing high the silver dew
> In whirls fantastically flew,
> And flung luxurious coolness round

The air, and verdure o'er the ground.
'Twas sweet, when cloudless stars were bright,
To view the wave of watery light,
And hear its melody by night.
And oft had Hassan's childhood played
Around the verge of that cascade;
And oft upon his mother's breast
That sound had harmonized his rest;
And oft had Hassan's Youth along
Its bank been soothed by Beauty's song ...

– *The Giaour*, 299-313

A little later in the poem the reader is shown the razor-thin bridge leading to the Muslim paradise:

Though on Al-Sirat's arch I stood,
Which totters o'er the fiery flood,
With Paradise within my view,
And all his Houris beckoning through ...

– *The Giaour*, 483-486

There is an overflow of non-Christian images and concepts. The poet does not feel obliged to intervene as an Englishman, though, and he has no interest in commenting critically on behalf of his Christian readership. He has simply packed the casket with eastern treasures for western readers to unlock for themselves and make of them what they will. Other contemporary writers were more eager to flatter English readers as members of the superior race, and believers in the one, true God. At the core of De Quincey's *Confessions of an English Opium-Eater*, for example, there is a visceral hatred of all things eastern, and the *English* opium-eater is keen to distance himself from his Oriental counterparts. De Quincey demonstrates his fear of becoming an Oriental (in taking opium), and of not doing any work at all. His opium-eater becomes an image for an alternative way of life that threatens nineteenth-century industrial European capitalism, so he ameliorates that threat by peppering his writing with references to the virtues of achievement, productivity and not wasting one's opportunities in life. De Quincey was very much of his time in that he carefully informed his readers that the consumption of opium in a British, Christian (as opposed to an eastern, god-forsaken) spirit was possible. Byron panders to no such prejudice because, as Bertrand Russell put it, 'he felt himself the equal of Satan' (Russell, 718). More cuttingly than De Quincey, Byron reaffirms Johnson's view of the vanity of human wishes ('from China to Peru').

The Giaour's alienation and his dark secret bring him by degrees to his death; but so too do his better qualities (a peculiarly Byronic caveat). In short, whatever combination of good and/or bad qualities one has, one will, with the very frictions of those qualities, reduce oneself to death, and then to dust, at the standard rate. As Robert Gleckner has put it, 'Man's violence ultimately produces his own defeat or decay, but what is more important is that man's virtues – courage, pride, love, loyalty – also lead him to destruction ... And it is this 'immutable law' which Byron seeks to dramatize for the first time in *The Giaour*. In finding expression for the "immutable law", he placed himself in a region of resplendent remoteness. The political concerns expressed by other writers could look dull and feel stiflingly familiar by comparison. The reader may attempt to trace Byron's predecessors, finding here and there recollections of Shakespeare, Milton, Pope or Congreve, but in the main the effect produced by those masters on Byron is insufficient to explain his achievement. He was the follower of no man. His work is the product of pain, and it is haunted by human love and human vices. One cannot but suspect that his work is also informed by abominations committed without enthusiasm, and without hope, and that the Hell now burning within him and all around him, and tempting him to self-destruct, is one of his own making:

> The Mind, that broods o'er guilty woes,
> Is like the Scorpion girt by fire;
> In circle narrowing as it glows,
> The flames around their captive close,
> Till inly searched by thousand throes,
> And maddening in her ire,
> One sad and sole relief she knows –
> The sting she nourished for her foes,
> Whose venom never yet was in vain,
> Gives but one pang, and cures all pain,
> And darts into her desperate brain:
> So do the dark in soul expire,
> Or live like Scorpion girt by fire;
> So writhes the mind Remorse hath riven,
> Unfit for earth, undoomed for heaven,
> Darkness above, despair beneath,
> Around it flame, within it death!
>
> – *The Giaour*, 422-438

Yet 'Byron's romanticism ... was only half sincere ... [and] The world insisted on simplifying him, and omitting the element of pose in his cosmic despair' (Russell, 721). The looseness of style promotes in the reader a more voracious openness to the flow of inexact rhymes ('beneath' and 'death') and repeated phrases ('Scorpion girt by fire'), and it all blends into something like an incantation. There breathes from the above passage a strange magic, a stir of echoes of interest to any reader ever troubled personally by guilt and regret.

As the Giaour makes his confession to the Friar, before dying of his wounds, there is an image of remorse which will have a reverberating impact upon such later writers as Baudelaire and Edgar Allan Poe:

> It is as if the dead could feel
> The icy worm around them steal,
> And shudder, as the reptiles creep
> To revel o'er their rotting sleep,
> Without the power to scare away
> The cold consumers of their clay!
>
>   – *The Giaour*, 945-950

The vision is cerebral, disturbed and gorgeous. Whereas in Johnson's world one could

> Fall in the gen'ral massacre of gold;
> Wide-wasting pest! that rages unconfined,
> And crowds with crimes the records of mankind
>   – 'The Vanity of Human Wishes'

in Byron's universe all energies seem to gravitate one towards the personalised charnel-house:

> Dark as to thee my deeds may seem:
> My memory now is but the tomb
> Of joys long dead
>
>   – *The Giaour*, 999-1001

In Byron's view, one could find oneself in a powerless position, forced to 'bear a life of lingering woes' (*The Giaour*, 1003), and 'to sustain/The searching throes of ceaseless pain' (*The Giaour*, 1005) precisely because, as there is no structure of things, one's mind will spin a structure for itself, with or without one's leave. Poetry will not come when called, and guilt will not go when shooed. The plates of the Italian engraver, Piranesi, showed surreal representations of vast classical dungeons, with endlessly labyrinthine combinations of staircases. De Quincey would famously compare the visions of Piranesi with the twistings and turnings performed again and again by his own troubled (and opium-vivified) conscience: 'With the same power of endless growth and self-reproduction did my architecture proceed in dreams'. But De Quincey was a Christian (albeit an eccentric one), with the moral duty to inform his readers that, although taking opium can be fun initially, the repercussions are so awful that it is not worth the candle. In contrast to that, when Byron's lucubration brings him, and his readers, within the pull of Hell or some other black hole, he has no Christian duty to prejudice and redirect that lucubration. Half horrified, half exhilarated, the reader is carried along (and sometimes dropped) by the poet, enchanted and repelled by the narrative concoction of fun and cruelty. Everything – the self, poetry, politics, the world, the universe – is disputable. Byron's poetry is often like a facetious illustration of the philosopher David Hume's theory, that the self is no more than 'a bundle or collection of different perspectives, which ... are in perpetual flux and movement' (*A Treatise of Human Nature*, Book II, Part IV, Section vi).

In Byron's view, there is no pattern out there to which we must adapt ourselves. We are, insofar as we know, alone in the universe, and therefore we must *make do*. When people perceive the universe to be godless, they tend to feel themselves subjected to unendurable agonies. Better to give a god full authority to sweep away all scorpion-venom and other pollutants. This is why people decide to allow a Christian, Kantian, Wordsworthian or other way of thinking into their lives. Byron rejects such prescriptions. In *Beppo* (1818), he flaunts the idea that he is making it up as he goes along:

> I've half a mind to tumble down to prose,
> But verse is more in fashion – so here goes!
>
> – *Beppo*, LII

There is only self-creativity and then death. It is better to imagine the universe not as a set of facts, nor a collection of lumps in space, nor three-dimensional entities bound together by certain unbreakable relations as taught by physics, chemistry or other natural sciences. The universe is a process which Byron thinks of as hostile to humans. If one tries to trick it, or organise it, or feel at home in it, or make some kind of comfortable pattern in which one can rest, the process will always overthrow one's efforts, and any noble notion about honour, or any desire to be awarded laurels, will hardly matter:

> I've braved [danger] – not for Honour's boast;
> I smile at laurels won or lost;
> To such let others carve their way,
> For high renown, or hireling pay ...
>
> – *The Giaour*, 1012-1015

All generalisations about the universe, all patterns put upon it, are forms of distortion. Politics offers rigorous generalisations of, to Byron, an external and empty kind. Love, not politics, was the force that motivated the Giaour to kill Hassan. (Remember the love that made Isabella put the head in the pot-plant.) The Giaour/Byron represents a depth, an elsewhere, unanswerable by schooled thinking. 'God' and 'Alla' provide blanket explanations for the west and east respectively:

> 'Yes Love indeed is light from Heaven;
> A spark of that immortal fire
> With angels shared, by Alla given,
> To lift from earth our low desire ...
>
> – *The Giaour*, 1131-1134

Byron later chronicles the intellectual development of young Don Juan, whose studies lead him to think about the questions that have exercised Greek philosophers and inky-fingered schoolboys. Does God exist? Where did the universe come from? But however strenuous one's intellectual labours, one's yearning for something *other* than the answers on offer to these hoary old questions rarely diminishes. In the following passage, Byron sees youth's furrowed brow, but he also identifies the precise spot (indicated by the dash, ' – ') at which Don Juan's love of a woman (Donna Julia) renders his love of wisdom (Philosophy) utterly irrelevant:

> He thought about himself, and the whole earth,
> Of man the wonderful, and of the stars,
> And how the deuce they ever could have birth;
> And then he thought of earthquakes, and of wars,
> How many miles the moon might have in girth,
> Of air-balloons, and of the many bars
> To perfect knowledge of the boundless skies; –
> And then he thought of Donna Julia's eyes.
>
> > – *Don Juan*, I, xcii

The dash has redirected the reader's attention in an instant to what really matters – to what means the most but can be neither explained nor quantified: love. Byron's heart was sick within him, but his courage as a writer did not fail him. He was, as Russell says, 'fierce' (Russell, 721). He took cognisance of the mundane world, and saw and felt the foulness that spreads through the lives of weak and corruptible people (himself included). But he knew love too, and he knew its power is uplifting.

His vision was by no means composed entirely of excrescences pulling him hellwards. It would take a Poe to refine this specific morbidity, and to aggravate this specific bizarreness:

> ... *no* event is so terribly well adapted to inspire the supremeness of bodily and of mental distress, as is burial before death. The unendurable oppression of the lungs – the stifling fumes of the

damp earth – the clinging to the death garments – the rigid embrace of the narrow house – the blackness of the absolute Night – the silence like a sea that overwhelms – the unseen but palpable presence of the Conqueror Worm – these things, with thoughts of the air and grass above, with memory of dear friends who would fly to save us if but informed of our fate, and with consciousness that of this fate they can *never* be informed – that our hopeless portion is that of the really dead – these considerations, I say, carry into the heart, which still palpitates, a degree of appalling and intolerable horror from which the most daring imagination must recoil.

– 'The Premature Burial'

Whereas Poe would persist in fine-tuning horrors and sharpening extremes, Byron had a more rounded sympathy with the emotional wounds that individuals inwardly sustain:

Alas! the breast that inly bleeds
Hath nought to dread from outward blow:
Who falls from all he knows of bliss,
Cares little into what abyss.

– *The Giaour*, 1155-1158

Byron followed the promptings not just of his melancholy, but also of his sense of identification with (even a scorpion's) suffering, and his sense of humour. As a writer in exile he would find his most exquisite balance. As a man in exile, however, he tended to be seen as perilously unbalanced.

15

Keats and non-being

WRITTEN IN JANUARY 1818, THE SAME month as the Lear sonnet, 'When I have fears that I may cease to be' shows Keats's fondness for the taste of antiquity in the cadences of a Shakespeare sonnet:

> When I do count the clock that tells the time,
> And see the brave day sunk in hideous night;
> When I behold the violet past prime,
> And sable curls all silvered o'er with white
>
> – Shakespeare, Sonnet 12

After what Keats himself called the 'ranting' of 'On Sitting Down to Read King Lear Once Again', 'When I have fears' turns a calmer focus down through the troubled mind, through lower levels where fears and fancies flourish, to a region (half in the dreaming, half in the waking mind) in which problems are frozen into 'naked and grecian' clarity. The deeper truth is, as Shakespeare said in *A Midsummer Night's Dream*, something of great constancy – and Keats is again trembling on the point of psychic discovery before creating a product of mind with the permanent urgency that remains in place despite receding in time, even after the artist himself has melted (as poor Yorick and Lorenzo have) back into the universal flux. His admiration of Shakespeare, as expressed in letters to friends, effects the prose backdrop to Keats's poetry at this time. Just as Shakespeare could spirit himself behind Cordelia's eyes, so Keats could spirit himself behind Isabella's.

Keats's fears that he might 'cease to be' may bring to mind the apprehension of death that has led countless individuals to total despair. Larkin's 'Aubade' (1977) is arguably now the most polished assertion of the secular terror of death. In this poem it is a given (rather than a fear) that each of us will 'cease to be' because on pronouncement of death we will have 'no sight, no sound,/No touch or taste or smell, nothing to think with,/Nothing to love or link with'. Keats, however, feels that imagination, though not material, is what we and our world are somehow made of. The more compelling the secular answers to the great mystery have been – for example, Larkin's declaration that death is the 'anaesthetic from which none come round' – the more hopelessly have people felt cut off in a material order uninformed by soul. Trelawney addressed this issue in a wonderfully spirited way on the poets' behalf:

> If our literature were confined to statistics and dry facts, it would be eternal winter. All our pains and aches and misadventures are dry facts, and all our pleasures spring from our imagination, which, like the sun, adorns everything. The poets create; they fill us with illusions which only Death proves delusions.
> – Preface, *Records of Shelley, Byron and the Author*

Keats's sun is maturing, and his life is getting autumnal. His brain is fruitful, misty and 'teeming', and there is still an abundance to be 'glean'd' before the winter sets in. Like Byron and Shelley, he knows he needs to get a move on.

16

Shelley's Queen

THE 21-YEAR-OLD BYRON HAD FIRED his luminous insults at specific public figures in *English Bards and Scotch Reviewers*. By contrast, Shelley's *Queen Mab: A Philosophical Poem* (1813) attacked types rather than individuals. For example,

> Those gilded flies
> That, basking in the sunshine of a court,
> Fatten on its corruption!
>
> – *Queen Mab*, III, 106-8

This is not so much the product of Shelley's personal desire to get even as it is the voice of the frank and naïve speculator singling out the rickety palaces to be razed before Jerusalem can be built. In a letter of 1811, Shelley had already recognised some key edifices of error in English society:

> Vile as aristocracy is, commerce, purse-proud ignorance & illiterateness is more contemptible. I still see Religion to be immoral – when I contemplate these gigantic piles of superstition, when I consider too the leisure for the exercise of mind, which the labor

which erected them annihilated, I set them down as so many retardations of the period when truth becomes omnipotent.

He has seen the appalling sum total of wasted time brought about by commerce, religion and superstition, but he can include also in his considerations the mizzling insignificant items, the heart-breaking fractions, the endless subdivisions of misery, that provoke him:

> Very useless ornament, the pillars, the iron railings, the juttings of wainscot, & ... the cleaning of grates are all exertions of bodily labor, which tho' trivial separately considered when united destroy a vast proportion of this valuable leisure – how many things could we do without, how unnecessary are *mahogany* tables, silver vases, myriads of viands & liquors, expensive printing that worst of all.
> – *Letters*, I, 151

The integrity of the poet is therefore far-reaching and thorough, working itself out into the details of mundane existence. Byron too complained about all the daily buttoning and unbuttoning and so on that leaves so little time in life to do other things. But Byron's complaint was the melancholy contemplation of an international celebrity. Shelley, by contrast, urgently recognises the opportunities missed to do higher work that really matters. Why *have* buttons, mahogany tables and silver vases? Why waste the time and the energy? The desire to live better which troubles us all a bit (if only vaguely and infrequently) exercises Shelley all his adult life. It is the spirit for whom he most wants to fight. He is at the side of the perceiving and presiding 'Spirit of Beauty' ('Hymn to Intellectual Beauty', II). In such a position, he can assess, for example, the specific political issue of social inequality as a tolerant and rational citizen:

> Nature rejects the monarch, not the man;
> The subject, not the citizen; for kings

> And subjects, mutual foes, forever play
> A losing game into each other's hands,
> Whose stakes are vice and misery.
>
> — *Queen Mab*, III, 170-4

Just as time ought not to be wasted with buttons, mahogany tables and silver vases, so too time ought not to be wasted on hierarchical procedures or systems of rules that have no basis in nature. Byron and Shelley can make very similar diagnoses of the ills of society, but where Byron is often pessimistic and blasé, Shelley is optimistic and anxiously solicitous.

The plot of *Queen Mab* does not, in itself, look particularly impressive. Mab, the omniscient queen of the fairies, is drawn in a magic car to the bedside of Ianthe, a sleeping girl. Ianthe is taken on a fantastic trip. Mab shows her what has gone wrong in the world in the past, and exhorts her to continue to fight against tyranny:

> ... thy will
> Is destined an eternal war to wage
> With tyranny and falsehood, and uproot
> The germs of misery from the human heart.
>
> — *Queen Mab*, IX, 189-92

Mab then re-deposits Ianthe in her bed.

The author would be denigrated both for the poem's 'airy-fairy' moments and the 'street-protest' republicanism of its main theme. Most people, on the waking realisation that they have had a dream about being shown what is wrong with the world by the Queen of the Fairies, would probably keep it to themselves. Dreams come to visit us and then go back to where they came from. They visit on a nightly, and are forgotten or repudiated on a daily, basis. But Shelley will not – cannot – forget or repudiate the strange and urgent energies that brought about *Queen Mab*.

Such a poem contributes significantly to the contrast between familiar eighteenth-century poetry (generally so accepting of the daily political order of things) and what is now known as Romanticism. With a self-soothingly charitable glance at a country churchyard in which underprivileged people were buried, Thomas Gray, a favourite poet of young Shelley, had already contemplated, with formal benevolence, the lower orders:

> Let not Ambition mock their useful toil,
> Their homely joys and destiny obscure;
> Nor Grandeur hear, with a disdainful smile,
> The short and simple annals of the poor ...
> — 'Elegy Written in a Country Churchyard'

Wordsworth perceived such showy open-mindedness as, really, rather far off and apathetic, so he responded with the cutting edge of his *Lyrical Ballads*: it was undoubtedly new for a poet to write with such genuinely sympathetic appreciation of what it might be like to experience the (unjust) world as an 'Idiot Boy', or a 'Mad Mother', or the poor little girl in 'We Are Seven' who actually wins an argument against the well-off, educated adult narrator of the poem.

But just over a decade after Wordsworth's revolution in poetry, Shelley cannot help but feel that Wordsworth has somehow gone astray, or lost faith in dreams, one might say. Wordsworth's long poem, *The Excursion* (1814), contained recollections of Joseph Fawcett and John Thelwall — French sympathisers he had known in the 1790s — as material for the failed revolutionary known as 'The Solitary'. Percy and Mary Shelley both read *The Excursion* in September 1814, and Mary recorded in her journal, 'Much disappointed. He [Wordsworth] is a slave.' (*Journal*, 15) Shelley would later write 'To Wordsworth' (1816) in which he would sadly recollect that the once radical poet 'stood/Above the blind and battling multitude', and that 'In honoured poverty [Wordsworth's] voice did weave/Songs consecrate to truth and liberty.' But now, no longer a radical force, Wordsworth has left Shelley 'to grieve,/Thus having been, that [Wordsworth should] cease to be.' As a result of the grief (and indeed the grievance), Shelley is even more inclined to press harder, continually reorienting himself in relation to the principals that Wordsworth has abandoned: 'truth and liberty.'

Shelley's work is not distant from what matters like Gray's, and it has not fallen away from what matters like Wordsworth's. Shelley looks unlikely to match Wordsworth's growing patience for political gradualism. Shelley's highest achievements have been viewed unsympathetically, or uncomprehendingly, by those grounded in conformist premises:

> Power, like a desolating pestilence,
> Pollutes whate'er it touches; and obedience,
> Bane of all genius, virtue, freedom, truth,
> Makes slaves of men, and of the human frame
> A mechanized automaton.
>
> – *Queen Mab*, III, 176-80

The poet argues that although 'every heart contains perfection's germ' (*Queen Mab*, V, 147), the prevailing money-worshipping way of life is 'Blunting the keenness of ... spiritual sense/With narrow schemings and unworthy cares' (*Queen Mab*, V, 162-3). *Queen Mab* has been called 'the most revolutionary document of the age in England' (Christiansen, 49), but some years after writing it Shelley would find himself worried by the poem. Perhaps his anxiety about a work now extant – at large, even – and beyond his control found its way into his wife's depiction of Frankenstein's troubles. Frankenstein recalled that after the 'infinite pains and care [he] had endeavoured to form [his creation]', and until just a split-second before he succeeded in 'infus[ing] a spark of being into' it, he had remained unaware of the misery awaiting him on the successful completion of his task. But from the moment the creature opened its dull yellow eye and breathed hard, Frankenstein found himself exiled forever from personal comfort or happiness, and it was the *autonomy* of the thing he had created – the actual embodiment of many fears, unexamined and discarded, but now returning to him in ghastly majesty – that shook him through so hard:

> His [the monster's] limbs were in proportion, and I had selected his features as beautiful. Beautiful! – Great God! His yellow skin scarcely covered the work of muscles and arteries beneath; his hair was of a lustrous black, and flowing; his teeth of a pearly whiteness; but these luxuriances only formed a more horrid contrast with his watery eyes, that seemed almost the same colour as the dim white sockets in which they were set, his shrivelled complexion and straight black lips.

As a young man, Shelley wished that he could transmute the 'withered leaves' of deciduous human hopes into an evergreen and graspable way of life. He wanted the sum force of his imagery and symbolism – carried on his rhythms of syntactic patterns and semantic complexes, and focused by the many other elements of his discourse – to infuse his work with soul, or 'to quicken a new birth!', as he would put it in 'Ode to the West Wind'. He would find out something important about the personal cost involved in gaining access to, and influencing, the intellectual universe. *Queen Mab* – 'written by me,' said Shelley, 'at the age of eighteen, I dare say in a sufficiently intemperate spirit' (*Letters*, II, 304) – was used against him at the trial which resulted in his losing custody of his children. The poem became for a time the backdrop against which Shelley would be brought into disrepute by his enemies. *Queen Mab* backfired on Shelley a little like *The Picture of Dorian Gray* would backfire on Wilde, and, for that matter, like Frankenstein's creation would backfire on Frankenstein: 'I had desired it with an ardour that far exceeded moderation; but now that I had finished, the beauty of the dream vanished, and breathless horror and disgust filled my heart.'

In the early 1790s, Britain's foremost conservative theorist, Edmund Burke, called the new French Republic a 'strange, nameless, wild, enthusiastic thing'. He had in mind the crowd – the rushing mob – on the streets of Paris, many-headed and pullulating, its component units seeming scarcely human and its aggregate lacking any noble features, its only language a roar. The 'withered leaves' of Shelley's writings could easily become the fodder of the latest politicised 'monster', on whose palate any perennial and Platonic niceties would be wasted. Even for years after Shelley's death, *Queen Mab* was an important influence on working-class radicals. In an accidental way that brings to mind alchemists inadvertently discovering gunpowder or the laws of gravity in their search for gold, Shelley created a monster in his search for something else.

Poetry lovers can be divided into two kinds: those who love it because it answers to their longing for beauty and wonder, and those who love it principally for its meaning. It has been possible for socialists to approve of Shelley's adolescent and political idealism, and to accept the poet's entranced lovers sailing in their magic boats. In *Red Shelley* (1980), Paul Foot has valiantly attempted to enlist the poet as an honorary socialist. For socialist readers of Shelley, the message of the 'Ode to the West Wind' is the harnessing of the 'impetuous one' in the cause of oppressed people. It is arguably a variation of Christianity that has been the new birth to be quickened. Shelley wanted to point out how far short of its potential society fell, his hope being that people might do something about it. In doing so, he found it absolutely necessary to discharge strong feelings and leave, for the attention of politically preoccupied reviewers, the incriminating singe marks on his labours:

> All things are sold: the very light of heaven
> Is venal; earth's unsparing gifts of love,
> The smallest and most despicable things
> That lurk in the abysses of the deep,
> All objects of our life, even life itself,
> And the poor pittance which the laws allow
> Of liberty ...
>
> – *Queen Mab*, V, 177-83

If Shakespeare criticised authority, he did it obliquely. Prospero can practise Shakespeare's magic all the more roughly on an island far, far from Shakespeare's London. King Lear can fall apart in front of a London audience because the legendary King of the Britons upon whom he is based (Leir) lived only in the remote past. *Queen Mab*, however, seems too immediate and transparent for its author's own good. The poet is exhaling grievances in the bell jar of contemporary Britain. He will soon have to leave and have his visions elsewhere.

17

Byron's Vision of Judgement

A S POET LAUREATE, SOUTHEY PRODUCED A long and ridiculous poem, *A Vision of Judgement* (1821), about King George III's entry into heaven:

> O'er the adamantine gates an Angel stood on the summit.
> Ho! he exclaimed, King George of England cometh to
>   judgement!
> Hear Heaven! Ye Angels hear! Souls of the good and the
>   Wicked
> Whom it concerns, attend!
>
> *– A Vision of Judgement*, IV

There was really no need for Byron to attack the poem. So many contemporaries were already pointing at it in hilarious disbelief that Southey's reputation was already taking a battering. Hartley Coleridge, known for being diffident to the point of characterlessness, expressed his opinion about Southey's poem with considerable force, in a letter to his brother, Derwent Coleridge, in 1821:

Have you seen Southey's Vision of Judgement!!!!! *O Tempora, O Mores* – And is it come to this? ... Seriously speaking, our late lamented Monarch did not deserve such an insult to his memory. And who, but a converted Revolutionist, would ever have dream'd of spurring the wind-gall'd, glander'd, stagger'd, bott-begrown, spavin'd ... broken-down gelding, that has turn'd blind with facing year after year the same round of Court Compliments – who, I say, but the Hexameter long trot; and so mounted as on another Rosinante, set off in search of adventures, in the world of spirits?

'Hexameter long trot' alludes to Southey's bizarre determination to use the classical hexameter, unsuited to the English language and therefore scarcely used in England.

Byron was only aroused when he read the paragraphs in Southey's preface that attacked him. So, in September 1821, Byron stepped in, invoking the words of Pope like a counter-spell to the evils emanating from Southey's sycophancy:

It has been wisely said, that 'One fool makes many' and it hath been poetically observed –
　　'[That] fools rush in where angels fear to tread.'
　　　　　　　　　　　– Pope's *Essay on Criticism*, line 625

If Mr Southey had not rushed in where he had no business, and where he never was before, and never will be again, the following poem would not have been written ... The gross flattery, the dull impudence, the renegado intolerance, and impious cant, of the poem by the author of 'Wat Tyler,' are something so stupendous as to form the sublime of himself – containing the quintessence of his own attributes.
　　　　　　　　　　　– Preface, *The Vision of Judgement*

Having set the spectacle of the Laureate stewing in his own wrongness, Byron proceeds to be cheerfully blasphemous in his own *Vision*. He outlines heaven as a sort of civil service environment, with Saint Peter as a bit like an under-worked petty

bureaucrat, 'yawn[ing]' (XVII) by the 'celestial gate' (XVI). Saint
Peter's obtuse underachiever's enquiries as to the identity of the
latest arrival show the immediacy with which Byron's humour
can outstrip Southey's rectitude:

> But ere he could return to his repose,
> A Cherub flapped his right wing o'er his eyes –
> At which Saint Peter yawned, and rubbed his nose:
> 'Saint porter,' said the angel, 'prithee rise!'
> Waving a goodly wing, which glowed, as glows
> An earthly peacock's tail, with heavenly dyes:
> To which the saint replied, 'Well, what's the matter?
> Is Lucifer come back with all this clatter?'
>
> – *The Vision of Judgement*, XVII

> 'No,' quoth the Cherub: 'George the Third is dead.'
> 'And who *is* George the Third?' replied the apostle:
> '*What George? What Third?*' 'The King of England,' said
> The angel.
>
> – *The Vision of Judgement*, XVIII

The members of the heavenly board look a little bored at their
workstations, toying idly with the cosmic components (as a minor
official at a loose end might twiddle with the boss's executive ball
clicker):

> The Angels all were singing out of tune,
> And hoarse with having little else to do,
> Excepting to wind up the sun and moon,
> Or curb a runaway young star or two ...
>
> – *The Vision of Judgement*, II

The poet knowingly situates his Satan in a pseudo-Miltonic
cosmos:

> Then Satan turned and waved his swarthy hand,
> Which stirred with its electric qualities

Clouds farther off than we can understand,
Although we find him sometimes in our skies;
Infernal thunder shook both sea and land
In all the planets – and Hell's batteries
Let off the artillery, which Milton mentions
As one of Satan's most sublime inventions.

— *The Vision of Judgement*, LII

For all this, Byron's intention is serious, and he means the poem to be like a fairground mirror in which society's distortions can be seen straight. Hence, his commentary on the funeral of George III:

... Of all
The fools who flock'd to swell or see the show,
Who cared about the corpse? The funeral
Made the attraction, and the black the woe.
There throbbed not there a thought which pierced the pall;
And when the gorgeous coffin was laid low,
It seemed the mockery of hell to fold
The rottenness of eighty years in gold.

— *The Vision of Judgement*, X

Byron refers not just to the dissolution and putrefaction of the corpse left behind by George III ('rottenness'), but also to the political corruption that has taken hold of England under that King's reign. The reign was long: 'He came to his sceptre young; he leaves it old' (*The Vision of Judgement*, XLIII). The legacy of oppressiveness will 'stink', as it were, until the deliquescence has been allowed to run its course, and until all pockets of vice and woe are dissolved. With such thoroughness the entire aberration will be reduced to inoffensive nothingness, but, regrettably, in Byron's view, the process will take time:

So mix his body with the dust! It might
Return to what it *must* far sooner, were

> The natural compound left alone to fight
> Its way back into earth, and fire, and air ...
> > – *The Vision of Judgement*, XI

The poet suggests that the efforts to preserve the royal body are synonymous with efforts to preserve bad kingship:

> But the unnatural balsams merely blight
> What Nature made him at his birth, as bare
> As the mere million's base unmummied clay –
> Yet all his spices but prolong decay.
> > – *The Vision of Judgement*, XI

When Byron attacks Southey, he attacks hypocrisy, because Southey is the very essence of that vice:

> He first sank to the bottom – like his works,
> But soon rose to the surface – like himself;
> For all corrupted things are buoyed like corks,
> By their own rottenness ...
> > – *The Vision of Judgement*, CV

At the height of the controversy over Byron's *Vision*, he wrote to Douglas Kinnaird on 2 May 1822:

> As to myself, I shall not be deterred by an outcry. They hate me, and I detest them, I mean your present public, but they shall not interrupt the march of my mind, nor prevent me from telling the tyrants who are attempting to trample upon all thought, that their thrones will yet be rocked to their foundation.
> > – *Correspondence*, II, 223

That letter is important with regard to our understanding of Byron's motivation for writing *The Vision*. He is not seeking merely to even the score with an adversary. He is fighting evil. Southey is evil because he eulogises a monarch and a regime responsible for deaths in America, France and Ireland. The concept of freedom has been, for Byron, unacceptably – even diabolically – reconfigured in Southey's *Vision* to look like something abhorrent in the mob rather than in the monarchy:

> And in the hubbub of senseless sounds the watchwords of
>   faction,
> Freedom, Invaded Rights, Corruption, and War, and
>   Oppression
> Loudly enounced were heard ...
>
> *– A Vision of Judgement,* V

Remarkably, Southey had once been a fanatical supporter of Robespierre, and declared, on hearing the news of Robespierre's death, that he would rather have heard of his own father's death and thought it 'the worst misfortune mankind could have sustained.' The fact that Southey's father was already dead indicates the thorough malleability of Southey's moral makeup. The Byron of *The Vision of Judgement* would give Southey much more reason to be worried than the Byron of *English Bards and Scotch Reviewers* did.

Southey's *Vision*, evokes the spectacle of the prompt, loyal Laureate attempting to squeeze through the pearly gates with the royal family:

> But the weight of the body withheld me. I stoopt to the
>   fountain,
> Eager to drink thereof, and to put away all that was earthly.
> Darkness came over me then at the chilling touch of the water,
> And my feet methought sunk, and I fell precipitate. Starting
> Then I awoke ...
>
> *– A Vision of Judgement,* XII

Byron's *Vision* evokes the more recognisable spectacle of Southey the hanger-on, the scavenger, animated purely by vanity, ingratiating and unscrupulous:

The varlet was not an ill-favoured knave;
A good deal like a vulture in the face,
With a hook nose and a hawk's eye, which gave
 A smart and sharper-looking sort of grace
To his whole aspect ...
                                        – *The Vision of Judgement*, XCIV

Byron has Southey 'plead[ing] his own bad cause,/With all the attitudes of self-applause.' (*The Vision of Judgement*, XCV) Byron witheringly summarises what Southey's plaints would be likely to sound like if he were compelled to appeal to the heavenly tribunal:

He said – (I only give the heads) – he said,
He meant no harm in scribbling; 'twas his way
Upon all topics; 'twas, besides, his bread,
Of which he buttered both sides; 'twould delay
Too long the assembly (he was pleased to dread),
And take up rather more time than a day,
To name his works – he would but cite a few –
'Wat Tyler' – 'Rhymes on Blenheim' – 'Waterloo.'
                                        – *The Vision of Judgement*, XCVI

Southey's *Vision* affected an elaborate salute over the coffin of George III. Byron's takes this to its logical conclusion in showing a Southey that would elaborately salute whoever was in the ascendant, or in authority:

He had written praises of a Regicide;
He had written praises of all kings whatever;
He had written for republics far and wide,
And then against them bitterer than ever ...
Then grew a hearty anti-jacobin –
Had turned his coat – and would have turned his skin.
                                        – *The Vision of Judgement*, XCVII

With a *coup de maître*, Byron has Southey the biographer place himself at Satan's disposal:

He had written Wesley's life: – here turning round
To Satan, 'Sir, I'm ready to write yours,
In two octavo volumes, nicely bound,
With notes and preface, all that most allures
The pious purchaser; and there's no ground
For fear, for I can choose my own reviewers:
So let me have the proper documents,
That I may add you to my other saints.'

– The Vision of Judgement, XCIX

The indignation has been finely and accurately controlled, like jets of fire. Byron's Southey looks so ludicrous and is totally convincing. It is almost as if a contemptible emperor has had his new clothes seen through and shouted about by an inconvenient child. A firebrand writer (rather like Hans Christian Andersen's legendary boy) can say a lot and not get into too much trouble if he can make everyone in the crowd laugh.

18

Shelley's Solitude

MARY SHELLEY SAID THAT *Alastor* is written in a very different tone from *Queen Mab*. In the latter, Shelley poured out all the cherished speculations of his youth – all the irrepressible emotions of sympathy, censure, and hope, to which the present suffering, and what he considers the proper destiny of his fellow-creatures, gave birth. *Alastor*, on the contrary, contains an individual interest only. A very few years, with their attendant events, had checked the ardour of Shelley's hopes ...

Alastor or The Spirit of Solitude tells the story of a young man who dies yearning for the woman he met in his dreams, for whom he can find no earthly match:

> ... He dreamed a veilèd maid
> Sate near him, talking in low solemn tones.
> Her voice was like the voice of his own soul ...
>
> – *Alastor*, 151-3

The poem's epigraph, from Saint Augustine's *Confessions* (Book III, Chapter 1), shows Shelley's awareness that he is not the first person to have been troubled by the presence in him of strong feelings and the absence of an external object corresponding to those feelings: 'I was not yet in love, but I was in love with love itself; and I sought for something to love, since I loved loving.'

There is something enclosed about the spirit in which this poem was written. The elusive love interest floats above the poet like a pale ghost, and its wavering existence seems to be drawn from each exhalation of the sleeping head. Shelley told Thomas Medwin about his dream journal:

> At this time Shelley was ever in a dreamy state, and he told me he was in the habit of noting down his dreams. The first day he said, they amounted to a page, the next to two, the third to several, till at last they constituted the greater part of his existence ... One morning he told me he was satisfied of the existence of two sorts of dreams, the Phrenic and the Psychic; and that he had witnessed a singular phenomenon, proving that the mind and soul were separate and different entities – that it had more than once happened to him to have a dream, which the mind was pleasantly and actively developing; in the midst of which, it was broken off by a *dream within a dream* – a dream of the soul, to which the mind was not privy; but that from the effect it produced – the start of horror with which he waked – must have been terrific. (Medwin, 89)

Shelley has become his own phantom, and is at once the haunting spirit and the haunted man:

> His strong heart sunk and sickened with excess
> Of love. He reared his shuddering limbs, and quelled
> His gasping breath, and spread his arms to meet
> Her panting bosom: – she drew back awhile,
> Then, yielding to the irresistible joy,
> With frantic gesture and short breathless cry
> Folded his frame in her dissolving arms.
> Now blackness veiled his dizzy eyes, and night
> Involved and swallowed up the vision; sleep,

> Like a dark flood suspended in its course,
> Rolled back its impulse on his vacant brain.
>
> *– Alastor*, 181-91

The lonely figure in *Alastor* is forced into the waking cold, rather like the narrator of Keats's 'La Belle Dame sans Merci' (written in 1819) finding himself 'Alone and palely loitering' on 'the cold hillside':

> Roused by the shock, he started from his trance –
> The cold white light of morning, the blue moon
> Low in the west, the clear and garish hills,
> The distinct valley and the vacant woods,
> Spread round him where he stood.
>
> *– Alastor*, 192-6

The political animal and incurable dreamer that published *Queen Mab* can no longer merely be accused of bleeding quite so unwisely in a shark-filled sea.

Alastor encourages the reader to interrogate a specific (though hard to define) inner tension: how could the youth in the poem turn away from the greater love to the less, from his dream lover to a natural lover? How is it that the mortal sleep must fall upon the individual, even when he has glimpsed immortal beauty? And why?

> Whither have fled
> The hues of heaven that canopied his bower
> Of yesternight? The sounds that soothed his sleep,
> The mystery and the majesty of Earth,
> The joy, the exultation? His wan eyes
> Gaze on the empty scene ...
>
> *– Alastor*, 196-201

Shelley is one of those individuals who is not allowed to forget. He is 'Obedient to the light/That [shines] within his soul' (*Alastor*,

493-4), and he is tempted to live in mourning for something great – 'That beautiful shape!' (*Alastor*, 211) – that has been 'Lost, lost, forever lost/In the wide pathless desert of dim sleep' (*Alastor*, 209-10), rather than cultivate, with Wordsworthian patience, an appreciation of lesser things in the light of common day.

> And now his limbs were lean; his scattered hair,
> Sered by the autumn of strange suffering,
> Sung dirges in the wind; his listless hand
> Hung like dead bone within its withered skin;
> Life, and the lustre that consumed it, shone,
> As in a furnace burning secretly,
> From his dark eyes alone.
>
> – *Alastor*, 248-54

The above lines tell of the listening look that poets have. Their nerves sensitise uniquely on the line that divides dreams from waking life and reality from reverie: 'Those who are subject to the state called reverie feel as if their nature were dissolved into the surrounding universe, or as if the surrounding universe were absorbed into their being. They are conscious of no distinction.' (Holmes, 298) Poets long to free themselves from the hereditary restrictions of their own nervous systems. They long to transcend themselves. A letter from Shelley to Hogg (8 May 1811) suggests as much:

> Solitude is most horrible; in despite of the [lack of self-love] which perhaps vanity has a great share in, but certainly not with my own good will I cannot endure the horror the evil which comes to *self* in solitude ... what strange being am I, how inconsistent, in spite of all my bo[a]sted hatred of self – this moment thinking I could so far overcome Natures law as to exist in complete seclusion, the next shrinking from a moment of solitude, starting from my own company as it were that of a fiend, seeking any thing rather than a continued communion with *self* – Unravel this mystery – but no.

I tell you to find the clue which even the bewildered explorer of the cavern cannot reach ...

— *Letters*, I, 77-8

Dictated by a frantic and obscure compulsion, the poet produces the howl that must go up from time to time from the heart of human nature. Individuals each carry the accumulating personal suffering about with them, and most of them do not know how to communicate that suffering. Many of them will not cry out to something outside them, that is, they will not try to pray, because they have no wish to find again only the depth inside, where the instincts writhe and wriggle without intermission, and without hope. Shelley expertly inspects the various cells in the mental prison-system of human nature:

> Those who, deluded by no generous error, instigated by no sacred thirst of doubtful knowledge, duped by no illustrious superstition, loving nothing on this earth, and cherishing no hopes beyond, yet keeping aloof from sympathies with their kind ... have their apportioned curse. They languish because none feel with them their common nature. They are morally dead ...
>
> — Preface, *Alastor*

Having read Wordsworth's *Excursion* before writing *Alastor*, Shelley perceived that 'self-centred [Wordsworthian] seclusion' leads to 'the vacancy of ... spirit ... mak[ing] itself felt.' In order to transcend 'the lasting misery and loneliness of the world', Shelley sought to unite the blind, confused and fragmentary elements of universal experience within the sacred circle of significance sadly vacated by Wordsworth. He knew that supreme openness was vital in order to assimilate and retain the 'things [that] depart which never may return:/Childhood and youth, friendship and love's first glow', which all flee 'like sweet dreams leaving [the dreamer] to mourn.' ('To Wordsworth') For Shelley,

Wordsworth's earlier work had been permeated with the wisdom of a fundamentally affectionate intellect, but *The Excursion* now revealed an unfortunate absence of that wisdom. Shelley knew that the poet's supreme task of synthesis – how to invoke the welding flame – could be taught and learned only by himself.

The poet recreates the youth's rapt inwardness –

> Oh, that the dream
> Of dark magician in his visioned cave,
> Raking the cinders of a crucible
> For life and power, even when his feeble hand
> Shakes in its last decay, were the true law
> Of this so lovely world!
>
> – *Alastor*, 681-6 –

but he also knows that the light of common day will disinterestedly excoriate the dreamer on his return:

> But thou art fled,
> Like some frail exhalation, which the dawn
> Robes in its golden beams, – ah! thou hast fled!
>
> – *Alastor*, 686-8

The poet diagnoses solitary idealism as the root of an unhappiness that is in himself and rife in Britain (assuming in the latter, national form an insularity that considers anything not the product of British effort to be a sort of moral lapse). In order to examine it, Shelley has involved himself productively with the sort of self-indulgence and narcissism avoided so evidently by other poets prouder of their plain living and high thinking. We do owe much to Wordsworth. His best poetry has not aged. His clear eye that sees Tintern Abbey sees more than ours do, even if there are (as Huxley pointed out, in 1929, in 'Wordsworth in the Tropics') walls which it cannot see through, and which now can be seen from the other side of time. Shelley was already beginning to see from the other side of time. For him, Wordsworth's choice to see in Nature a divine, Anglican unity was just the creation of yet another false universe which (as it has turned out) would become densely populated by Wordsworthians. One key Wordsworthian, Arnold, would write, in an essay on Byron, that Shelley was a 'beautiful but ineffectual angel, beating in the void his luminous wings in vain'. The implication was that the best, and only, way to live one's life was with one's feet firmly on the ground.

Shelley's challenge was always to keep his judgement, and to keep his language from being clouded by his anger. He knew that most people – including the eminent and ageing Wordsworth – cultivate heartfelt associations with parts, not the whole of life. He knew that these parts are fetishes – 'Commerce' (*Queen Mab*, V, 53), 'Obedience' (Wroe, 19), or 'stones, stones, stones; nothing but stones!' (Peck, I, 72) – or as Thomas Taylor would have called them, 'phantoms of false enthusiasm', invariable particularities which furnish hell on earth. Wordsworth's memory, once his greatest resource, would become his worry. Coleridge, too, would struggle with himself. His over-developed self-analytical habits are legendarily masochistic:

> For not to think of what I needs must feel,
>   But to be still and patient, all I can;
> And haply by abstruse research to steal
>   From my own nature all the natural man –
>   This was my sole resource, my only plan:
> Till that which suits a part infects the whole,
> And now is almost grown the habit of my soul.
>   – 'Dejection: An Ode', VI

Shelley's sympathy with the plight of a fellow visionary ensnared by the contingencies of life's surface appearances is moving:

Ah! wherefore didst thou build thine hope
On the false earth's inconstancy?
Did thine own mind afford no scope
Of love, or moving thoughts to thee?
That natural scenes or human smiles
Could steal the power to wind thee in their wiles.

– 'To Coleridge'

The author of *Alastor* is feeling the full burden of existence, and he is paying the cost involved in assembling the disparate rags of experience when life's terrible energies are blowing around and through him, and when 'faithless smiles' and 'falsehood' ('To Coleridge') are pervasive in society. He tries to realise on paper his existence. So what if the author of *Alastor* is egotistical and self-absorbed? The point is that he has grasped something hard to define, yet ultimately definite, and he has the uplifting sense of having against great odds saved something from eternity. To make that something touchable, or to render it visible – whatever *it* is – will always seem to the majority of readers a vain task. As the professor says in C.S. Lewis's *The Lion, the Witch and the Wardrobe* (1950), 'I wonder what they *do* teach them at these schools.' (Chapter 5) Maddeningly, for the poet also, the resumption of normal consciousness is too often accompanied by the painful sense of vanity, a pain that would provoke Arthur Rimbaud to abjure his art, and Hart Crane to take his own life (and Wordsworth to write the politically self-correcting *Excursion* and *Peter Bell*). The poet's exaltation must fade away, and the moment must become immersed again in its customary insipidity: 'The glory of the moon is dead;/Night's ghosts and dreams have now departed' ('To Coleridge'). Shelley knows well enough that his soaring birds, blasting trumpets, surging and breaking waves, howling and driving storms, and erupting volcanoes will be, *even to him sometimes, as well as to his harshest critics*, questionable fragments, trickeries, fantasies and guesses leaving him bored, leaving him awake, and leaving him alone. He knows that an important part of what he wants to say is neither resistant nor palpable, and that the unsettling absence of edges around it can push poets into insanity or send them back to the 'safer' regions (really, though, fetishes) of naturalistic description or correct politics. Shelley's poetry carries the echoes and harmonies of greater things, and though the concluding lines of *Alastor* concede that there are concrete reasons for pessimism, something between those lines is the uplift of a mood music most people thought was lost in the dissonance and bloodshed in Paris between 2 and 6 September 1792:

> Art and eloquence,
> And all the shows o' the world, are frail and vain
> To weep a loss that turns their lights to shade.
> It is a woe too 'deep for tears', when all
> Is reft at once, when some surpassing Spirit,
> Whose light adorned the world around it, leaves
> Those who remain behind, not sobs or groans,
> The passionate tumult of a clinging hope;
> But pale despair and cold tranquillity,
> Nature's vast frame, the web of human things,
> Birth and the grave, that are not as they were. (710-20)

He knows that 'the deep truth is imageless', and that he has a real poet's work to do, not just in translating deep, imageless truth into images, but in keeping and conveying, somehow, the fructifying spirit of the encounter:

> Oh! there are spirits of the air,
> And genii of the evening breeze,
> And gentle ghosts, with eyes as fair
> As starbeams among twilight trees ...

With mountain winds, and babbling springs,
And moonlight seas, that are the voice
Of these inexplicable things,
Thou didst hold commune, and rejoice
When they did answer thee ...

– 'To Coleridge'

19

Byron's *Manfred*

E.J. Trelawney records that in 1822 Byron told Shelley of the criticisms John Murray, Byron's publisher, had of his dramas. Murray thought them unstageable and, worse, unmarketable, and urged Byron in the double interest of art and commerce to resume his 'Corsair style, to please the ladies.'

– Frank D. McConnell, 'Byron as Antipoet'

BYRON'S *MANFRED* (1817), THE VERSE PLAY that inspired Schumann's musical poem and Tchaikovsky's *Manfred* symphony, was written in the wake of war across Europe. Empires fell, and charismatic leaders liberated old nations and declared new ones. Arguably, the outer turmoil compelled artists to turn even more inward. Byron's Manfred is introspective. He shuts himself away from society because of a dreadful but unnamed deed that caused the death of his beloved:

> My solitude is solitude no more,
> But peopled with the Furies; – I have gnashed
> My teeth in darkness till returning morn,
> Then cursed myself till sunset; – I have prayed

For madness as a blessing – 'tis denied me.
I have affronted Death – but in the war
Of elements the waters shrunk from me,
And fatal things passed harmless; the cold hand
Of an all-pitiless Demon held me back ...

– *Manfred*, II, ii, 139-147

Manfred looks only for death, but death on his own terms, rather than those of the Christian church. He has reached his own understanding of life by taking a path of personal suffering, as the spirits of destiny acknowledge:

... This man
Is of no common order, as his port
And presence here denote: his sufferings
Have been of an immortal nature – like
Our own; his knowledge, and his powers and will,
As far as is compatible with clay,
Which clogs the ethereal essence, have been such
As clay has seldom borne; his aspirations
Have been beyond the dwellers of the earth,
And they have only taught him what we know –
That knowledge is not happiness, and science
But an exchange of ignorance for that
Which is another kind of ignorance.

– *Manfred*, II, iv, 64-76

Byron can be seen in the character of Manfred. Both are wilful, passionate and prone to despair. Even the poet's incestuous love affair with his half-sister, Augusta, might be the unnamed deed that drives Manfred to suicide. Mario Praz has argued that the affinities between Byron, Manfred and the Marquis de Sade are very strong:

What Manfred said of Astarte ('I loved her, and destroy'd her'), what Byron wished to be able to say of Augusta and of Annabella (see the Incantation in *Manfred*), was to become the motto of the 'fatal' heroes of Romantic literature. They diffuse all round them the curse which weighs upon their destiny, they blast, like the simoom, those who have the misfortune to meet with them (the image is from *Manfred*, III, i); they destroy themselves, and destroy the unlucky women who come within their orbit. Their relations with their mistresses are those of an incubus-devil with his victim. (Praz, 1933)

In a weary letter from Italy, Byron tells Augusta that despite his love of nature, even the spectacular scenery fails to console him: 'The mountains, the glacier, the forest nor the cloud can for one moment lighten the weight upon my heart, nor enable me to lose my own wretched identity in the majesty and power and the glory around, above, beneath me.' Russell has recognised the importance to Byron of Augusta. She was the only person who could give him what he wanted:

His shyness and sense of friendlessness made him look for comfort in love affairs, but as he was unconsciously seeking a mother rather than a mistress, all disappointed him except Augusta. Calvinism, which he never shook off ... made him feel that his manner of life was wicked; but wickedness, he told himself, was a hereditary curse in his blood, an evil fate to which he was predestined by the Almighty ... He loved Augusta genuinely because she was of his blood ... and also, more simply, because she had an elder sister's kindly care for his daily welfare. But this was not all she had to offer him. Through her simplicity and her obliging good-nature, she became the means of providing him with the most delicious self-congratulatory remorse. He could feel himself the equal of the greatest sinners – the peer of Manfred ... (Russell, 718)

20

Keats's *Hyperion*

WRITTEN MOSTLY BETWEEN SEPTEMBER AND December 1818, in blank verse (which had freed Milton from 'the bondage of rhyming'), *Hyperion* represents the filling out of Keats's potential into the substantiality of great achievement. Making good his earlier claim of independence from the classically trained critics, Keats again found his theme in Greek mythology. Saturn is introduced as a 'fallen divinity' (*Hyperion*, I, 12) like Milton's Lucifer, damaged and darkened by his fall, and contagious – 'Spreading a shade' (*Hyperion*, I, 13). In these opening lines the usual traffic of the elements has been stilled and silenced – 'No stir of air' (*Hyperion* I, 7), 'A stream went voiceless by, still deadened more' (*Hyperion* I, 11).

The natural world will allow itself to be darkened and quietened for a time, but then it will realign its loyalties to a new cohort of gods, the Olympians. Such are the unbreakable laws of organic existence, including also, emphatically, the spiritual evolution believed in by the poet: 'it must/Be of ripe progress' (*Hyperion*, I, 124-5). In this scheme of things, as if he has inscribed it in marble

on behalf of the incoming gods, Keats tells us that the Titans have
not got what it takes to admit the reality of, and therefore adapt
to, the changing environment, so they naturally gravitate to minor
roles. When the self-motivated Apollo arrives, the Titans are a bit
like Chekhov's aristocrats who, on finding themselves dispensable
in the new meritocratic world, have to allow themselves to be
dismantled and put away. Keats would never let this happen, nor
allow a layer of dust settle on him: 'Scarce images of life, one
here, one there,/Lay vast and edgeways; like a dismal cirque/Of
Druid stones, upon a forlorn moor ... ' (*Hyperion*, II, 33-5). The
gods (and their drones) of the past no longer exist as any part of
the vital force of life. In Keats's time, science has killed the old
gods and myths – or at any rate made the atmosphere unpropitious
to them – so new ones have to be invented. Saturn and Thea are
in what Keats has called, elsewhere, the 'Vale of Soul-making'
(*Letters*, I, 102). In this region, 'cruel pain' (*Hyperion*, I, 44) is
the stuff one must use to make one's soul. Titans refuse, and
remain ignorant, and become angry. Hyperion himself is one such
case:

> Fall! No, by Tellus and her briny robes!
> Over the fiery frontier of my realms
> I will advance a terrible right arm
> Shall scare that infant thunderer, rebel Jove,
> And bid old Saturn take his throne again.
>
> – *Hyperion*, I, 246-50

Similarly, Saturn, in bewildered envy, hopes to create another
world, but without in any way changing his approach:

> A little time, and then again he snatch'd
> Utterance thus. – 'But cannot I create?
> Cannot I form? Cannot I fashion forth
> Another world, another universe,

> To overbear and crumble this to naught?
> Where is another chaos? Where?'
>
> – *Hyperion*, I, 140-5

One might be reminded of Lear and Kent unprepared for the new era in which Goneril and Regan acquired metaphorical serpents' teeth with which to see their hollowed father off once and for all. Saturn could scarcely survive, let alone triumph, in the 'fierce convulse' (*Hyperion*, III, 129) through which only the strong and properly prepared (because transformable) soul can 'Die into life' (*Hyperion*, III, 130). Keats has answered the call from his higher self, and his higher self has come to collect him: 'Soon wild commotions shook him, and made flush/All the immortal fairness of his limbs;/Most like the struggle at the gate of death ... ' (*Hyperion*, III, 124-6). Many people refuse the call, because the realm from which it is sent to them is supposed not to exist. Sherlock Holmes, for whom there was always a logical explanation, would never bother about it. C.G. Jung would bother about it, but he would be dismissed by the prevailing intellectualism of the twentieth century, mainly for arguing consistently that non-physical, psychic phenomena should be analysed as rigorously as physical phenomena. (Any intellectual conceding that non-physical, psychic phenomena are real runs the risk of being labelled unaccountably medieval – as if Diderot et al had not ridden roughshod over ancient puerilities.)

Hyperion, with all his hang ups, is the quintessence of the essentially healthy yet neurotic individual whose blackest thoughts have made necessary, and possible, the Prozac and CBT phenomena that have busied countless medical professionals, social workers and their administrators. With *Hyperion*, Keats wrote the Hyperion (the 'sober-sadness' he recognised in himself that he knew could be 'laughed at' with some justice [*Letters*, II,

174]) out of himself. He said to Reynolds (on 3 May 1818) that
'until we are sick, we understand not; in fine, as Byron says,
"Knowledge is sorrow", and I go on to say that "sorrow is
wisdom".' In the greatest poetry, personal and universal sufferings
are inextricably combined. Keats knew that more, and stronger,
pain was on its way to him. He eulogised it in advance. He knew
the worms that would devour him had already hatched, so he saw
to their – and many of the great mystery's other agents' –
beautification.

21

Shelley's Radical *Islam*

DURING SHELLEY'S SCHOOLDAYS AT ETON (1804-10), he was goaded and tormented by the other children:

> The particular name of some particular boy would be sounded by one, taken up by another and another, until hundreds echoed and echoed the name ... The Shelley! Shelley! Shelley! which was thundered in the cloisters was but too often accompanied by practical jokes, – such as knocking his books from under his arm, seizing them as he stooped to recover them, pulling and tearing his clothes, or pointing with the finger, as one Neapolitan maddens another. The result was ... a paroxysm of anger which made his eyes flash like a tiger's, his cheeks grow pale as death, his limbs quiver, and his hair stand on end. (Holmes, 20)

Despite the environment unpropitious to learning, Shelley's hatred of tyranny, intensified by his first-hand exposure to it, spurred him to learn things tyrants did not know:

> Yes, from the records of my youthful state,
> And from the lore of bards and sages old,
> From whatso'er my wakened thoughts create
> Out of the hopes of thine aspirings bold,

Have I collected language to unfold
Truth to my countrymen; from shore to shore
Doctrines of human power my words have told;
They have been heard, and men aspire to more
Than they have ever gained or ever lost of yore.

– Revolt of Islam, IV, xii

This epic poem (at nearly 5000 lines, the longest Shelley ever wrote) is not about Islam. It is about revolution. One must understand the poet in a non-literal way. As Peacock said, 'His imagination often presented past events to him as they might have been, not as they were' (Wroe, 7). At Eton, Shelley may or may not have hit back against one of the bullies by stabbing him with a fork – or possibly a knife, depending on which of his accounts one believes (Holmes, 20) – but by his mid-twenties, in writing *Laon and Cythna*, he was hitting out at the establishment with sustained and concentrated radical force:

For me the world is grown too void and cold,
Since hope pursues immortal destiny
With steps thus slow – therefore shall ye behold
How Atheists and Republicans can die;
Tell your children this!

– Laon and Cythna, XII, 30

Many passages like this had to be diluted, possibly as a result of Shelley's amendments for the sake of his nervous publisher, Ollier, and his printer, Buchanan McMillan; or possibly as a result of someone else making the amendments. The fourth line of the above excerpt became 'How those who love, yet fear not, dare to die', which is obscure by comparison. The re-worked poem, *The Revolt of Islam*, lost many of its more piquant political passages, and modified its underlying tolerance of incest, as the loss of the stanza beginning with the following lines shows: 'I had a little sister, whose fair eyes/Were loadstars of delight, which drew me home' (*Laon and Cythna*, II, xxi).

In the Preface, Shelley explains his choice of the Spenserian stanza, a form he will use again in *Adonais* (1821): 'I have adopted the stanza of Spenser (a measure inexpressibly beautiful) not because I consider it a finer model of poetical harmony than the blank verse of Shakespeare and Milton, but because in the latter there is no shelter for mediocrity; you must either succeed or fail.' He has something to prove, both to himself and to 'those whom I now address':

> This perhaps an aspiring spirit should desire. But I was enticed also by the brilliancy and magnificence of sound which a mind that has been nourished upon musical thoughts can produce by a just and harmonious arrangement of the pauses of this measure.

He means to somehow mimetically represent the eternal fugue from which the ceaselessly fluctuating temporal world issues. Neville Rogers's *Shelley at Work: A Critical Study* (1967) justly makes much of the fact that the manuscript drafts of Shelley's poems show a musical composer at work as much as a poet.

Even after the editorial work necessary in order to get the poem published, there is still considerable power in *The Revolt of Islam*. The poet is forceful enough about the poem's political purpose in the Preface: 'the awakening of an immense nation from their slavery and degradation to a true sense of moral dignity and freedom; the bloodless dethronement of their oppressors and the unveiling of the religious frauds by which they had been deluded into submission'. In the Preface, the prose is beautiful and powerfully flowing, and it feels in kilter with the convulsions of the French Revolution and its sequent wars:

> It has ceased to be believed that whole generations of mankind

ought to consign themselves to a hopeless inheritance of ignorance and misery because a nation of men who have been dupes and slaves for centuries were incapable of conducting themselves with the wisdom and tranquillity of freemen so soon as some of their fetters were partially loosened.

– Preface, *Revolt of Islam*

There is something persuasive and even faintly addictive about the poet's impetuosity, and, further, his way of raising and navigating the swells of rhetoric that seem to come through him from what he calls the 'master-theme of the epoch' – the French Revolution: 'There is a reflux in the tide of human things which bears the shipwrecked hopes of men into a secure haven after the storms are past. Methinks those who now live have survived an age of despair.' He investigates the very poetic machinery with which he sends the sparks of his individuality into the universal imagination, which he trusts will be combustible:

I have sought to enlist the harmony of metrical language, the ethereal combinations of the fancy, the rapid and subtle transitions of human passion, all those elements which essentially compose a poem, in the cause of a liberal and comprehensive morality; and in the view of kindling within the bosoms of my readers a virtuous enthusiasm for those doctrines of liberty and justice, that *faith and hope in something good, which neither violence nor misrepresentation nor prejudice can ever totally extinguish* among mankind. (italics added)

During the narration of the spiritual and sexual union of brother-and-sister lovers Laon and Cythna, one senses the ache, not just for flesh, but for something deeper, beyond materiality, of which the flesh is just a symbol:

The Meteor showed the leaves on which we sate,
And Cythna's glowing arms, and the thick ties

Of her soft hair which bent with gathered weight
My neck near hers; her dark and deepening eyes,
Which, as twin phantoms of one star that lies
O'er a dim well move though the star reposes,
Swam in our mute and liquid ecstasies;
Her marble brow, and eager lips, like roses,
With their own fragrance pale, which Spring
    but half uncloses.

The Meteor to its far morass returned.
The beating of our veins one interval
Made still; and then I felt the blood that burned
Within her frame mingle with mine, and fall
Around my heart like fire; and over all
A mist was spread, the sickness of a deep
And speechless swoon of joy, as might befall
Two disunited spirits when they leap
In union from this earth's obscure and fading sleep.
             – *Revolt of Islam*, VI, xxxiii-xxxiv

But the poem does sprawl in many different other directions, and fails to achieve the cohesion of a *Paradise Lost*. *The Revolt of Islam* is a repository for many of Shelley's personal and public interests at the time. The poem is (like *Queen Mab*) influenced by Godwin's *Political Justice* (1793), a key left-wing book of the time, including Godwin's hatred of all forms of tyranny. Shelley explores the more personal nature of the relationship between himself and the older political thinker:

A course precipitous, of dizzy speed,
Suspending thought and breath; a monstrous sight!
For in the air do I behold indeed
An Eagle [Godwin] and a Serpent [Shelley] wreathed in fight: –
And now relaxing its impetuous flight,
Before the aëreal rock on which I stood,
The Eagle, hovering, wheeled to left and right,

And hung with lingering wings over the flood,
And startled with its yells the wide air's solitude.

– *Revolt of Islam*, I, viii

The poem has affinities with Spenser's *Faery Queene*. Like Spenser's, Shelley's descriptions are not picturesque, but they are more like dreams in their independence from specific geographical, historical or political realities. Shelley, like Spenser, puts nothing in the poem, not even the concept of the French Revolution, without keeping about it the frisson of the unknown from which dreams and actual events alike emerge:

Thus, the dark tale which history doth unfold
I knew, but not, methinks, as others know ...
So that when Hope's deep source in fullest flow,
Like earthquake did uplift the stagnant ocean
Of human thoughts – mine shook beneath the wide emotion.

When first the living blood through all these veins
Kindled a thought in sense, great France sprang forth,
And seized, as if to break, the ponderous chains
Which bind in woe the nations of the earth.

– *Revolt of Islam*, I, xxxviii-xxxix

The poet has some of Godwin's rationalist belief in the benevolence of mankind, and he shares Godwin's wish to sweep away the restraints of social institutions, but he has in addition something of the Spenserian touch (such as unobtrusive but intentional alliterativeness helping to conjure hard-to-paraphrase dreamscapes) that had already reached *Paradise Lost* and 'The Rime of the Ancient Mariner'.

The poet also keeps the frisson of the unknown, into which all must return:

We know not where we go, or what sweet dream

May pilot us through caverns strange and fair
Of far and pathless passion, while the stream
Of life our bark doth in its whirlpools bear ...

– Revolt of Islam, VI, xxix

His short poem, 'Death', posthumously published by his wife in 1824, appears to be a balder statement of the problem:

Death is here, and death is there,
Death is busy everywhere,
All around, within, beneath,
Above, is death – and we are death ...

First our pleasures die – and then
Our hopes, and then our fears – and when
These are dead, the debt is due,
Dust claims dust – and we die too.

– 'Death'

In such a situation as this, as in the Thousand and One Nights, we (who must die) are left (in the meantime) with stories. Stories, of course, are made of words, and, as Shelley says, *poets'* words 'unveil the permanent analogy of things by images which participate in the light of truth; but as their periods are harmonious and rhythmical, and contain in themselves the elements of verse; being the echo of the eternal music.' (*A Defence of Poetry*) So all must depend on how the stories are told. That is, all must depend on poetry. Shelley tells *The Revolt of Islam* with gusto, in a Preface and 12 cantos with (unlike *Queen Mab*) no notes. The villain of the story is the Establishment, which (for example) in the poet's view denies men freedom as long as it denies women freedom:

Can man be free if woman be a slave?
Chain one who lives, and breathes this boundless air
To the corruption of a closèd grave!
Can they whose mates are beasts, condemned to bear

> Scorn, heavier far than toil or anguish, dare
> To trample their oppressors? In their home
> Among their babes, thou knowest a curse would wear
> The shape of woman ...
>
> – *Revolt of Islam*, II, xliii

It may seem difficult sometimes to disagree with Paul Johnson that evildoers are portrayed merely as embodied evil in *The Revolt of Islam* (and 'The Masque of Anarchy'):

> The Tyrant peoples dungeons with his prey,
> Pale victims on the guarded scaffold smile
> Because they cannot speak ...
>
> – *Revolt of Islam*, IX, xxiv

But Shelley instructively appreciates the efficiency with which those in control parcel out the miseries that regulate the status quo, here to a recalcitrant journalist (like Peter Finnerty) languishing in a prison-cell, and there to an anonymous boy begging on the chartered streets:

>   and, day by day,
> The moon of wasting Science wanes away
> Among her stars, and in that darkness vast
> The sons of earth to their foul idols pray,
> And gray Priests triumph, and like blight or blast
> A shade of selfish care o'er human looks is cast.
>
> – *Revolt of Islam*, IX, xxiv

Again, as Shelley put it in the notes of *Queen Mab*, the wrongness of the imposed and maintained order of things looks even more wrong in juxtaposition with the 'vast' mystery of the cosmos. But in *The Revolt of Islam* at its best, the poet's continuing blend of rebellion and wonder finds expression in an impressive flow of Spenserian stanzas. The authority with which Shelley now handles the notoriously difficult Spenserian form frees him from the need for a supplementary commentary in the manner of Erasmus Darwin's *Botanic Garden*. That is, since registering his debt to Darwin, Shelley has evolved, despite (or because of) a political environment where 'truth and liberty' are no longer vital forces in Wordsworth:

> This is the winter of the world; – and here
> We die, even as the winds of Autumn fade,
> Expiring in the frore and foggy air. –
> Behold! Spring comes, though we must pass, who made
> The promise of its birth ...
>
> – *Revolt of Islam*, IX, xxv

With the subtlety and strength of a martial artist, the poet uses tyranny's own weight against it, presenting a nightmare the reader will recognise has been burned into the dreaming brain by actual wrong governance:

> Famine, than whom Misrule no deadlier daughter
> Feeds from her thousand breasts, though sleeping there
> With lidless eyes lie Faith and Plague and Slaughter –
> A ghastly brood conceived of Lethe's sullen water.
>
> – *Revolt of Islam*, X, xvii

Shelley had seen for himself the appalling state of post-Revolutionary France in 1814. He wrote from France to Harriet Shelley in August 1814:

> We came 120 miles in four days. The last two days we past over the country that was the seat of war. I cannot describe to you the frightful desolation of this scene. Village after village entirely ruined & burned; the white ruins towering in innumerable forms of destruction among the beautiful trees. The inhabitants were famished; families once perfectly independent now beg their bread ... No provisions, no accom[m]odation; filth, misery & famine everywhere.
>
> – *Letters*, I, 392

He had heard horrible stories about innocent people having to
resort to prostitution, and even cannibalism:

> There was no corn – in the wide marketplace
> All loathliest things, even human flesh, was sold;
> They weighed it in small scales – and many a face
> Was fixed in eager horror then. His gold
> The miser bought; the tender maid, grown bold
> Through hunger, bared her scornèd charms in vain ...
> — *Revolt of Islam*, X, xix

In Shelley's vision, a nation's citizens have been tyrannised into
insanity:

> It was not hunger now, but thirst. Each well
> Was choked with rotting corpses, and became
> A cauldron of green mist made visible
> At sunrise. Thither still the myriads came,
> Seeking to quench the agony of the flame
> Which raged like poison through their bursting veins;
> Naked they were from torture, without shame,
> Spotted with nameless scars and lurid blaines –
> Childhood, and youth, and age, writhing in savage pains.
> — *Revolt of Islam*, X, xxi

This is far from simplistic. The poet does retain his hope for society,
but not in any context of foursquare republicanism, and certainly
not to the beat of the busy Parisian guillotine. The tall shadow of
the guillotine (and of the gunman) has spindled across time from
Burke all the way to the modern reactionary's ideological slit-
window: if one squints just so, one might make out the continuum
of left-wing malevolence lurking in widespread tolerance of
thinkers from Rousseau to Sartre.

Nuances get lost in dogmatic definitions. If anything, the
analysis of *The Revolt of Islam* offered by the first president of

the Shelley Society, the Reverend Stopford Brooke, in *Naturalism in English Poetry* (1820), is more attuned to the poet's frustrated power and fragmented compactness:

> [Shelley] tried to be real and to embody with temperance his ideas on the progress of mankind, but was continually swept in spite of himself into an impassioned idealism and fury; but where, feeling himself lost and uncontrolled, he tried to get back again into temperance and reality, and only half succeeded, so that the poem is broken, unequal, unsatisfactory from want of unity of impression. (Peck, II, 42)

Despite the poet's distemper, the slaughter of the multitude at the gates of the Golden City resonates uncannily with the use in England in 1817 of cavalry and yeomanry to break up public meetings and subdue dissatisfaction. Dissatisfaction expressed in print, such as Richard Carlile's working-class periodical, *The Republican*, was also vigorously checked. Carlile would be tried for blasphemous libel in October 1819. The charge was based on several passages in Paine's *Age of Reason*. For this, and also for the republication of Palmer's *Principles of Nature*, Carlile was fined £1,500 and put in Dorchester Gaol for three years. In a masterly letter to Hunt intended for publication in the *Examiner*, Shelley showed that the authorities' sentencing of Carlile was a symptom of their ingrained intolerance:

> the prosecutors care little for religion, or care for it only as it is the mask & the garment by which they are invested with the symbols of worldly power. In prosecuting Carlile they have used the superstition of the Jury as their instrument for crushing a political enemy, or rather they strike in his person at all their political enemies. They know that the Established Church is based upon the belief in certain events of a supernatural character having occurred in Judea eighteen centuries ago; that but for this belief the farmer would refuse to pay the tenth of the produce of his

labours to maintain its numbness and idleness; that this class of persons if not maintained in idleness would have something else to do than to divert the attention of the people from obtaining a Reform in their oppressive government, & that consequently the government would be reformed, & that the people would receive a just price for their labours, a consummation incompatible with the luxurious idleness in which their rulers esteem it in their interest to live.

– Letters, II, 143

That is, the mania of inequality has been carefully inculcated by Christian education. And when the conditioning is not enough, there is always supplementary treachery: in 1817, the Habeas Corpus was suspended and *agents provocateurs* were planted to find people guilty of subversive activity. If they failed to find them, they framed them. Still hanging in the air was the miserable injustice meted out that year to the Pentrich leaders, Brandreth, Ludlam and Turner (Holmes, 384-6).

One considerable strength of *The Revolt of Islam* is that Shelley superimposes his supernatural labyrinth upon post-Revolutionary Europe, and the device, looking eerie and sounding exaggerated, yet ringing true, gives a poet's definition to the consequences of dogma – whatever species of political animal is guilty of it:

> It was not thirst, but madness! Many saw
> Their own lean image everywhere – it went
> A ghastlier self beside them, till the awe
> Of that dread sight to self-destruction sent
> Those shrieking victims ...
>   ... and cried aloud, 'We tread
> On fire! the avenging Power his hell on earth has spread.'
>
> *– Revolt of Islam*, X, xxii

This epic poem shows that what has looked like the defeat of Liberty is by no means conclusive. Laon and Cythna are, finally, burnt at the stake, but the music suggests something other than death:

> And is this death? – The pyre has disappeared,
> The Pestilence, the Tyrant, and the throng;
> The flames grow silent – slowly there is heard
> The music of a breath-suspending song,
> Which, like the kiss of love when life is young,
> Steeps the faint eyes in darkness sweet and deep;
> With ever-changing notes it floats along,
> Till on my passive soul there seemed to creep
> A melody, like waves on wrinkled sands that leap.
>
> – *Revolt of Islam*, XII, xvii

The mysterious something-or-other present in music and poetry is the antidote to the 'infectious gloom' the poet complained about in the Preface. The 'kiss of love when life is young' cannot be quantified. Its power and beauty, however, can make things happen. A brother and sister can love and resolve to live together, and if the authorities will not let them live together, they can die together. The authorities can kill people, but they cannot kill what people have already thought and done, and continue to think and do, in the context of love's power and beauty. Like love, music cannot be quantified, and yet its power and beauty can make things happen. Music is present in the best poetry, which is, for Plato, 'divine insanity' and for Shelley 'harmonious madness'. The absence of an uplifting *je ne sais quoi* in a civilization's arts can suit tyrants and their drones down to the ground: 'gloom and misanthropy ... the solace of a disappointment that unconsciously finds relief only in the wilful exaggeration of its own despair.' (Preface, *Revolt of Islam*) Peacock called it a 'conspiracy against cheerfulness.' It became the general pessimism of succeeding ages, and it has been excellent as a means of restraining insubordination without the need for state violence. An efficient government will be utterly dedicated to conducting detailed and ongoing management of the *zeitgeist*. Such a government cultivates control over people by propagating emotive or palliative messages via entertainments to harmonise, and when necessary mobilise, mass opinion. If a government does this effectively enough, it can keep its use of batons, guns and tear gas to an election-minded minimum. Hence the social realism, sex and sentimental trash sharing almost total domination over our commercial media. The idea of something important, magical or shamanic in the arts has come to seem at least as passé as manned barricades. Poets' harmoniousness is too often drowned out by state-sponsored noise, and men's madness too often steps forward to seize the day.

22

Byron Venetianising

With all its sinful doings, I must say,
That Italy's a pleasant place to me,
Who love to see the Sun shine every day ...

– Beppo, XLI

I like on Autumn evenings to ride out,
Without being forced to bid my groom be sure
My cloak is round his middle strapped about,
Because the skies are not the most secure;
I know too that, if stopped upon my route,
Where the green alleys windingly allure,
Reeling with grapes red wagons choke the way, –
In England 'twould be dung, dust, or a dray.

– Beppo, XLII

BEPPO (1818) SHOWS THAT BYRON PREFERS Italy to England. It also shows that the poet will not follow the example of other Romantics who had got hold of philosophical tenets and tried to combine the authentic lyrical spasm with a metaphysical explanation of the universe.

Beppo was the poem in which Byron made comic, rather than

hid, his difficulty in finding rhymes for the *ottava rima* metre. He began to twist the necks of accepted epithets in order to make poetry splutter and screech instead of twittering:

> I love the language, that soft bastard Latin,
> Which melts like kisses from a female mouth,
> And sounds as if it should be writ on satin,
> With syllables which breathe of the sweet South,
> And gentle liquids gliding all so pat in,
> That not a single accent seems uncouth,
> Like our harsh northern whistling, grunting, gutteral,
> Which we're obliged to hiss, and spit, and sputter all.
>
>   – *Beppo*, XLIV

Having been through the darkness and depression from his marriage and its breakup, he found a new lightness with which he could respond to his new environment:

> Didst ever see a Gondola? For fear
> You should not, I'll describe it you exactly:
> 'Tis a long covered boat that's common here,
> Carved at the prow, built lightly, but compactly,
> Rowed by two rowers, each called 'Gondolier,'
> It glides along the water looking blackly,
> Just like a coffin clapt in a canoe,
> Where none can make out what you say or do.
>
>   – *Beppo*, XIX

(One wonders what he said and did in gondolas.) The poem is modelled on the style of the serio-comic Italian poet, Luigi Pulci, whose masterpiece is the *Morgante Maggiore* (1483). Byron found the perfect vehicle in which he could practice a newly nimble disrespect for anything with hypocrisy in it:

> She was a married woman; 'tis convenient,
> Because in Christian countries 'tis a rule

To view their little slips with eyes more lenient;
Whereas if single ladies play the fool,
(Unless within the period intervenient
A well-timed wedding makes the scandal cool)
I don't know how they ever can get over it.
Except they manage never to discover it.

– *Beppo*, XXIV

Byron wrote *Beppo* during September and early October 1817. On 12 October he told Murray: 'I have written a poem (of 84 octave stanzas) humorous ... on a Venetian anecdote which amused me.' The amusing anecdote was that a man had been away at sea for so long that his wife believed him to be dead. However, the man returned to find his wife and her new lover at a ball. To conclude the anecdote, all three had coffee at the new lover's house. That simple plot suited Byron's imagination in the same way that a large, uncluttered stage might suit a brilliant, restless solo dancer. Byron's heterogeneous, hyperactive thoughts are allowed to find intelligible and easy expression, and even unfold and move about with grace in *Beppo*. The mode of expression is Byronically unbuttoned. *Beppo* displays the poet creating and inhabiting the idiom in which he can best perform. No writer before Byron had ever referred to *Macbeth* humorously, but Byron points out that if the reader is thinking of coming to Venice as a recognisable non-Catholic, he will risk being 'haul[ed].. o'er the coals' by the clergy, who will 'No[t] say one mass to cool the cauldron's bubble/That boiled your bones unless you paid them double.' There is such a sense of relish in the poet's candour. He runs amok, saying just what he likes about, say, the transparently brutal Catholic fanaticism in Italy, or the ridiculous charade acted out, back in England, by young Protestant women:

> 'Tis true, your budding Miss is very charming,
> But shy and awkward at first coming out,
> So much alarmed, that she is quite alarming,
> All Giggle, Blush – half Pertness, and half Pout;
> And glancing at *Mamma*, for fear there's harm in
> What you, she, it, or they, may be about:
> The Nursery still lisps out in all they utter –
> Besides, they always smell of bread and butter.
>
> – *Beppo*, XXXIX

The poetic fountain has begun to overflow, and Byron will not try to regulate it, but will allow himself be buffeted between the gay and the grave:

> I fear I have a little turn for Satire,
> And yet methinks the older that one grows
> Inclines us more to laugh than scold, though Laughter
> Leaves us so doubly serious shortly after.
>
> – *Beppo*, LXXIX

He would indicate his fondness for England by alluding to William Cowper's poem, *The Task*, II, and Charles Churchill's poem, 'The Farewell' ('Be England what she will,/With all her faults, she is my Country still'), and then allow it to become comically apparent that, as he says he likes everything, it must follow that his 'fondness' for his country means nothing at all:

> 'England! with all thy faults I love thee still,'
> I said at Calais, and have not forgot it;
> I like to speak and lucubrate my fill;
> I like the government (but that is not it);
> I like the freedom of the press and quill;
> I like the Habeas Corpus (when we've got it);
> I like a Parliamentary debate,
> Particularly when 'tis not too late;
>
> – *Beppo*, XLVII

I like the taxes, when they're not too many;
I like a seacoal fire, when not too dear;
I like a beef-steak, too, as well as any;
Have no objection to a pot of beer;
I like the weather, – when it is not rainy,
That is, I like two months of every year.
And so God save the Regent, Church, and King!
Which means that I like all and every thing.

— *Beppo*, XLVIII

He then begins to enumerate his 'beloved' country's 'little' blemishes, and does so for the length of another stanza before 'repudiating' himself for his digression:

Our [England's] standing army, and disbanded seamen,
Poor's rate, Reform, my own, the nation's debt,
Our little riots, just to show we're free men,
Our trifling bankruptcies in the Gazette,
Our cloudy climate, and our chilly women,
All these I can forgive, and those forget,
And greatly venerate our recent glories,
And wish they were not owing to the Tories.

— *Beppo*, XLIX

But to my tale of Laura, – for I find
Digression is a sin ...

— *Beppo*, L

Digression, like sin, is at the heart of Byron's work: not only can digression serve as structure; it in fact constitutes the very structure of human consciousness:

Of the Immortality of the Soul, it appears to me that there can be little doubt, if we attend for a moment to the action of the Mind. It is in perpetual activity. I used to doubt of it, but reflection has taught me better. It acts also very independent of body; in dreams for instance incoherently and madly, I grant

you; but still it is *Mind*, and much more *Mind* than when we
are awake ...

– Detached Thoughts

His knowledge of 'the actions of the Mind' gives Byron the
confidence that his poetry does possess the wealth and weight of
thought that gives brevity to his style, making it concise and
pregnant. He discusses digression in another digression:

> ... by degrees [digression]
> Becomes exceeding tedious to my mind,
> And, therefore, may the reader too displease –
> The gentle reader, who may wax unkind,
> And caring little for the Author's ease,
> Insist on knowing what he means – a hard
> And hapless situation for a Bard.

– Beppo, L

In yet another digression, he hammily laments the limitations on
his talents as a poet:

> Oh! that I had the art of easy writing
> What should be easy reading! could I scale
> Parnassus, where the Muses sit inditing
> Those pretty poems never known to fail,
> How quickly would I print (the world delighting)
> A Grecian, Syrian, or *As*syrian tale;
> And sell you, mixed with western Sentimentalism,
> Some samples of the *finest Orientalism*!

– Beppo, LI

Byron has already quickly printed, and had large readerships
delight in, his 'samples of ... *Orientalism*' (for example, *The Giaour*
and 'The Bride of Abydos'), yet it is as if those achievements are
of little account to him:

> But I am but a nameless sort of person,
> (A broken Dandy lately on my travels)
> And take for rhyme, to hook my rambling verse on,
> The first that Walker's Lexicon unravels,
> And when I can't find that, I put a worse on,
> Not caring as I ought for critics' cavils ...
>
> – *Beppo*, LII

Compare the above description of the writer at work with, say, Wordsworth's lifelong effort to convince the world that he never actually *wrote* a word of poetry, but that it came to him on the breezes as he walked over the moors and mountains of the Lake District. Byron refused to put any of the usual disguises on the creative impulses behind his poems. This meant that his creativity was allowed to grow without constantly being pruned and qualified for tidy inclusion in some impressive, but ultimately life-distorting scheme of thought.

> To turn, – and to return; – the Devil take it!
> This story slips for ever through my fingers,
> Because, just as the stanza likes to make it,
> It needs must be – and so it rather lingers;
> This form of verse began, I can't well break it,
> But must keep time and tune like public singers ...
>
> – *Beppo*, LXIII

Lesser writers often try to feign control over their writing. They are forced at the outset to give up any attempt at being frank or naïve. They are unable to write what they think, because if they did, their work would look unsophisticated. So, they try to make readers believe that their thoughts have gone much deeper than is really the case. Their works draw attention because they say things in forced, unnatural ways, trembling between the two separate aims of communicating what they want to say and of concealing it. Their object is to dress up their ideas in order to give people the impression that there is very much more to them than for the moment meets the eye.

At the age of forty-seven, Wordsworth would publish the poem, 'Composed on an Evening of Extraordinary Beauty' (1817), which includes such lines as 'Thine is the tranquil hour, purpureal eve', and prayers to God. Byron perceived in Wordsworth's, and other writers' strained, vague, prolix and cumbrous styles not just a waste of words, but also the trick of concealing poverty of thought under a stupefying farrago of never-ending chatter. The following, from *Detached Thoughts* illustrates Byron's concern: 'One of my notions, different from those of my contemporaries, is, that the present is not a high age of English Poetry: there are *more* poets ... than ever there were, and proportionally *less* poetry.' Byron was a ferocious castigator of humbug, as the following attack on the poet William Sotheby ('*Botherby*') demonstrates:

> No solemn, antique gentleman of rhyme,
> Who having angled all his life for Fame,
> And getting but a nibble at a time,
> Still fussily keeps fishing on, the same
> Small 'Triton of the minnows', the sublime
> Of Mediocrity, the furious tame,
> The Echo's echo, usher of the school
> Of female wits, boy bards – in short, a fool!
>
> – *Beppo*, LXXIII

> A stalking oracle of awful phrase,
> The approving '*Good!*' (by no means GOOD in law)
> Humming like flies around the newest blaze,
> The bluest of bluebottles you e'er saw,
> Teasing with blame, excruciating with praise,
> Gorging the little fame he gets all raw,

Translating tongues he knows not even by letter,
And sweating plays so middling, bad were better.

                                              – *Beppo*, LXXIV

Away from England, Byron's poetry was becoming more riotously clever. He was giving the English – 'so suspicious,' as Marsha Rowe has said, 'of cleverness, fearing it to be superficial' (*So Very English*, 9) – even less reason to approve of him.

23

Keats Peeping Between the Curtains

THE POWER AND RADIANCE OF 'THE Eve of St Agnes' seem to have left some key nineteenth- and twentieth-century commentators untouched. Jeffrey's synopsis of the poem is useful up to a point for its first-class succinctness:

> The superstition is that if a maiden goes to bed on that night [St Agnes's Eve], without supper, and never looks up after saying her prayers, till she falls asleep, she will see her destined husband by her bedside the moment she opens her eyes. The fair Madeline, who was in love with the gentle Porphyro, but thwarted by an imperious guardian, resolves to try this spell: and Porphyro, who has a suspicion of her purpose, naturally determines to do what he can to help it to a happy issue; and accordingly prevails on her ancient nurse to admit him to her virgin bower; where he watches reverently, till she sinks in slumber; and then, arranging a most elegant dessert by her couch, and gently rousing her with a tender and favourite air, finally reveals himself, and persuades her to steal from the castle under his protection.

But such a summing-up can serve also to ironically display (in displaying Jeffrey's striking unawareness of it) the poem's abounding moral ambivalence. There is a sexual *frisson* in the poem, and the reader preferring his sensual nature to be left undisturbed may find Keats's key ingredient distasteful, or perhaps even distastefully delicious. Is it possible to read stanzas XXV and XXVI feelingly without indulging in a kind of voyeurism? Byron's jibe about 'this miserable Self-polluter of the human mind' (*Keats: The Critical Heritage*, 129) was well-aimed (not least at Byron's own experience as a reader of 'The Eve of St Agnes'?): 'such writing is a sort of mental masturbation ... I don't mean he is *indecent*, but viciously soliciting his own ideas into a state, which is neither poetry nor any thing else but a Bedlam vision produced by raw pork and opium.' (*Keats: The Critical Heritage*, 129) Even more worryingly (because more titillatingly?), the lovely Madeline is the unsuspecting performer, spied upon by Porphyro (and the reader) from the closet in the bedroom:

> Full on this casement shone the wintry moon,
> And threw warm gules on Madeline's fair breast,
> As down she knelt for heaven's grace and boon;
> Rose-bloom fell on her hands, together prest,
> And on her silver cross soft amethyst,
> And on her hair a glory, like a saint:
> She seem'd a splendid angel, newly drest,
> Save wings, for heaven: – Porphyro grew faint:
> She knelt, so pure a thing, so free from mortal taint.
>
> – *Eve of St Agnes*, XXV

The contemporary reader may have found in the above stanza what Coleridge called the 'vicious taste of our modern ... Monk Lewis' (*Coleridge Notebooks*, 3449). Coleridge had in mind Matthew Lewis, whose sensational Gothic novel, *The Monk* (1796), contained many passages suggesting irresistibly that the author had been shockingly transfixed by his own violent, youthful aching for female flesh:

> ... [Matilda] lifted her arm, and made a motion as if to stab herself. The friar's eyes followed with dread the course of the dagger. She had torn open her habit, and her bosom was half exposed. The weapon's point rested upon her left breast: and, oh! that was such a breast! The moon-beams darting full upon it enabled the monk to observe its dazzling whiteness: his eye dwelt with insatiable avidity upon the beauteous orb: a sensation till then unknown filled his heart with a mixture of anxiety and delight; a raging fire shot through every limb; the blood boiled in his veins, and a thousand wild wishes bewildered his imagination.
>
> – *The Monk*, I, ii

The intentions of Keats's Porphyro do not appear to be as bad – but this too could be self-deception:

> 'I will not harm her; by all saints I swear,'
> Quoth Porphyro: 'O may I ne'er find grace
> 'When my weak voice shall whisper its last prayer;
> 'If one of her soft ringlets I displace,
> 'Or look with ruffian passion in her face ...
>
> – *Eve of St Agnes*, XVII

That is, it is better to look through a keyhole. However, rather unsettlingly, Porphyro's feelings are clear, without his intentions being clearly defined. The lack of definition is part of the point. The reader's experience of Keats's best poetry depends upon incomplete and uncertain knowledge. Remember that Shakespeare never advises readers whether his Hamlet, or his Richard III, is good or bad. Keats's works, like Shakespeare's, are distinguished by the conspicuous absence of moral directives. The 'poetical Character,' says Keats, 'has as much delight in conceiving an Iago as an Imogen. What shocks the virtuous philosopher, delights the chameleon Poet. It does no harm from its relish of the dark side of things any more than from its taste for the bright one.' Madeline performs a striptease without knowing it:

> Anon his heart revives: her vespers done,
> Of all its wreathed pearls her hair she frees;
> Unclasps her warmed jewels one by one;
> Loosens her fragrant bodice; by degrees
> Her rich attire creeps rustling to her knees:
> Half-hidden, like a mermaid in sea-weed ...
>
> – *Eve of St Agnes*, XXVI

Is there not something silkily, and sinfully, indulgent about the above passage? Dare one enjoy the passage as a porously receptive reader? Or would one have to emerge in shame from the experience? The poem is a guilty pleasure.

Keats has draped the boundaries of good taste with sweet-scented Spenserian stanzas, and it is harder for the reader to perceive precisely how the boundaries are being pushed, or dissolved – though s/he does sense that they are being changed in some way. Having written his way through strange psychic territories where personal and universal concerns overlap, Keats now has the practiced boldness to generate a sort of verbal Eden. Is there not a serpent present too? The poem is intensely erotic. 'The Imagination may be compared to Adam's dream – he awoke and found it truth.' (*Letters*, I, 185) Can the fumes of a personal Hell be detected through the poppied air of 'The Eve of St Agnes'? A letter from Keats to Benjamin Bailey (July 1818) is remarkably revealing:

> I am certain I have not a right feeling towards Women – at this moment I am striving to be just to them but I cannot – Is it because they fall so far beneath my Boyish imagination? ... When among men I have no evil thoughts, no malice, no spleen – I feel free to speak or to be silent – I can listen and from everyone I can learn –

my hands are in my pockets, I am free from all suspicion and comfortable. When I am among Women I have evil thoughts, malice spleen – I cannot speak or be silent – I am full of Suspicions and therefore listen to no thing – I am in a hurry to be gone –

– *Letters*, I, 341

Whether or not one forgets that one is, at some level, spying (with Porphyro) on Madeline, it is difficult to envisage a more prodigiously dreamlike – and at the same time delicately precise – combination of words with which to recreate the occasion of a beautiful young girl getting into a cold bed, heating it with her own body warmth, and going to sleep:

> Soon, trembling in her soft and chilly nest,
> In sort of wakeful swoon, perplex'd she lay,
> Until the poppied warmth of sleep oppress'd
> Her soothed limbs, and soul fatigued away;
> Flown, like a thought, until the morrow-day;
> Blissfully haven'd both from joy and pain;
> Blinded alike from sunshine and from rain,
> As though a rose should shut, and be a bud again.
>
> – *Eve of St Agnes*, XXVII

It could be that Porphyro (like his creator, not wanting 'to think insults in a Lady's Company' but thinking them nevertheless?) is in some sense the serpent:

> Stol'n to this paradise, and so entranced,
> Porphyro gazed upon her empty dress,
> And listen'd to her breathing, if it chanced
> To wake into a slumberous tenderness;
> Which when he heard, that minute did he bless,
> And breath'd himself: then from the closet crept,
> Noiseless as fear in a wide wilderness,
> And over the hush'd carpet, silent, stept,
> And 'tween the curtains peep'd, where, lo! – how fast she slept.
>
> – *Eve of St Agnes*, XXV, III

The depth of Keats's appreciation for Book IV of *Paradise Lost*, in which Satan gazes in unhappiness at Adam and Eve's uncorrupted circumstances, is clear:

> Under a tuft of shade that on a green
> Stood whispering soft, by a fresh fountain side
> They sat them down, and after no more toil
> Of their sweet gardening labour than sufficed
> To recommend cool zephyr, and made ease
> More easy, wholesome thirst and appetite
> More grateful, to their supper fruits they fell,
> Nectarine fruits which the compliant boughs
> Yielded them, sidelong as they sat recline
> On the soft downy bank damasked with flowers:
> The savoury pulp they chew, and in the rind
> Still as they thirsted scoop the brimming stream ...
>
> – *Paradise Lost*, IV, 325-36

The fragrant textures in Keats's versification are Miltonic:

> And still she slept an azure-lidded sleep,
> In blanched lined, smooth, and lavender'd,
> While he from forth the closet brought a heap
> Of candied apple, quince, and plum, and gourd;
> With jellies soother than the creamy curd,
> And lucent syrops, tinct with cinnamon;
> Manna and dates, in argosy transferr'd
> From Fez; and spiced dainties, every one,
> From silken Samarcand to cedar'd Lebanon.
>
> – *Eve of St Agnes*, XXX

The word 'dainties' – used, less felicitously, not so long ago in stanza XLVII of 'Isabella' – is now an integral part of one of the mature poet's greatest works. Keats does not waste words now, much less deploy them to unwittingly comic effect. Even the above adjective-rich ('spiced', 'silken', 'cedar'd') passage does not cloy, possibly because Samarkand (one of the oldest cities of Asia, once the capital of Tamerlane's Mongol empire) and Lebanon (part of the Ottoman Empire from the early sixteenth century, and with a coastline on the Mediterranean Sea) are ingredients too far-flung to blend in the mind as Carlyle's alleged 'world of treacle!'

Arguably, Keats's 'Life of Sensations' (*Letters*, I, 185) heightens the reader's sensual pleasure whilst simultaneously etherising his morals. Porphyro gets into bed with Madeline:

> Beyond a mortal man impassion'd far
> At these voluptuous accents, he arose,
> Ethereal, flush'd, and like a throbbing star
> Seen mid the sapphire heaven's deep repose;
> Into her dream he melted, as the rose
> Blendeth its odour with the violet, –
> Solution sweet ...
>
> – *Eve of St Agnes*, XXXVI

He seems to make love to her. Is it rape? The reader has been inundated with 'woofed phantasies' and 'voluptuous accents', and may feel more inclined to 'look ... dreamingly' than judge soberly. The presence of a sort of narcoleptic cocoon inhabited by Madeline and Porphyro (and the reader) is somehow confirmed, rather than dispelled, by the pattering upon it of 'the flaw-blown sleet'. The experience so far is of haziness, warmth, and low-level sexual tension, like the gradually unfocused masturbation of a young man (Keats?) about to fall asleep. The reader does not have to strain to imagine why Byron sneered at 'Johnny Keats's *p-ss a bed* poetry.' (*Letters and Journals*, VII, 200)

Madeline and Porphyro escape from the castle, and in the process the reader is treated to a masterful display of familiar Gothic scenery. The restless chilly breezes agitate the castle's interior, including the lamplight, the hanging embroidery and the carpeting:

> She hurried at his words, beset with fears,
> For there were sleeping dragons all around,
> At glaring watch, perhaps, with ready spears –
> Down the wide stairs a darkling way they found.–
> In all the house was heard no human sound.
> A chain-droop'd lamp was flickering by each door;
> The arras, rich with horseman, hawk, and hound,
> Flutter'd in the besieging wind's uproar;
> And the long carpets rose along the gusty floor.
>
> — *Eve of St Agnes*, XL

Against this backdrop, the momentum of the spectral, escaping lovers – and the images and sounds accompanying their flight – is almost cinematic:

> They glide, like phantoms, into the wide hall;
> Like phantoms, to the iron porch, they glide;
> Where lay the porter in uneasy sprawl,
> With a huge empty flagon by his side:
> The wakeful boodhound rose, and shook his hide,
> But his sagacious eye an inmate owns:
> By one, and one, the bolts full easy slide: –
> The chains lie silent on the footworn stones; –
> The key turns, and the door upon its hinges groans.
>
> — *Eve of St Agnes*, XLI

Now that the lovers – the dreamers – have gone from the castle, death and decay (the 'large coffin-worm' and the 'ashes cold') close in like Blake's, or Shelley's, shades of death.

> All things that we love and cherish,
> Like ourselves, must fade and perish;
> Such is our rude mortal lot –
> Love itself would, did they not.
>
> — Shelley, 'Death'

We are left with nothing but the story, and, most importantly, how that story has been told. Of old Angela, the Baron and the Beadsman posterity can only have the names. (It looks unlikely that there will be any records.) Despite the warm and sensible motions of those who dance and drink and sing 'Amid the timbrels, and the throng'd resort/Of whisperers in anger, or in sport;/'Mid looks of love, defiance, hate, and scorn' (*Eve of St Agnes*, VIII), the vast majority of them are 'Hoodwink'd with faery fancy', chasing 'all the bliss to be', instead of finding fulfilment in the moment, now: 'Sudden a thought came like a full-blown rose,/ Flushing his brow, and in his pained heart/Made purple riot ... ' (*Eve of St Agnes*, XVI). In these lines, the thought that suddenly occurs to Porphyro is that he will persuade Angela to sneak him into Madeline's bedroom; but, of course, the thought has occurred to Porphyro's creator, the poet with the dendritic imagination to feel the mucky provenance – not just see the nice effect – of a 'full-blown rose'. The poet is now writing consistently at his best; and further, the poetry his pen has yet to glean from his teeming brain will not need to be explainable to be immortal. 'The faint conceptions I have of Poems to come brings the blood frequently into my forehead'.

24

Shelley Asleep in Italy

CHANCELLOR ELDON HAD RULED AGAINST Shelley in the matter of taking away his children by his first wife. By the time Shelley had married Mary and had two children with her, he was worried that they too would be taken away from him. This is why he was, as the first line of 'The Masque of Anarchy' reveals, 'in Italy' at the time he heard the news of the Peterloo Massacre in September 1819: 'The same day that your letter came, came the news of the Manchester work, & the torrent of indignation has not yet done boiling in my veins. I wait anxiously [to] hear how the Country will express its sense of this bloody murderous oppression of its destroyers.' (*Letters*, II, 117) Shelley then quoted from his own work, *The Cenci* (1819): 'Something must be done ... What yet I know not.'

Two weeks later, he was sending 'The Masque of Anarchy' to Hunt, with a view to publishing it in *The Examiner*. Hunt did not publish it at the time. Had he done so, it is almost certain that both editor and poet would have faced prison sentences for sedition. The poem would not be published until ten years after

Shelley's death, when it would be less dangerous to make public such an outburst.

The poem is influenced by 'The Rime of the Ancient Mariner', but it is arguably a rougher reading, or listening, experience than the contemporary ballad-reading public would have been used to:

> Next came Fraud, and he had on,
> Like Eldon, an ermined gown;
> His big tears, for he wept well,
> Turned to mill-stones as they fell;
>
> And the little children, who
> Round his feet played to and fro,
> Thinking every tear a gem,
> Had their brains knocked out by them.
>
> – 'Masque of Anarchy', IV-V

Admittedly, Shelley included personal antipathy, and this does account for the abrasive feel of many of the lines. But the overall achievement of the poem is in its capacity to convey the rightness of very strong feelings against a government demonstrably capable of murdering its own citizens, and standing over the corpse of Liberty. The poem's advice to the remaining citizens has the thrill of ambiguity:

> Rise like lions after slumber,
> In unvanquishable number;
> Shake your chains to earth like dew
> Which in sleep had fallen on you –
> Ye are many, they are few.
>
> – 'Masque of Anarchy', XXXVIII

This is exactly the kind of exhortation that will incense some people and incite others to salute the poet. On the one hand, it seems clear that Shelley is advocating revolutionary violence: there is no such thing as a vegetarian lion. On the other hand, the poet is walking 'in the visions of Poesy' ('Masque of Anarchy', I), and therefore not to be taken literally. The above lines could be said to exist somewhere between implosion and hallucination; they appear to have been uttered by the collective spirit of a people oppressed that has just found the strength to fight for its rights. The argument could go on indefinitely about how, literally and precisely, Shelley thought the fight should be conducted. Just as it never occurred to Blake to adhere to the facts when he included, say, the lion and the wolf in the same region of the planet (in 'To the Evening Star'), so Shelley naturally prioritised the refinement of a different mode of accuracy when he addressed the 'Men of England, heirs of glory,/Heroes of unwritten story' ('Masque of Anarchy', XXXVII). Any passive supporter of authority today, any somnambular consumer, could potentially – or so Shelley ardently hoped – be jarred into fuller consciousness by the following words:

> What is Freedom? – Ye can tell
> That which Slavery is too well,
> For its very name has grown
> To an echo of your own.
>
> 'Tis to work, and have such pay
> As just keeps life from day to day
> In your limbs, as in a cell,
> For the tyrants' use to dwell,
>
> So that ye are for them made
> Loom, and plough, and sword, and spade –
> With or without your own will bent
> To their defence and nourishment.

'Tis to see your children weak
With their mothers pine and peak,
When the winter winds are bleak –
They are dying whilst I speak.

– 'Masque of Anarchy', XXXIX-XLII

Shelley pummels the reader with raw political realities. The
stranglehold that money asserts on human freedom is made vivid
in the following three stanzas:

'Tis to let the Ghost of Gold
Take from toil a thousand-fold
More than e'er its substance could
In the tyrannies of old;

Paper coin – that forgery
Of the title deeds which ye
Hold to something of the worth
Of the inheritance of Earth.

'Tis to be a slave in soul,
And to hold no strong control
Over your own wills but be
All that others make of ye.

– 'Masque of Anarchy', XLIV-XLVI

The card-carrying employee might feel in no real position to
exercise rights whenever those in power diminish rights further
and further. But Shelley has a special power with which to remind
the reader that hypocrisy does not only exist in those in authority.
He also reminds the reader that rights need to be fought (in *some*
way) for, and won.

It may even seem unnecessary, *de trop*, to discuss what is
repellent about gratuitously wasteful capitalism. Many people feel
that it is wrong, and even fundamentally stupid, to work for bosses

they despise, but they simply have to get on with it, as there are things to be paid for, and the money is not going to fall from the sky. One stark example of the sort of worker that gets on with things unquestioningly is the soldier, as Shelley would suggest in his *Philosophical View of Reform* (1820), 'more degraded than a murderer', and 'like the bloody knife which has stabbed and feels not ... beyond abhorrence and below contempt.' (It is worth noting that Shelley wrote this piece in response to contemporary political economists, such as Thomas Malthus, who thought that poor people should solve their country's problems by not having children.) Most people will stifle their own sighs after a fairer life. To do so – one is encouraged, if one is detected struggling with the concept during one's school and university days – is to discover a degree of political maturity as a naturalised citizen of Babylon. Shelley's words carry a truth inconvenient for probationary Babylonians. The poet has the power to weaken any faith a worker might have in the ideology convenient to his employer. He can make workers ashamed of the conformist clichés that paper over the unholy pact with the enemy. He can resuscitate drowned hopes with the galvanic battery of his ballad's rhythm. The thumping music heightens and metabolises sensations that many workers (or those workers aware of them) would prefer to keep dormant in themselves, because of the certainty of their being left intellectually more scrupulous and therefore feeling even more defenceless. If you read Shelley 'too much', you become a 'danger' to yourself and to your co-workers, because Shelley's lines have the power to release in readers' minds the natural opiates that promote in individuals the natural wish to band together and do something about injustice:

And at length when ye complain
With a murmur weak and vain,
'Tis to see the Tyrant's crew
Ride over your wives and you –
Blood is on the grass like dew!

– 'Masque of Anarchy', XLVII

One could almost catch an intimation of an understandably incensed, rapidly coalescing mob.

Of course, the strike-breakers can arrive and smash protesters' heads in with clubs as and when necessary, but Shelley has helped people shine a clear light on the science of media-manipulation, propaganda and control of the public mind – 'Like a dream's dim imagery' ('Masque of Anarchy', LII) – long before Theodor Adorno or Noam Chomsky thought of such things, or were thought of themselves. There are lessons to be learned from the universal indifference that greets the extraordinary efforts of a figure like Shelley (be it remembered, born to an aristocratic heritage). And there are lessons to be learned from the (understandably) muted enthusiasm of publishers like Hunt and Ollier. If the *An Address to the People on the Death of the Princess Charlotte* was published in 1817-18, there are no reviews of the pamphlet in any of the newspapers of the time. It was as late as 1843 when Thomas Rodd issued it as a stabbed octavo pamphlet of 16 pages. If it was published before 1843, it must have been limited and given exclusively to the parliamentarians Shelley most wanted (fondly) to influence – just as he had contrived to bring 'The Necessity of Atheism' to the attention of the bishops of heads of colleges at Oxford. 'The Masque of Anarchy' would not be published until 1832, and Shelley's 'Song to the Men of England' (1819) would not be published until 1839:

Men of England, wherefore plough
For the lords who lay ye low?
Wherefore weave with toil and care
The rich robes your tyrants wear?

Wherefore feed, and clothe, and save,
From the cradle to the grave,
Those ungrateful drones who would
Drain your sweat – nay, drink your blood?

Wherefore, Bees of England, forge
Many a weapon, chain, and scourge,
That these stingless drones may spoil
The forced produce of your toil?

Have ye leisure, comfort, calm,
Shelter, food, love's gentle balm?
Or what is it ye buy so dear
With your pain and with your fear?

– 'Song to the Men of England'

The questions the poet asks of the men of England are limpid.
The advice offered is enlivening in its simplicity:

The seed ye sow, another reaps;
The wealth ye find, another keeps;
The robes ye weave, another wears;
The arms ye forge, another bears.

Sow seed, – but let no tyrant reap;
Find wealth, – let no impostor heap;
Weave robes, – let not the idle wear;
Forge arms, – in your defence to bear ...

– 'Song to the Men of England'

Radical action is needed. Better to be a rugged responsible workman
reaping, keeping, wearing and bearing the products of your own

labour, than a sleeping cog in a machine that benefits someone else. The concept of workers providing slavishly for the benefit of others did exercise the poet years earlier in *Queen Mab*:

> what are they? –
> – The drones of the community; they feed
> On the mechanic's labour; the starved hind
> For them compels the stubborn glebe to yield
> Its unshared harvests; and yon squalid form,
> Leaner than fleshless misery, that wastes
> A sunless life in the unwholesome mine,
> Drags out in labour a protracted death
> To glut their grandeur; many faint with toil
> That few may know the cares and woe of sloth.
>
> – *Queen Mab*, III, 108-17

But by 1820, the more mature poet wishes to hear from Hunt 'of any bookseller who would like to publish a little volume of *popular songs* wholly political, & destined to awaken & direct the imagination of the reformers.' (*Letters*, II, 191) Shelley knows well enough that his hope will be considered a fond one. 'I see you smile,' he continues to Hunt, 'but answer my question.' (*Letters*, II, 191) Having already served time in prison, Hunt is probably very thoughtful about what he will say and do next. No wonder Shelley notices that 'Of the politics of the day you never speak' (*Letters*, II, 191).

However, there was still a fundamental misunderstanding between Shelley and most readers. His '*popular songs*' provided food for the radical thinking anterior to revolutionary action. And again here is the rub. How many readers are going to think along the same lines as Shelley when deciding what to do?

> We are all Greeks. Our laws, our literature, our religion, our arts, have their root in Greece. But for Greece, Rome, the instructor,

the conqueror, or the metropolis of our ancestors, would have spread no illumination with her arms, and we might still have been savages and idolaters; or, what is worse, might have arrived at such a stagnant and miserable state of social institution as China and Japan possess.

The human form and the human mind attained to a perfection in Greece, which has impressed its image on the faultless productions whose very fragments are the despair of modern art, and has propagated impulses which cannot cease, through a thousand channels of manifest or imperceptible operation, to ennoble and delight mankind until the extinction of the race.

– Preface, *Hellas*

The poet's descriptions (of, say, the west wind, or a skylark) and his exhortations (to men to rise up against tyranny) can work very powerfully at a superficial level. His strength is also his weakness. In one sense, readers know where they stand. They know that the poet has a passionate love of liberty and a passionate hatred of tyranny, and that the intense emotional significance which the French Revolution had for him was that it meant the liberation of that which he most loved from that which he most hated. However, many readers have found inspiration in Shelley without further investigation of the real point or lodestar from which the poet takes his bearings: ancient Greece.

25

Byron's *Hebrew Melodies* and *Domestic Pieces*

MANY PEOPLE ASSUME THAT AT BYRON'S core there is merely the smashy pith of superficial talent rather than the solidity of real genius. His reputation as a lyric poet has been neglected because of his personality. We are over-supplied with information, and it runs away with the topic. Sometimes we are invited to admire his non-conformity, and sometimes we are encouraged to censure him as no more than a self-indulgent aristocratic pervert with little control over his lusts. The available cradle-to-grave biographies, and the other accounts, tend to perpetuate the arbitrariness and circularity, and in that sense they are fictions revealing to us our fantasies about what we want Byron to be. It was like that during his day too. When Byron, and Percy and Mary Shelley, stayed in Switzerland in 1816, the local inhabitants suspected the strangers in their midst of orgiastic practices, and worse. 'They looked upon me as a man-monster,' complained Byron, who was, indeed, literally being looked upon. A local hotelier hired out telescopes so that British tourists could spy on the Byron household. Some of those tourists returned to

Britain with colourful accounts of what they had 'seen'. In 1817, Southey commandeered the bandwagon, and announced that Byron and Shelley 'had formed a league of incest'. If there is anything that the twenty-first-century reader knows about Byron, it is that he was – in the words of Lady Caroline Lamb – 'mad – bad – & dangerous to know'. Yet his lyric poetry might make one ask: what was he really like?

His *Hebrew Melodies* are important pieces because of what, and whom, they relate to – the suffering of the Hebrews, 'Israel's scattered race' that 'cannot quit its place of birth' and 'will not live' elsewhere:

> But we must wander witheringly,
> In other lands to die;
> And where our fathers' ashes be,
> Our own may never lie:
> Our temple hath not left a stone,
> And Mockery sits on Salem's throne.

– 'The Wild Gazelle'

In *Hebrew Melodies*, two different plights – the one of a famous, persecuted race and the other of a famous, persecuted poet – fuse:

> And where shall Israel lave her bleeding feet?
> And when shall Zion's songs again seem sweet?
> And Judah's melody once more rejoice
> The hearts that leaped before its heavenly voice?
>
> Tribes of the wandering foot and weary breast,
> How shall ye flee away and be at rest!
> The wild-dove hath her nest, the fox his cave,
> Mankind their country – Israel but the grave!

– 'Oh! Weep For Those'

So it was not just in satire that Byron achieved greatness. His lyric poetry shows his other gift. 'She Walks in Beauty' opens with a phenomenal phrase: 'She walks in Beauty, like the night'. This line has an exclamatory element, and from such an exclamation it is impossible for the poet to carry on at the same lyrical altitude. But there is also the necessity for the poet to *go into* the issue, and to explore the idea raised by the first line. In this way, Byron makes the poem complete:

> And on that cheek, and o'er that brow,
> So soft, so calm, yet eloquent,
> The smiles that win, the tints that glow,
> But tell of days in goodness spent ...
>
> – 'She Walks in Beauty'

Byron knows about physiognomy, and knows that the prevailing facial expression of an individual (in this case, of 'she' that 'walks in beauty') is the result of a gradual process of innumerable, fleeting and characteristic contractions of the features. Yet Byron's knowledge does not drive him to deliver a self-explanatory and self-extinguishing poem. W.H. Auden often quenched his own flame almost as soon as he had kindled it. Auden could introduce a poem with a spark of verbal magic ('Lay your sleeping head, my love,/Human on my faithless arm', or 'Out on the lawn I lie in bed'), only to end up ranting about the political ideas exchanged and received so routinely amongst the Oxbridge set of the 1930s:

> And, gentle, do not care to know,
> Where Poland draws her Eastern bow,
> What violence is done;
> Nor ask what doubtful acts allows
> Our freedom in this English house,
> Our picnics in the sun.
>
> – 'Out on the lawn I lie in bed'

Auden had considerable ability as a lyric poet, but he never knew

the love of a woman. Byron did exist in a homo-erotic society –
where men associated with men – but that was not what his life
was really about. He needed women.

As so many aristocrats were, Byron was abandoned by his
parents. He did not often come across women of capacious minds.
All men had that problem. His half-sister had enough in common
with him for them to be interested in each other; and she was
different enough from him for them to be attracted to each other
sexually:

> I feel almost at times as I have felt
> In happy childhood; trees, and flowers, and brooks,
> Which do remember me of where I dwelt,
> Ere my young mind was sacrificed to books,
> Come as of yore upon me, and can melt
> My heart with recognition of their looks;
> And even at moments I could think I see
> Some living thing to love – but none like thee.
> > – 'Epistle to Augusta', VII

When Byron says to Augusta, 'Oh that thou wert but with me!'
('Epistle to Augusta', VIII), it is easy to think of Wordsworth's
loving address to his sister, Dorothy, in 'Lines composed a few
miles above Tintern Abbey':

> For thou art with me here upon the banks
> Of this fair river; thou my dearest Friend,
> My dear, dear Friend; and in thy voice I catch
> The language of my former heart, and read
> My former pleasures in the shooting lights
> Of thy wild eyes. Oh! yet a little while
> May I behold in thee what I was once,
> My dear, dear Sister!

Arguably, tender love, with the sexual component, is often behind the best lyric poetry produced by Byron and Wordsworth. To imagine what it would be like to receive the following from a lover now exiled in Italy is to form some sense of the pangs of star-crossed love:

> Though the rock of my last Hope is shivered,
> And its fragments are sunk in the wave,
> Though I feel that my soul is delivered
> To Pain – it shall not be its slave.
> There is many a pang to pursue me:
> They may crush, but they shall not contemn –
> They may torture, but shall not subdue me –
> 'Tis of *Thee* that I think – not of them.
>
> Though human, thou didst not deceive me,
> Though woman, thou didst not forsake,
> Though loved, thou forborest to grieve me,
> Though slandered, thou never couldst shake, –
> Though trusted, thou didst not betray me,
> Though parted, it was not to fly,
> Though watchful, 'twas not to defame me,
> Nor mute, that the world might belie.
>
> Yet I blame not the World, nor despise it,
> Nor the war of the many with one;
> If my Soul was not fitted to prize it,
> 'Twas folly not sooner to shun:
> And if dearly that error hath cost me,
> And more than I once could foresee,
> I have found that, whatever it lost me,
> It could not deprive me of *Thee*.
>
>   – 'Stanzas to Augusta', July 1816

There is no hint of contrivance. The pain of separation, and yet the simultaneous pleasure of being able to think of one's lover so vividly, is encapsulated with a poet's total and natural confidence in his powers. When a poet has something to say, and says it, there is an instantly recognisable authenticity about the poem, which looks like an inevitable occurrence, like something we all knew, but had not yet happened in a poem.

There is a consistency about the vast achievement of Byron's work. He stood before the mystery of existence, knowing how to give utterance to his non-knowledge of what existence is. He stood up to what was wrong with people, including himself, and society, and faced his world's faults in all their glaring enormity. He laughed raucously at the corrective systems of thought on offer. He wove lyrical spells, whose magic conveys that he loved tenderly, and powerfully, and was himself loved:

> There be none of Beauty's daughters
> With a magic like thee;
> And like music on the waters
> Is thy sweet voice to me:
> When, as if its sound were causing
> The charmed Ocean's pausing
> The waves lie still and gleaming,
> And the lulled winds seem dreaming ...
>
> – 'Stanzas for Music', March 1816

26

Keats's Nightingale

TO SOME READERS, KEATS'S STATE OF mind after writing *Hyperion* can seem as lacking in robustness as it did beforehand. In 'Ode to a Nightingale' (1819), having complained that 'My heart aches, and a drowsy numbness pains/My sense, as though of hemlock I had drunk', Keats claims to 'have been half in love with easeful Death,/Call'd him soft names in many a mused rhyme,/To take into the air my quiet breath'. Why 'half in love'? The young poet is like most of us, in that he keenly feels the pain of consciousness and yet has not entirely objective grounds for putting an end to his existence. He has by now absorbed and accommodated the 'death wish' as many people do. As a great poet, he has anatomised it even as it has melted and mutated in the most fugitive mode.

Not all readers have had the patience (or courage) to follow half-thoughts through the shades evoked – or invoked – by Keats. Could he not have tried to define his negative emotions more sharply? This is what Sylvia Plath would do, with the result that many readers would avert their gaze in horror, though prepared to recognise Plath's disturbed brilliance. The delight of seeing Keats achieving such a grasp of his unalterable personal circumstances is not cancelled by the terrible nature of those circumstances and his use of them as a poet. Yes, Keats has a very sore throat when writing the poem, but his 'light-winged Dryad of the trees' sings 'of summer in full-throated ease'. The poet, like some kind of metaphysical amphibian, or, for that matter, like a shaman, can inhabit his sore-throated or full-throated self almost at will; he can 'Fade far away, dissolve, and quite forget' (rather like the Titans in *Hyperion*) the pain that flesh is heir to, or he can remain present and improvable.

There are passages in this poem whose omission would not have seemed to damage the central theme, but which can touch and transform the reader, as if in passing, like the hem of some wonderful garment flowing behind a ritual magician on the move. For example, in

> O for a beaker full of the warm South,
> > Full of the true, the blushful Hippocrene,
> > > With beaded bubbles winking at the brim,
> > > > And purple-stained mouth

the reader can see a whole evening of drinking, and how enjoyable such an evening can seem *at the time* is encapsulated with pristine empathy – and yet one also recognises, if one is honest with oneself, that one has often acquired a purple-stained mouth in pursuit of a few hours' peace from pain- and death-related emotions.

Keats explores a state of mind known to anyone who has ever wanted to – while at the same time knowing they cannot – retreat from the world. The desire to 'Fade far away, dissolve' echoes Hamlet's wish to 'melt,/Thaw, and resolve ... into a dew' (*Hamlet* I,2,29-30), and foreshadows Thomas Hood's *Bridge of Sighs*

(1844), which Baudelaire translated, finding in it the phrase 'Anywhere out of the world' to borrow as the title for a prose poem of his own. Baudelaire expressed his vision of the world as a hospital ward with brilliant bitterness. But the same human predicament as expressed by Keats has no mention of a hospital, and yet a whole ward-full of suffering is revealed in one glance at the convex reflection of one of his freshly beaded lyric teardrops: 'The weariness, the fever, and the fret/Here where men sit and hear each other groan' (III). The reader instinctively knows that the writer capable of generating a panoptic moment such as this one will have the power and magic to create yet more liberating mental spaciousness.

Symbolically, the bird is inextinguishable ('Thou wast not born for death, immortal Bird!'), beyond the reach of human destructiveness and rapacity ('No hungry generations tread thee down'). Again, Keats provides a miniature picture – this time a flash from the remote past – which magically presents the nightingale's perennial quintessence: 'The voice I hear this passing night was heard/In ancient days by emperor and clown'. Magic showings have usurped empirical evidence in this stanza (VII), which culminates in Keats's bird being said to have 'Charm'd magic casements, opening on the foam/Of perilous seas, in faery lands forlorn.' The alliteration itself foams, and the feel of the poet's language has become almost completely immersive, almost as if we would wish to stay there forever. But – and this is an important part of the point – we are not there, and it will only be a matter of time before some happenstance word, in the very flow of words required to promote the mood and contrive the vision, will puncture and pucker the whole seductive sphere, letting the atmosphere of the unimaginative world back in. For Keats, 'forlorn' does it: 'Forlorn! the very word is like a bell/To toll me back from thee to my sole self!' Just as the flaw-blown sleet pattering on the windowpane gave heightened definition to the vision involving Madeline and Porphyro in 'The Eve of St Agnes', so the return to diminished consciousness from poetic vision in 'Ode to a Nightingale' serves to enhance the otherworldly colour and power. The bell-sound grows: 'forlorn' – with its small 'f' at the end of stanza VII, and swelling to 'Forlorn!' at the beginning of the concluding stanza with a capital 'F' and an exclamation mark. Similarly, the fading from the vision is represented by 'Adieu! adieu!', and one is not quite sure whether it is the vision or the speaker himself who is retreating 'Up the hill-side' like unaccountable Lakeland vapours. The ambivalence the reader is left with is lingeringly provocative: 'Fled is that music: – Do I wake or sleep?' There is no moral pressure at any point. (The pressure of being mortal, however, needles the poet's attention like a fishbone.) Vapours and visions come and go as they will, when they will, and Keats knows that however strenuously some of his contemporaries might squint for a desired result, Shakespeare was always clear- and open-eyed – yet knowing that even supreme clarity and openness is no guarantee of any human being's actual independence from the binding mammalian dream.

Drug, or alcohol, addiction can be an avoidance of consciousness of mortality – 'Now more than ever seems it rich to die,/To cease upon the midnight with no pain' – and Keats's sense of his own mortality, particularly since expectorating and recognising his own arterial blood during a tubercular coughing-fit in February 1820 (*Letters*, II, 251 and 254), would give him anything but ease.

27

Keats's Indolence

KEATS COULD ALSO FIND OPULENT EXPRESSION for his most lethargic moods, as in the following stanza from 'Ode On Indolence':

> They faded, and, forsooth! I wanted wings:
>   O folly! What is love! and where is it?
> And for that poor Ambition! it springs
>   From a man's little heart's short fever-fit;
> For Poesy! – no, – she has not a joy, –
>   At least for me, – so sweet as drowsy noons,
>   And evenings steep'd in honied indolence;
> O, for an age so shelter'd from annoy,
>   That I may never know how change the moons,
>   Or hear the voice of busy common-sense!

A man of character is, by his very nature, 'incapable of remaining Content with half-knowledge' (*Letters*, I, 194). For Keats, Wordsworth was a man of character, preaching from within his impressive – but in the end wooden and unworkable – system of thought. By 1817-18, Keats's imaginative orientation in the direction of the unspecific – his glorious courage of his lack of conviction – took shape, and it is as if there emerged over his art the transformative power of a new sunrise, leaving in shade what his art was not:

> We hate poetry that has a palpable design upon us – and if we do not agree, seems to put its hand in its breeches pocket. Poetry should be great & unobtrusive, a thing which enters into one's soul, and does not startle it or amaze it with itself but with its subject. – How beautiful are the retired flowers! how they would lose their beauty were they to throng into the highway crying out, 'admire me I am a violet! dote upon me I am a primrose!'
>
> – *Letters*, I, 224

In anatomising his own talent and temperament, Keats continued to reaffirm that he had more in common with Shakespeare – 'Chief Poet!' (*Letters*, I, 215) – than with Wordsworth:

> Modern poets differ from the Elizabethans in this. Each of the moderns like an Elector of Hanover governs his petty state, & knows how many straws are swept daily from the Causeways in all his dominions ... I will cut all this – I will have no more of Wordsworth ... why should we kick against the Pricks, when we can walk on Roses? ... – Why with Wordsworth's 'Matthew with a bough of wilding in his hand' when we can have Jacques [from Shakespeare's *As You Like It* II i 31] 'under an oak &c' ... '
>
> – *Letters*, I, 224

In his copy of *Paradise Lost*, Keats made some notes: 'What creates the intense pleasure of not knowing? A sense of independence, of power, from the fancy's creating a world of its own by the sense of probabilities.' Books IV and VII of *Paradise Lost* – 'two specimens of very extraordinary beauty ... better described in themselves than by a volume' (Gittings, 262-3) – boosted Keats's imagination in a way that no other writing apart from Shakespeare's could: 'Nothing is finer for the purposes of great productions, than a very gradual ripening of the intellectual powers ... ' (*Letters*, I, 214).

To denigrate Keats on the grounds that he had no character – or at any rate not enough character to rank alongside the greatest poets – would involve forgetting all about the greatest poets, namely Milton and Shakespeare. Keats knew this, and could articulate it in his prose as clearly and magically as he could create his poetry: ' ... several things dovetailed in my mind, & at once it struck me, what quality went to form a Man of Achievement especially in Literature & which Shakespeare possessed so enormously – I mean *Negative Capability*, that is when a man is capable of being in uncertainties, Mysteries, doubts, without any irritable reaching after fact & reason ... ' (*Letters*, I, 193). Keats's '*Negative Capability*' involves passive achievement – a suspension of judgment so that ideas and feelings can be creatively explored. Keats's letters refer to the various 'Chambers' of his own imagination which, when it received sense impressions from the outside world, could produce poetry as organically as 'the Leaves of a tree' (*Letters*, I, 238). He felt that he was tapping into a power that all humans had in them, but very few (except, for example, Shakespeare) realised. 'Now it appears to me that almost any Man may like the spider spin from his own inwards his own airy Citadel – the points of the leaves and twigs on which the spider begins her work are few, and she fills the air with a beautiful circuiting: man should be content with as few points to top with the fine Webb of his Soul and weave a tapestry empyrean – full of Symbols for his spiritual eye, of softness for his spiritual touch, of space for his wandering of distinctness for his Luxury.' (*Letters*, I, 231-2) He knew himself, in the fullest sense of the phrase – physiologically and temperamentally, as the following exegesis of an isolated episode of his own 'laziness' shows:

This morning I am in a sort of temper indolent and supremely careless: I long after a stanza or two of Thompson's Castle of indolence – My passions are all asleep from my having slumbered till nearly eleven and weakened the animal fibre all over me to a delightful sensation about three degrees on this side of faintness – if I had teeth of pearl and the breath of lilies I should call it languor – but as I am ... I must call it Laziness – In this state of effeminacy the fibres of the brain are relaxed in common with the rest of the body, and to such a happy degree that pleasure has no show of enticement and pain no unbearable frown. Neither Poetry, nor Ambition, nor Love have any alertness of countenance as they pass by me: they seem rather like three figures on a greek vase – a Man and two women – whom no one but myself could distinguish in their disguisement. This is the only happiness; and is a rare instance of advantage in the body overpowering the Mind.

– *Letters*, II, 78-9

One thinks of Keats's 'Ode on a Grecian Urn' as etched in marble, so it feels like an unusual privilege and pleasure to catch a glimpse of 'a greek vase' in prose pre-dating that ode.

As he continued to feel his poetic potential gathering in him, Keats's anxieties about the past or the future did not, he said, contaminate the purity of his contemplation. He wrote to Benjamin Bailey in November 1817: 'you perhaps at one time thought there was such a thing as Worldly Happiness to be arrived at, at certain periods of time marked out – you have of necessity from your disposition been thus led away – I scarcely remember counting upon any Happiness – I look not for it if it be not in the present hour – nothing startles me beyond the Moment.' (*Letters*, I, 186) He wanted to savour each moment, to live in it, not through it. How many of today's enthusiasts of Eckhart Tolle (1948-), recently released from remorse about the past and anxiety about the future, and intoxicated on 'the power of now', are aware that such ideas were formulated – though by no means originated –

by Keats? 'When Man has arrived at a certain ripeness in intellect any one grand and spiritual passage serves him as a starting post towards all "the two-and thirty Pallaces". How happy is such a "voyage of conception", what delicious diligent Indolence! A doze upon a sofa does not hinder it, and a nap upon Clover engenders ethereal finger-pointings' (*Letters*, I, 231-2).

According to Richard Woodhouse, Keats had only to see a billiard ball in order to 'conceive ... that it may have a sense of delight from its own roundness, smoothness volubility & the rapidity of its motion' (Bate, 261). Keats could accept the incomplete knowledge that 'Beauty is truth, truth beauty' as 'all [he needed] to know', without attempting to orientate the insight any further in order to meet any intellectual impatience on its own terms: 'I have an idea that a Man might pass a very pleasant life in this manner – let him on any certain day read a certain Page of full Poesy or distilled Prose, and let him wander with it, and muse upon it, and reflect from it, and bring home to it, and prophesy upon it, and dream upon it' (*Letters*, I, 231-2). The poet could dilate even the smallest chamber of mental freedom into a dreamscape.

28

Keats's Grecian Urn

FOLLOWING BLAKE'S EXAMPLE OF THE interrogative, exclamatory approach in a poem ('Did he who made the lamb make thee?'), Keats asks questions too, but of what or whom it is unclear: it is not the case that he is actually affecting to ask the Grecian urn itself – 'What men or gods are these? What maidens loth?/What mad pursuit? What struggle to escape?/What pipes and timbrels? What wild ecstasy?' – about the scenes depicted on it. Rather, the urn serves as the medium for the expression of a mode of life and culture long vanished, yet still accessible to the open, dreaming mind touchable by poetry. Just as a new 'planet' can swim into one's ken (but not one's control), so too can music seem to find its way to a point just beyond the reach, and the perishing touch, of 'the sensual ear'. Keats, for all his self-knowledge, is still experiencing some revulsion for the inescapable, irreversible process of change and decay – the arrow of time. In indulging that fearful, futile Hyperion-self still in him, he can also watch it as it welcomes each static scene depicted on the urn as some sort of suggestion of the possibility of literally stopping the arrow of time. The fearful, yearning self in Keats – in us all – then relishes the imaginary prospect of a changeless universe in which, for example, one's lover's personal beauty remains eternally intact, or one never wearies of, say, music, or the company of one's lover, and one never has to see the leaves falling from the trees telling one that winter is on its way. Again, the profusion of imagery becomes immersive, and it is almost as if the reader has become a naturalised inhabitant of this strange dimension where nothing changes, looking back almost with pity at 'All breathing human passions' which leave poor mortals 'high-sorrowful and cloy'd', their foreheads 'burning' and their tongues 'parching'.

Planets are left pockmarked, or even destroyed utterly, by the impacts of other huge, hurling, whirling lumps in space. The human body inherits what Shakespeare calls the thousand natural shocks. Any attempt to avoid the pockmarks, the shocks or the ultimate destruction of one's self as one thinks one knows it is as certain of failing as trying to make a square triangle, or even trying to imagine one. The arrow of time cannot be reversed, or stopped, and Keats – for all his searching and shape-shifting between warm mammal and 'Cold Pastoral', between 'truth' and 'beauty' – is of course unable to shift anything outside his own dream.

What is there, though, outside the dream – the poetic vision – worth bothering about?

29

Keats's Psyche

PSYCHE IS THE GODDESS OF THE soul, and Keats's ode to her is a warm act of advocacy for the least worshipped divine being in the Greek pantheon. No longer is the poet apologising ('Like a sick eagle looking at the sky') for his interest in Greek ideas: 'Yet even in these days so far retir'd/From happy pieties ... I see, and sing, by my own eyes inspir'd.' There is an enriching ambivalence about the means with which he has had his vision: 'Surely I dreamt to-day, or did I see/The winged Psyche with awaken'd eyes?' The levelling of dreams and waking thought is not second, but first, nature to the poet. There is no discernible anxiety to show that he has outgrown his cockney contemporary. He remains in Hunt's debt: the 'hush'd, cool-rooted flowers, fragrant-eyed,/Blue, silver-white, and budded Tyrian' could easily have been found in *The Story of Rimini*. But the power and compactness is his own, and he has, by the time of writing this first of his great odes, in April 1819, become what Shelley will say (in *A Defence of Poetry*) a true poet is – a hierophant of unapprehended wisdom: 'Yes, I will be thy priest, and build a fane/In some untrodden region of my mind,/Where branched thoughts, new growth with pleasant pain,/Instead of pines shall murmur in the wind ... ' Eight lines after 'pain', there emerges 'the wreath'd trellis of a working brain'. Those eight lines could represent the 'Vale of Soul-making' in which personal suffering has been approached as the raw material and worked into the worthiness of the poet *par excellence.*

The poem has an achieved greatness accompanied by a giddiness of vision comparable with Shelley's 'Triumph of Life' (1822). Keats demanded of himself – his individuality and his use of personal suffering – 'a greater system of salvation than the Christian religion.' Hunt had attacked, in journalism, the Prince Regent, but Keats was attacking, in poetry, the religion of the Establishment. He had already done this in, for example, his sonnet 'Written in disgust of vulgar superstition' ('Surely the mind of man is closely bound/In some black spell'), but now he was throwing back the curtain to reveal a genuinely uplifting alternative.

30

Autumnal Keats

H E HAD LOOKED UP INTO THE night sky, and he had looked into Chapman's Homer, and found – himself. It is significant to remember that one of the passages of Chapman's Homer that most excited Keats involved the planet Jupiter rising in an Autumn sky. Now, in 'To Autumn', the 'I' – the personal pronoun – has been shed like a full-grown and withered leaf, because the poet is prepared to see life's deciduousness through in order to transcend it by accessing – and even himself becoming – a special kind of objectivity. It is an objectivity that, unlike the kind taught by the French philosophers, does not aspire to absolute detachment from, or superiority to, the individual experience of the material world and its wearisome, feverish and fretful irrationalities. As merely descriptive poetry, 'To Autumn' is famously sensual and vivid: many readers will savour the 'mists and mellow fruitfulness', the 'hair soft-lifted by the winnowing wind', and the 'wailful choir' of 'small gnats' that mourns 'Among the river sallows, borne aloft/Or sinking as the light wind lives or dies'. But this poetry promotes an osmosis of feeling and meaning in the mutual involvement of personal and universal concerns. The year – like the writer, to say nothing of the reader – is dying. The flourishing features of the physical world suggest some source of their own nourishment that is metaphysical.

In this zone of consciousness, reality that is not material is given definition it does not often enjoy in the industrializing culture Keats finds himself living in: 'Where are the songs of Spring? Ay, where are they?' (They are in the imagination, or nowhere.) 'Hedge-crickets sing', the 'red-breast whistles' and 'gathering swallows twitter in the skies.' Remember, the year is dying. But there is an impulse (symbolised by the mysteriously energised swallows) to move out of the gathering shadow of death – to go south, like Porphyro and Madeline. When one is sick, one may long (though perhaps in vain) to get well, even as one gets worse. If the reader of the poem is familiar with Keats's personal circumstances, the phrase 'Thou watchest the last oozings hours by hours' might bring to mind Joseph Severn's sketch of the poet on his deathbed, and the artist's note below that sketch: '28 Janry 3 o'clock mng. Drawn to keep me awake – a deadly sweat was on him all this night'.

Part of the poet's point is that everything that lives dies. Gnats die, and humans die, but sensed in the special atmosphere of Keats's zone of symbols, the 'choir' of one species is no more affectingly 'wailful' than the choir of the other. We do not think small gnats ever mourn. The question provoked in us by the poem is not, however, What do we think gnats do? but What do we think we do? ('Think not of them'.) Medieval man saw himself in all things and all things in himself, bearing, this 'correspondence within him,' as Jung would put it, 'by virtue of his reflecting consciousness, on the one hand, and, on the other, thanks to the hereditary, archetypal nature of his instincts, which bind him to his environment.' (*The Undiscovered Self*, 1958) 'Enlightened' intellectuals will scorn any idea that the appearance of a comet in the sky has anything to do with the squabbles and other trivialities on earth: is it not my boundless ego, ignorance and vanity that prompt me to write into my own story the distant flight of a thunderbolt? No. And 'To Autumn' shows why not.

The sun is not maturing; the year is, and I am. But like Wallace Stevens's blackbird, the sun 'is involved in what I know', whether I am a thirteenth-century peasant or the most up-to-date astronomer. When Shelley called Keats 'a portion of that loveliness/Which once he made more lovely', he had in mind the imperishable radiance Keats never failed to behold beyond all perishable things – including his own autumnal, tubercular body.

31

Keats's Melancholy

ONE OF KEATS'S GREAT ODES WAS to the Greek goddess, Psyche. Another was to a Greek vase. Another was to a season, autumn. Another was to a bird, the nightingale. The 'Ode on Melancholy' shows the poet opening some metaphorical casements on a mood that, like the sea, has been much written about yet still remains mysterious. Melancholy can come as suddenly as a storm-blast on the Ancient Mariner's ocean: 'the melancholy fit shall fall/Sudden from heaven like a weeping cloud'. Or it can, more gradually, turn 'aching Pleasure ... to Poison'. Where does it come from? Where does it go to? Any answer, of course, is not located in space and time – and the only way an answer could be conceived is in terms of some of the familiar specifics of the material world – such as yew-berries and peonies (not to mention the familiar specifics of literary culture such as Lethe and Proserpine):

> Make not your rosary of yew-berries,
> Nor let the beetle, nor the death-moth be

Your mournful Psyche, nor the downy owl
A partner in your sorrow's mysteries.

Keats does not want to 'drown the wakeful anguish of the soul', because, however unpleasant, this is the medium in which transformation happens. If you 'go ... to Lethe', you will lose the wit to follow 'ethereal finger-pointings', and you will forfeit the natural human right to transformation.

Again, the detached voice – a detached voice unafraid of declaring itself situated inside individual human experience – knows what it is like to 'glut thy sorrow on a morning rose,/Or on the rainbow of the salt sand-wave'. There is not necessarily any lack of respect for empirical evidence. Keats knows as well as any learned disciple of Isaac Newton what salt crystals do to light. There is most definitely a sense of wonder, as exemplified by the 'wealth of globed peonies.' A peony can be, to Keats, a whole (other) world – and he can bring its whole other worldliness into being in the reader's imagination by spinning the suggestive 'globe' on a different – though unforced – axis of discourse. To the literal-minded, the double-exposure of microcosm and macrocosm can seem unhelpful. But Blake spoke a visionary language closely-related to Keats's when he saw a world in a grain of sand.

Keats sees transience everywhere, but looks past it to what it symbolises ('Ay, in the very temple of delight/Veil'd Melancholy has her Sovran shrine,/Though seen of none ... ') just as the philosopher looks past the astronomer's stars and statistics to what they symbolise. Again, Blake knew, and said, as much:

Joy and woe are woven fine,
A clothing for the soul divine.
Under every grief and pine
Runs a joy with silken twine.

– *Auguries of Innocence*

A trophy is something to be won – a material object to be hoisted aloft in triumph in front of cheering spectators. At the conclusion of 'Ode on Melancholy', the reader is left with 'cloudy trophies hung' in the mind. In protecting the purity of the unspecific, the poet has left no metaphorical mantelpiece upon which these prizes would otherwise have been obliged to be displayed, sooner or later having their nimbus dissolved by the inevitable dust-layer of familiarity. Shelley used clouds as the very image of mutability ('We are as clouds that veil the midnight moon;/How restlessly they speed, and gleam, and quiver'); Hamlet saw in a cloud the shape of a camel one moment, a weasel the next moment, and a whale the next. Clouds have a poetic pedigree that goes at least as far back as Aristophanes. Poets' language can be cloudy, simultaneously concealing and revealing reality. In 'To Autumn', the poet invokes the slanting rays of an autumnal sun which at once veils and venerates ('mists' and 'fruitfulness') what it shines upon: 'barred clouds bloom the soft-dying day'. Even the most impressive trophies of the material world will be changed as the light by which they are beheld changes – and, not least, as the beholder changes, as s/he is inextricably involved in the being of what s/he beholds. The trophies of the imagination gleam by what Thomas Traherne thought of as the 'ministry of inward light' ('The Circulation', V).

32

Shelley's Concern
About a Little Soul

IN DECEMBER 1820, SHELLEY MET EMILIA Viviani, the eldest daughter of Count Viviani, a nobleman of Pisa, and she became the inspiration for Shelley's greatest love poem (though Shelley's interest in Emilia herself would be outstripped by the mystical nature of the poem). Shelley said to Gisborne in October 1821: 'The *Epipsychidion* is a mystery; as to real flesh and blood, you know that I do not deal in those articles ... The person whom [the poem] celebrates was a cloud instead of a Juno, and poor Ixion starts from the centaur that was the offspring of his own embrace.' (*Letters*, II, 363) The object of Shelley's love changed 'as clouds that veil the midnight moon' (to borrow from his poem, 'Mutability'), and the poet's belief in free love – and his opposition to the idea of marriage – is expressed most eloquently in the following lines:

> I never was attached to that great sect,
> Whose doctrine is that each one should select
> Out of the crowd a mistress or a friend,
> And all the rest, though fair and wise, commend

> To cold oblivion, though 'tis in the code
> Of modern morals, and the beaten road
> Which those poor slaves with weary footsteps tread
> Who travel to their home among the dead
> By the broad highway of the world, and so
> With one chained friend, perhaps a jealous foe,
> The dreariest and the longest journey go.
>
>   – *Epipsychidion*, 149-159

The poet's passion seems to burn with the goal of spiritual purity in mind rather than carnal longing, and this for many readers has made Shelley too remote to listen to when he is not addressing the 'Men of England' in plainer speech. The poem was published anonymously in 1821, and the strongest view of it, which appeared in a satirical piece in the little-known periodical, *The Gossip*, was on its incomprehensibleness. 'It [*Epipsychidion*] is an idealized history of my life and feelings,' he told Gisborne, in June 1822: 'I think one is always in love with something or other; the error, and I confess it is not easy for spirits cased in flesh and blood to avoid it, consists in seeking in a mortal image the likeness of what is perhaps eternal.' (*Letters*, II, 434)

Shelley can only temporarily believe that in Emilia he has found at last the woman of his dreams, but the joy of such a discovery (however short-lived) is given a sort of permanence by the following lines:

> There was a Being whom my spirit oft
> Met on its visioned wanderings, far aloft,
> In the clear golden prime of my youth's dawn,
> Upon the fairy isles of sunny lawn,
> Amid the enchanted mountains, and the caves
> Of divine sleep, and on the air-like waves
> Of wonder-level dream, whose tremulous floor
> Paved her light steps. On an imagined shore,

Under the gray beak of some promontory
She met me, robed in such exceeding glory
That I beheld her not. In solitudes
Her voice came to me through the whispering woods,
And from the fountains and the odours deep
Of flowers, which, like lips murmuring in their sleep
Of the sweet kisses which had lulled them there,
Breathed but of *her* to the enamoured air;
And from the breezes whether low or loud,
And from the rain of every passing cloud,
And from the singing of the summer birds,
And from all sounds, all silence ...
Her spirit was the harmony of truth.

— *Epipsychidion*, 190-216

Wordsworth had done something similar with his 'Lines written a few miles above Tintern Abbey', his poem of love to his sister Dorothy; Byron, too, had felt, somehow, in the natural world around him the presence of the love of his life, Augusta Leigh, from whom he had been physically separated:

In the Desert a fountain is springing,
In the wide waste there still is a tree,
And a bird in the solitude singing,
Which speaks to my spirit of *Thee*.

— 'Stanzas to Augusta', July 1816

Shelley says in his 'Ode to a Skylark' that we look before and after and pine for what is not, and so his exploratory yearnings have left many readers looking at the discoveries with pleasure or in perplexity:

Warm fragrance seems to fall from her light dress,
    And her loose hair; and from some heavy tress
The air of her own speed has disentwined,
    Her sweetness seems to satiate the faint wind;

> And in the soul a wild odour is felt,
> Beyond the sense, like fiery dews that melt
> Into the bosom of a frozen bud.
> See where she stands! a mortal shape indued
> With love and life and light and deity,
> And motion which may change but cannot die;
> An image of some bright Eternity;
> A shadow of some golden dream ...
>
> – *Epipsychidion*, 105-16

Just as Shelley had watched the skylark fly up into the deep sky and melt into the 'pale purple', so the actual – and therefore temporary – object of his love refines itself into consistent invisibility:

> ... a Splendour
> Leaving the third sphere pilotless; a tender
> Reflection of the eternal Moon of Love,
> Under whose motions life's dull billows move;
> A metaphor of Spring and Youth and Morning;
> A vision like incarnate April, warning,
> With smiles and tears, Frost the Anatomy
> Into his summer grave.
>
> – *Epipsychidion*, 116-23

Having made the natural world – 'Of waves, flowers, clouds, woods, rocks' (511) and 'quick bats in their twilight dance' (532) and 'spotted deer' (533) – shine in the implosive aureole of his vision, the poet who fell upon the thorns of life and bled (in 'Ode to the West Wind') is now enduring the death throes of a martyr:

> One Heaven, one Hell, one immortality,
> And one annihilation. Woe is me!
> The wingèd words on which my soul would pierce
> Into the height of Love's rare Universe,

Are chains of lead around its flight of fire.
I pant, I sink, I tremble, I expire!

– *Epipsychidion*, 586-91

Even at the height of his powers, Shelley continues to provide his detractors with ammunition. 'I expire!' might seem hammy to readers over-supplied with information about the poet's personality and encouraged to censure him. Hamlet's 'Horatio, I am dead' and 'O, I die, Horatrio!' (*Hamlet*, V, ii) tend to be received less incredulously because critics know nothing of the author's actual life: for all they know, Shakespeare might have been every bit as delicate and *farouche* as Shelley the public schoolboy, and every bit as callous a user of women and as 'simplistic' a polemicist as Shelley the adult. But Shakespeare is completely hidden behind his art. If he was bad to his wife, no evidence of it remains to inform our reading of Hamlet's treatment of Ophelia. If he had a silly voice, no remembrance of it interferes with the shudder that Hamlet's gazing into the late Yorick's skull brings on in the reader. In the fullness of time, Shakespeare's contribution to thought has been declared elemental and set free. In the meantime, Shelley's had to remain on remand until the arrival of an unbiased tribunal.

33

Byron's *Don Juan*

L ANGLEY MOORE HAS OFFERED A PLAUSIBLE
speculation as to *Don Juan*'s uncatchable oscillation between
the sublime and the ridiculous:

> Byron was assiduous in the study of boxing, shooting and fencing,
> partly because he would naturally wish to master those physical
> accomplishments which, like swimming and horsemanship, could
> be practised despite his handicap, and partly because they were
> sporting activities of a man-about-town, and this was an aspect of
> his life that he had cultivated from early youth. It has seemed to
> some critics unworthy of a poet to care about the world of fashion,
> but his genius derived its sustenance from the variety of his
> experiences and all the contrasts they provided, which gives *Don
> Juan* its flashing interplay of poetical and mundane images. (Langley
> Moore, 190)

Don Juan is the most Byronic poem because of all the varied moods
– ecstasy, flippancy, indignation, pride, self-immersion, self-
assertion, guilt, insouciance, sentimentality, nostalgia, optimism,
pessimism. Byron took a poet's liberties with an old idea. The
joke in *Don Juan* is that it is based on the myth of Don Giovanni,

but instead of the great seducer of the traditional tale, there is a hero who in fact finds himself seduced by one woman after another. He is much more of a passive character than the active rake that audiences and readers were used to. The interesting thing about *Don Juan* is that, in it, Byron deconstructs the earlier poem, *Childe Harold*, the poem which had made women throw themselves at him, because they confused the writer with the hero he had created. The impact was made by the image of the romantic hero who was mysterious, gloomy, brooding and handsome. The gloomy, reflecting hero suddenly becomes the hero of *Don Juan* who has no kind of inner life or sense of memory at all. Don Juan spends the first part of Canto II in a state of melancholy at his departure from his native country, and weeping over the love letter he has received from one of the women who has seduced him:

> 'Farewell, my Spain! a long farewell!' he cried,
> 'Perhaps I may revisit thee no more,
> But die, as many an exiled heart hath died,
> Of its own thirst to see again thy shore:
> Farewell, where Guadalquiver's waters glide!
> Farewell, my mother! and, since all is o'er,
> Farewell too, dearest Julia! – (here he drew
> Her letter out again, and read it through.)
>
> 'And oh! if e'er I should forget, I swear –
> But that's impossible, and cannot be –
> Sooner shall this blue Ocean melt to air,
> Sooner shall Earth resolve itself to sea,
> Than I resign thine image, oh, my fair!
> Or think of anything, excepting thee ...

A little later in the canto the letter is being torn up to be used as lots to decide who is going to be the person that is eaten (the crew and passengers are stranded upon the ocean, out of food, and about to engage in cannibalism):

> And none to be the sacrifice would choose;
> At length the lots were torn up, and prepared,
> But of materials that must shock the Muse –
> Having no paper, for the want of better,
> They took by force from Juan Julia's letter ...

The poem thoroughly debunks any pious or precious idea about human dignity, and it completely mystified Byron's readers. This is one of the reasons why Hazlitt was unable to stand Byron:

> The solemn hero of tragedy plays *Scrub* in the farce ... The Noble Lord is almost the only writer who has prostituted his talents in this way. He hallows in order to desecrate; takes a pleasure in defacing the images of beauty his hands have wrought; and raises our hopes and our beliefs in goodness only to dash them to the earth again, and break them in pieces the more effectively from the height they have fallen.
>
> – *Spirit of the Age*

Hazlitt saw Byron as not having high seriousness. Byron takes the reader up, and then knocks him down – in the cannibal episode, right down: Byron takes the reader from the first to the seventh circle of hell, and the manner in which he does it can look far too morally careless to a Christian reader:

> The lots were made, and marked, and mixed, and handed,
> In silent horror, and their distribution
> Lulled even the savage hunger which demanded,
> Like the Promethean vulture , this pollution;
> None in particular has sought or planned it,
> 'Twas Nature gnawed them to this resolution,
> By which none were permitted to be neuter –
> And the lot fell on Juan's luckless tutor.

He but requested to be bled to death:
The surgeon had his instruments, and bled
Pedrillo, and so gently ebbed his breath,
You hardly could perceive when he was dead.
He died as born, a Catholic in faith,
Like most in the belief in which they're bred,
And first a little crucifix he kissed,
And then held out his jugular and wrist.

The surgeon, as there was no other fee,
Had his first choice of morsels for his pains;
But being thirstiest at the moment, he
Preferred a draught from the fast-flowing veins:
Part was divided, part thrown in the sea,
And such things as the entrails and the brains
Regaled two sharks, who followed o'er the billow –
The sailors ate the rest of poor Pedrillo.

– Don Juan, II, lxxv-lxxvii

The above passage does not merely illustrate a poet's fascination with morbid detail. Byron the satirist had the ability to capture the mental realities in human beings, and he could capture them with the ferocity of a collector driving his pins through social butterflies.

Hazlitt was unable to appreciate that although the character of Don Juan is central, the bigger character was Byron, avoiding the easy option of playing the moralist, and instead showing readers in Regency England the infallibility of their own appetites' pursuit of gratification. Earlier in the poem, Byron shows the surface stillness of Julia's temperament beginning to register the first tremors of desires gathering below:

Juan she saw, and, as a pretty child,
Caressed him often – such a thing might be
Quite innocently done, and harmless styled,
When she had twenty years, and thirteen he;

But I am not so sure I should have smiled
When he was sixteen, Julia twenty-three;
These few short years make wondrous alterations,
Particularly amongst sun-burnt nations.

                 – *Don Juan*, I, lxviii

Whate'er the cause might be, they had become
Changed; for the dame grew distant, the youth shy,
Their looks cast down, their greetings almost dumb,
And much embarrassment in either eye;
There surely will be little doubt with some
That Donna Julia knew the reason why,
But as for Juan, he had no more notion
Than he who never saw the sea of Ocean.

                 – *Don Juan*, I, lxx

The poet traces very closely Donna Julia's silent explosion of inner lust. The passage is particularly subversive. It is one thing for a lady to look demure and practice piety, but it is another for her to contain entirely her own unstoppable passions:

And if she met him, though she smiled no more,
She looked a sadness sweeter than her smile,
As if her heart had deeper thoughts in store
She must not own, but cherished more the while
For that compression in its burning core;
Even Innocence itself has many a wile,
And will not dare to trust itself with truth,
And Love is taught hypocrisy from youth.

                 – *Don Juan*, I, lxxii

The above stanza encapsulates the mechanism by which the respectable individual maintains her respectability, even when rattled by feelings that she simultaneously wants and does not want to have. Byron remains focused on this concept, and does not interrupt himself with the usual digression:

But Passion most dissembles, yet betrays
Even by its darkness; as the blackest sky
Foretells the heaviest tempest, it displays
Its workings through the vainly guarded eye,
And in whatever aspect it arrays
Itself, 't is still the same hypocrisy;
Coldness or Anger, even Disdain or Hate,
Are masks it often wears, and still too late.

— *Don Juan*, I, lxxiii

His focus still uninterrupted, the poet ratchets up the sense of Julia's sexual tension. One realises the reason for the sustained focus: the stanzas are gathering like a judgment on the conventional concept of monogamy:

Then there were sighs, the deeper for suppression,
And stolen glances, sweeter for the theft,
And burning blushes, though for no transgression
Tremblings when met, and restlessness when left;
All these are little preludes to possession,
Of which young Passion cannot be bereft ...

— *Don Juan*, I, lxxiv

Becoming fully strident now, Byron demonstrates that human desires will flow despite the traditions built by humans to dam them:

Poor Julia's heart was in an awkward state;
She felt it going, and resolved to make
The noblest efforts for herself and mate,
For Honour's, Pride's, Religion's, Virtue's sake:
Her resolutions were most truly great,
And almost might have made a Tarquin quake:
She prayed the Virgin Mary for her grace,
As being the best judge of a lady's case.

— *Don Juan*, I, lxxv

She vowed she never would see Juan more,
And next day paid a visit to his mother,
And looked extremely at the opening door,
Which, by the Virgin's grace, let in another;
Grateful she was, and yet a little sore –
Again it opens, it can be no other,
'Tis surely Juan now – No! I'm afraid
That night the Virgin was no further prayed.

— *Don Juan*, I, lxxvi

The poet has brought Julia to look over the moral precipice:

She now determined that a virtuous woman
Should rather face and overcome temptation,
That flight was base and dastardly, and no man
Should ever give her heart the least sensation,
That is to say, a thought beyond the common
Preference, that we must feel, upon occasion,
For people who are pleasanter than others,
But then they only seem so many brothers.

— *Don Juan*, I, lxxvii

When Julia and Juan next meet, Byron again sustains his focus on Julia's inner struggle, and the precariously thin line that can divide 'Platonic' and sexual enthusiasm:

Julia had honour, virtue, truth, and love
For Don Alfonso; and she inly swore,
By all the vows below to Powers above,
She never would disgrace the ring she wore,
Nor leave a wish which wisdom might reprove;
And while she pondered this, besides much more,
One hand on Juan's carelessly was thrown,
Quite by mistake – she thought it was her own ...

— *Don Juan*, I, cix

Unconsciously she leaned upon the other,
Which played within the tangles of her hair;
And to contend with thoughts she could not smother
She seemed by the distraction of her air ...

– Don Juan, I, cx

The hand which still held Juan's, by degrees
Gently, but palpably confirmed its grasp,
As if it said, 'Detain me, if you please';
Yet there's no doubt she only meant to clasp
His fingers with a pure Platonic squeeze ...

– Don Juan, I, cxi

... she must have thought there was no harm,
Or else 't were easy to withdraw her waist;
But then the situation had its charm,
And then – God knows what next – I can't go on;
I'm almost sorry that I e'er begun.

– Don Juan, I, cxv

Byron inhabits a twilight region between comedy and high seriousness, which, because it cannot be cleanly identified as one or the other, has not had the attention it deserves:

Oh Plato! Plato! you have paved the way,
With your confounded fantasies, to more
Immoral conduct by the fancied sway
Your system feigns o'er the controlless core
Of human hearts ...

– Don Juan, I, cxvi

The poet's challenging of received wisdom has made his work perennially important. People still believe things – not to mention die, kill, starve, marry, work for them – that are not necessarily true. Byron is special because he reminds us of what we thought we knew, and he does it with a texture of imagination that feels plastic and fun to play with. No new commandments can be chiselled because all is constantly changing, and is, in short, irregularly *alive*. He did not stop, having attacked 'History, Tradition .../newspapers ... ' (*Don Juan*, I, cciii), but worked on to reveal a reality wondrous beyond the ken of tradition:

> But now at thirty years my hair is grey –
> (I wonder what it will be like at forty?
> I thought of a peruke the other day –)
> My heart is not much greener; and, in short, I
> Have squandered my whole summer while 't was May,
> And feel no more the spirit to retort; I
> Have spent my life, both interest and principal,
> And deem not, what I deemed – my soul invincible.
>
>   – *Don Juan*, I, ccxiii

> No more – no more – Oh! never more on me
> The freshness of the heart can fall like dew,
> Which out of all the lovely things we see
> Extracts emotions beautiful and new,
> Hived in our bosoms like the bag o' the bee.
> Think'st thou the honey with these objects grew?
> Alas! 't was not in them, but in thy power
> To double even the sweetness of a flower.
>
>   – *Don Juan*, I, ccxiv

> No more – no more – Oh! never more, my heart,
> Canst thou be my sole world, my universe!
> Once all in all, but now a thing apart,
> Thou canst not be my blessing or my curse ...
>
>   – *Don Juan*, I, ccxv

Even when the poet feels scorched by reality's aridity, he paradoxically teems as a creative force:

> What is the end of fame? 'tis but to fill
> A certain portion of uncertain paper:

Some liken it to climbing up a hill,
Whose summit, like all hills, is lost in vapour;
For this men write, speak, preach, and heroes kill,
And bards burn what they call their 'midnight taper',
To have, when the original is dust,
A name, a wretched picture and worse bust.

— *Don Juan*, I, ccxviii

34

Byromania

BYRON WAS GIVEN A ROUGH TIME, and it has to be said that it was mainly because of prudery. His achievements make up a complex picture. He was a lyric poet in a way that Pope was not. At the same time, he had the wit, and the impatience with existence, that urged him to write more straightforwardly than the other Romantic poets.

Why were the critics so hostile? When Byron's body was returned from Greece – 'the only place I ever was contented in' – to England, his reputation was so bad that he could not possibly have been buried in Westminster Abbey or St Paul's Cathedral. The paper, *John Bull,* jeered that the poet had 'quitted the world at the most unfortunate period of his career, and in the most unsatisfactory manner – in voluntary exile, where his mind, debased by evil associations and the malignant brooding over imaginary ills, has been devoted to the construction of elaborate lampoons.' His body was returned to Nottinghamshire. At his funeral, on 12 July 1824, the multitude of spectators did not care about the achievement of *Don Juan,* the Hebrew Melodies, or the Turkish Tales. But they did care about tales of incest and sodomy.

Some literary historians have made bold to suggest that the poetry has great merit, but the condemnation of the moralists found an influential voice. In 1924, Bishop Herbert E. Ryle effectively stymied another attempt to get Byron a place in Poets' Corner in Westminster:

> Byron, partly by his own openly dissolute life and partly by the influence of licentious verse, earned a worldwide reputation for immorality among English-speaking people. A man who outraged the laws of our Divine Lord, and whose treatment of women violated the Christian principles of purity and honor, should not be commemorated in Westminster Abbey.

Ryle spoke on behalf of the established church, which would not change the decision, despite the publication in the *Times* of a letter, in defence of Byron, from a group of people including Thomas Hardy, Rudyard Kipling and three former Prime Ministers (Asquith, Balfour and Lloyd George).

Byron's work is a fascinating blend of real feeling *and* real sharpness. Coleridge said: 'according to the noble wont of the English people, Byron's literary merits would seem continually to rise, while his personal errors, if not denied, or altogether forgotten, would be little noticed, & would be treated with ever softening gentleness.' (*Coleridge Collected Letters*, edited E.L. Griggs, V, 207) He was not sexually repressed. He was sexually troubled, and driven irresistibly from within to anatomise that trouble. He did not have the inner serenity to retire and cultivate his spirit in silence. The unwieldy swirl in him of dust and deity precluded the recollection of emotion in tranquillity – as it precludes such recollection in most human beings.

There are writers who systematise and preach their systems.

When we read their works, and when we are greatly impressed, we sometimes try to live our lives by those writers' precepts. But we often find that, for us, there is something wooden and unworkable about living one's life in accordance with, say, the teachings of Wordsworth, or Christ. To have one's behaviour and thoughts regulated by the general rules of someone else is to continually remind oneself that one is not good enough as one is. To have to act better than one is, is like walking with a pebble in one's shoe in order to remember to play the part of someone with a limp – it is false and painful. One absolutely must, from time to time, flex oneself out of constraints.

Byron is such an exuberant expression of the impulse in us all towards *freedom*, that churchmen, critics, literary theorists, and other people with wooden agendas have not been very passionate about informing readers of the extents of Byron's two geniuses – as a lyric poet –

> My soul is dark – Oh! quickly string
> The harp I yet can brook to hear;
> And let thy gentle fingers fling
> Its melting murmurs o'er mine ear.
> If in this heart a hope be dear,
> That sound shall charm it forth again:
> If in these eyes there lurk a tear
> 'Twill flow, and cease to burn my brain.
>
> But bid the strain be wild and deep,
> Nor let thy notes of joy be first:
> I tell thee, minstrel, I must weep,
> Or else this heavy heart will burst;
> For it hath been by sorrow nursed,
> And ached in sleepless silence long;
> And now 'tis doomed to know the worst,
> And breaks at once – or yield to song.
>
> – 'My Soul is Dark', *Hebrew Melodies*

– and as a satirist:

> But let it go: – it will one day be found
> With other relics of 'a former World',
> When this World shall be *former*, underground,
> Thrown topsy-turvy, twisted, crisped, and curled,
> Baked, fried, or burnt, turned inside-out, or drowned,
> Like all the worlds before, which have been hurled
> First out of, and then back again to chaos –
> The superstratum which will overlay us.
>
> – *Don Juan*, IX, xxxvii

While the detractors, and the purveyors of faint praise, have been busy reducing the poet to something they could understand, his work has joyously persisted on its own terms. To read his work is to know that the verbal universe he created has its own patterns of interconnectivity, its own laws, and its own life:

> The mind can make
> Substance, and people planets of its own
> With beings brighter than have been, and give
> A breath to forms which can outlive all flesh.
>
> – *The Dream*, 1816

35

Keats's Bright Star

IN 'BRIGHT STAR! WOULD I WERE steadfast as thou art'
(1819) Keats's star, like the scenes on the urn, looks 'steadfast'
– something that we poor human beings, destined to ride the
roller-coaster of emotions and then die, can never be. Keats,
however, is a true poet, and so his *aspiration* to be steadfast is
troubling in its burning intensity. 'I have felt/A presence that
disturbs me with the joy/Of elevated thoughts,' said Wordsworth
in his 'Lines written a few miles above Tintern Abbey', in which
he expressed his deep love for his sister. Keats too expresses his
love for Fanny Brawne, but whereas Wordsworth had recognised
something of his former self in the shooting lights of Dorothy's
wild eyes, Keats is contemplating abdicating (remember Lear) his
former self in order simply to be 'Pillow'd upon my fair love's
ripening breast,/To feel for ever its soft fall and swell,/Awake for
ever in a sweet unrest,/Still, still to hear her tender-taken breath,/
And so live ever – or else swoon to death.' The desire to regress
into childhood innocence is what Keats is observing in himself. It
is not a desire that has taken possession of him entirely. He is

demonstrating his uncanny capacity for ambivalent attention to his own doubleness. He is at once like one of the figures on the urn, 'for ever' with his head resting childishly on his lover's bosom, *and* the higher, brighter other co-ordinate to which humanity will owe the debt of gratitude.

36

Keats's Living Hand

O N READING KEATS'S POSTHUMOUS FRAGMENT, 'This Living Hand', one may be reminded of Porphyro's 'glowing hand' in stanza XXXI of 'The Eve of St Agnes' (and his unsettlingly vague intentions in Madeline's bedroom), and one may also catch an echo of Shakespeare's Claudio expressing his fear of death to his sister Isabella: 'To lie in cold obstruction and to rot;/This sensible warm motion to become/A kneaded clod ... ' (*Measure For Measure* III,1,122-4). The tyrannical Angelo has told Isabella that if she refuses to grant him his sexual wishes, he will have Claudio killed. On hearing of this, Claudio is understandably keen for Isabella to prioritise his life above her own virtue. As it happens, she does not. This is another wintry blast of Shakespearean wisdom. Actions and destinies are determined by characters' own flawed passions and points of view. Isabella (reacting to her brother's 'cowardice'), like Cordelia (reacting to her father's foolish request for confirmation of her love for him), is trying to live by her own lights and do the right thing – but the reader is never told what is really 'right'. Fanny

Brawne's refusal to comply with Keats's wishes may echo, for the poet, Shakespeare's revelations. If this is the case, then the pressure of meaning behind the following words has resonances of Claudio's pressure on Isabella, and Lear's on Cordelia: 'thou would wish thine own heart dry of blood/So in my veins red life might stream again,/And thou be conscience-calm'd ... ' However, Keats completes this short poem with an extraordinary gesture of his 'living hand': ' – see here it is – /I hold it before you.' It feels as if the gesture is made towards the reader of distant posterity – as if the hand is being outstretched, not just through time and space then and there, but through the dream connecting readers and writers scattered in time and space – indeed the dream we all live in – by way of a greeting. James Elroy Flecker would surely find in this symbol the inspiration to write 'To a Poet a Thousand Years Hence':

> O friend unseen, unborn, unknown,
> Student of our sweet English tongue,
> Read out my words at night, alone:
> I was a poet, I was young.
>
> Since I can never see your face,
> And never shake you by the hand,
> I send my soul through time and space
> To greet you. You will understand.

37

Keats's Reptile Woman

APOLLONIUS STANDS FOR INTELLECT AND REASON;
Lamia stands for emotion and sensation. Lamia can devour
men. One thing that gives 'Lamia' (1819) its power is that Keats
has never felt more divided: he knows that the grand findings of
scientists such as Newton and philosophers such as Godwin can
be used for the greater good of society. He also knows that poetry
is not science or philosophy, and therefore the good of poetry is
harder to identify – if it really exists at all, except in the (vain?)
poet's imagination.

As John Whale has said, 'In giving the poem her name, Keats declares
his interest in the nature of his Lamia.' (Whale, 79) The following
famous passage suggests that Keats's sympathies lie with Lamia:

> Do not all charms fly
> At the mere touch of cold philosophy?
> There was an awful rainbow once in heaven:
> We know her woof, her texture; she is given
> In the dull catalogue of common things.
> Philosophy will clip an Angel's wings,

Conquer all mysteries by rule and line,
Empty the haunted air, and gnomed mine –
Unweave a rainbow, as it erewhile made
The tender-person'd Lamia melt into a shade.

— *Lamia*, II, 229-38

The beauty and acuity in Keats's poetry will, like Lamia, 'melt into ... shade' if it is elucidated only by school inspectors or other professionals with the crude, insistent passion to hold their ground and register their disrespect for the 'bad' and the 'weak'. The 'progress' of place-hunting humanity can often look impressive (or imposing) on state-generated charts; but *is* the education available in the western world blameless for the masses of uninteresting adults? To enumerate the amount of Angels' wings that have been clipped, and the weightless mental riches that have been confiscated, would be, of course, impossible. At the time of writing 'Lamia', Keats (like the other great English Romantics) perceived 'progress' to be proliferating like cancer cells into the collective mind from the central theses of educationists.

Lamia's metamorphosis from a serpent into a woman displays again Keats's impressive rapport with *Paradise Lost*:

Left to herself, the serpent now began
To change; her elfin blood in madness ran,
Her mouth foam'd, and the grass, therewith besprent,
Wither'd at dew so sweet and virulent;
Her eyes in torture fix'd, and anguish drear,
Hot, glaz'd, and wide, with lid-lashes all sear,
Flash'd phosphor and sharp sparks, without one cooling tear.
The colours all inflam'd throughout her train,
She writh'd about, convuls'd with scarlet pain:
A deep volcanian yellow took the place
Of all her milder-mooned body's grace;
And, as the lava ravishes the mead,
Spoilt all her silver mail, and golden brede;

Made gloom of all her frecklings, streaks and bars,
Eclips'd her crescents, and lick'd up her stars:
So that, in moments few, she was undrest
Of all her sapphires, greens, and amethyst,
And rubious-argent: of all these bereft,
Nothing but pain and ugliness were left.
Still shone her crown; that vanished, also she
Melted and disappear'd as suddenly ...

        – *Lamia*, I, 146-66

Whale is insightful: 'There's a disturbing inversion at work here: in a story of a man-eating predatory lamia one might legitimately expect the narrative to begin with the putting on of a disguise of false beauty with which to lure and deceive the hapless male prey. Instead, Keats has his creature lose its dazzling beauty so as to become a woman.' (Whale, 81) The tonal instability, over which the immature author of *Endymion* and 'Isabella' had significantly less control, is now fixedly and fluidly part of the mature poet's repertoire. Lamia is only *confoundingly* multi-faceted because that, for Keats, is the point:

She was a Gordian shape of dazzling hue,
Vermillion-spotted, golden, green, and blue;
Striped like a zebra, freckled like a pard,
Eyed like a peacock, and all crimson barr'd;
And full of silver moons, that, as she breathed,
Dissolv'd, or brighter shone, or interwreathed
Their lustres with the gloomier tapestries –
So rainbow-sided, touch'd with miseries,
She seem'd, at once, some penanced lady elf,
Some demon's mistress, or the demon's self.
Upon her crest she wore a wannish fire
Sprinkled with stars, like Ariadne's tiar:
Her head was serpent, but ah, bitter-sweet!
She had a woman's mouth ...

        – *Lamia*, I, 47-60

The apparently unfixed subjects of Keats's poetry can find a different mode of definition against the backdrop of his letters:

> ... I do not think myself more in the right than other people and ... nothing in the world is provable ... I am sometimes so very sceptical as to think Poetry itself a mere Jack a lanthern to amuse whoever may chance to be struck with its brilliance – As Tradesmen say every thing is worth what it will fetch, so probably every mental pursuit takes its reality and worth from the ardour of the pursuer – being in itself a nothing – Ethereal things may at least be thus real, divided under three heads – Things real – things semireal – and no things – Things real – such as existences of Sun Moon & Stars and passages of Shakspeare – Things semireal such as Love, the Clouds &c which require a greeting of the Spirit to make them wholly exist – and Nothings which are made Great and dignified by ardent pursuit ...
>
> – *Letters*, I, 242-3

In light of this passage, from Keats's letter of March 1818 to Bailey, perhaps it would not be sensible or appropriate to inquire what 'Lamia' is 'of' or 'about', in the way, say, that one might interrogate Wordsworth's narrative poems such as 'The Mad Mother', 'The Idiot Boy', and 'We Are Seven', and find that they are 'of' and 'about' the thoughts and feelings of Britain's poorest and least articulate citizens.

Keats told his brother he was 'certain there is that sort of fire in it which must take hold of people in some way – give them either pleasant or unpleasant sensation. What they want is sensation of some sort' (*Letters*, II, 189). Keats saw himself as a provider of this need: 'A Poet is the most unpoetical of any thing in existence; because he has no Identity – he is continually in for – and filling some other Body – The Sun, the Moon, the Sea and Men and Women who are creatures of impulse are poetical and have about them an unchangeable attribute – the poet has

none; no identity ... ' (*Letters*, I, 387). But he knew that his
'Lamia' was – howsoever inspired, like the rest of his best poetry
– not fiery in a way that would quickly cut through the hard,
passionless clatter of contemporary thinking, and win him the
recognition he deserved.

38

Keats's Pitiless Woman

'LA BELLE DAME SANS MERCI' MEANS 'Beautiful Lady Without Pity'. For poets, death is a lady who must finally come for you. This poem is about death and the dying, and the dead. Keats wrote about what he saw in a dream. The poem is about him, and so deeply personal that he did not want to publish it. He is too young to die. He will not have achieved, in his mind, what he set out to do:

> And this is why I sojourn here
>   Alone and palely loitering,
> Though the sedge has wither'd from the lake,
>   And no birds sing.
>
> — 'La Belle Dame Sans Merci', XII

The phrase 'Alone and palely loitering' is as haunting as Coleridge's 'Alone, alone all, all alone' – as if it has been echoing, all along, through the unsounded reaches of one's nervous system until a Keats, or a Coleridge, got it to come into one's ken.

The spirit of the German love poet Tannhäuser informs this magical, mysterious and painful ballad. The poem seems to be a –

if not the – source of the Pre-Raphaelites such as Algernon Charles Swinburne and the Symbolists such as Gustave Moreau. In 1887, William Michael Rossetti appreciated the charm of the poem: 'This is a poem of *impression*. The impression is immediate, final, and permanent; and words would be more than wasted upon pointing out to the reader that such and such are the details which have conduced to impress him ... ' (*Keats: Narrative Poems*, 65).

The reader may learn the poem by heart easily enough, and possess it, and be possessed by it, allowing the incantation to find its full psychic purchase in the combination of imagination, intellect and nervous energy that characterises a reader's receptivity to poetry. However, as is the case with Coleridge's 'Kubla Khan' and 'The Rime of the Ancient Mariner', whenever one tries to understand the poem, one discovers that one is trying to apply a formula to something that evades the formula. To ask what it 'means' is as misguided an approach as asking what a dream 'means' – or what a new planet that swims into one's ken means. It shape-shifts actively and echoically, and will not passively have its shape shifted into a final, defining passage of prose.

On one level, there appears to be a clash of discourses between the Belle Dame and the knight: 'She look'd at me as she did love,/ And made sweet moan.' ('La Belle Dame Sans Merci', VI) *Did* she love? What did the moan mean? (Does the presence of the adjective 'sweet' really do anything to answer the question?) If the reader is inclined to accept that the poem is about sex and death, s/he will understand that 'She' is coming – *le petit mort*. Does 'She' love him? (Does the presence of the word 'sure' really do anything to answer the question?) 'And sure in language strange she said – /"I love thee true."' ('La Belle Dame Sans Merci', VII) When did the dream begin? At what exact moment did the real turn into the unreal, reality into reverie? Where was the border? Where is the border?

The pressure of unanswered questions is like the presence of the dark – and death – that envelopes the figures in Rembrandt's 'Anatomy Lesson of Dr Tulp' (1632) or 'Night Watch' (1642). We are surrounded at all times by Mystery. We live in – and only in – Mystery. And we feel – or *will* feel – pain frequently: 'And I awoke, and found me here/On the cold hill's side.' ('La Belle Dame Sans Merci', XI) We do not know why we are here (to say nothing of the question of *if* we are here, or anywhere, or if the question why? has any meaning).

When one experiences the desolation of being left by one's lover for ever, one is not actually left on a hill side; but one may recognise – having palely loitered on one's own version of it, perhaps – Keats's hill side. Shakespeare caught it earlier: Juliet was Romeo's 'Sun', and her extinction meant his extinction. Such a metaphor never – like a material reality – loses its lustre or shape over the centuries, or even millennia, but keeps all its value, and even retains and renews it. This is what Keats has in mind in the following letter:

> I will call the *world* a School instituted for the purpose of teaching little children to read – I will call the *human heart* the *horn Book* used in that School – and I will call the *Child able to read, the Soul* made from that *school* and its *hornbook*. Do you not see how necessary a World of Pains and troubles is to school an Intelligence and make it a soul? A Place where the heart must feel and suffer in a thousand diverse ways!
>
> – *Letters*, II, 102

Like Frank Osbaldistone in Scott's novel, *Rob Roy* (1817), many young people find themselves accountable to their parents – as, later on, they will find themselves accountable to the other funders of their activities. In the exacting realm of utility, mono-dimensional reading habits are often instilled in people. So it is all the more remarkable that poems such as the 'Ode to a Nightingale', 'To Autumn' or 'La Belle Dame Sans Merci' show the irreducibility of fine Romantic art to one 'meaning'. Keats's poetry is indicative of his (and the Romantic Movement's) resistance to an ethos unpropitious to all human beings but those who conceive themselves in terms of a mechanistic science. Keats has been in the grip of the muse, and living in a state of imaginative exaltation deriving in part from his visionary sense, and the rising towards the surface of unconscious themes. In 'La Belle Dame Sans Merci', he gives utterance to the unformulated content of the unconscious state of many individuals, a mélange of mortal anxiety and somnambulist eroticism. He felt 'more and more every day, as my imagination strengthens, that I do not live in this world alone but in a thousand worlds' (*Letters*, I, 403). As Jung would put it in *The Undiscovered Self*, 'Such a condition cries out for order and synthesis.' Keats has answered the cries with some of the most beautiful and powerful poetry ever composed.

39

Shelley's Triumph

SHELLEY'S USE OF THE DANTESQUE *TERZA rima* is well-known: in the 'Ode to the West Wind' (1819), the poet used the form to convey the onward rush of autumn leaves, and political and spiritual hopes. In his last poem, *The Triumph of Life*, he sets a scene of strange beauty that proves a perfect environment in which to experience a vision:

> Swift as a spirit hastening to his task
> Of glory and of good, the Sun sprang forth
> Rejoicing in his splendour, and the mask
>
> Of darkness fell from the awakened Earth;
> The smokeless altars of the mountain snows
> Flamed above crimson clouds, and at the birth
>
> Of light the Ocean's orison arose,
> To which the birds tempered their matin lay.
> All flowers in field or forest, which unclose
>
> Their trembling eyelids to the kiss of day,

Swinging their censers in the element,
With orient incense lit by the new ray

Burned slow and inconsumably, and sent
Their odorous sighs up to the smiling air ...

— *Triumph of Life*, 1-14

Within the larger unity of nature, each hub of life unfolds its own unity of form in perfect, minute precision. The fragrance of the flowers and the light toward which the flowers turn are, in a reductive sense, merely among the many parts of the blind mechanism that most people take the world to be. For the conventionally educated mind, the atoms making up the external scene, supposedly no different from the atoms making up the observer (or participant), are inert, and driven hither and thither by external forces. Not for Shelley. On receiving 'the kiss of day', the flowers swing their 'censers'. The rite of the morning is *observed* – by the Sun, the Ocean, the birds, and even the 'smiling' air. The second and third stanzas quoted above fill the reader's beholding like a rose window in a cathedral. The one permanent reality, the underlying principle, is shining through the details of the world's phenomena:

Before me fled
The night; behind me rose the day; the deep
Was at my feet, and Heaven above my head; –
When a strange trance over my fancy grew
Which was not slumber ...

Poetic vision is inevitable:

... for the shade it spread

Was so transparent that the scene came through,

As clear as when a veil of light is drawn
O'er evening hills ...

– Triumph of Life, 26-33

All the outward circumstances and actual reality have become necessary as the laws and conditions of the visible world into which the invisible world is translated. Nature, where everything is fleeting, and everything hangs together in the deepest sense, can become the screen for vision:

The birds, the fountains and the oceans hold
Sweet talk in music through the enamoured air.
And then a vision on my brain was rolled.

– Triumph of Life, 38-40

Giving expression to his sense of the beautiful has by now become Shelley's chief occupation and delight. Mary Shelley remembered the triumphant spirit of the poet at this time:

In the wild but beautiful Bay of Spezzia the winds and waves became his playmates. His days were chiefly spent on the water ... At night, when the unclouded moon shone on the calm sea, he often went alone in his little shallop to the rocky caves that bordered it, and sitting beneath their shelter wrote *The Triumph of Life*, the last of his productions. The beauty but strangeness of this lonely place, the refined pleasure which he felt in the companionship of a few selected friends, our entire sequestration from the rest of the world, all contributed to render this period of his life one of continual enjoyment. I am convinced that the two months we passed there were the happiest he had ever known ...

The poet's happiness can be explained: he knows that the materialists are wrong, and he knows they are wrong because they discard love and imagination. They put their trust entirely in reason in order to deal with life's challenges:

> ... they who wore
> Mitres and helms and crowns, or wreaths of light,
> Signs of thought's empire over thought; their lore
>
> Taught them not this, to know themselves; their might
> Could not repress the mystery within,
> And, for the morn of truth they feigned, deep night
>
> 'Caught them ere evening.'
>
>   – *Triumph of Life*, 209-15

Their thoughts are so fixed upon literal ends that they see nothing in between. Shelley wants to reintroduce passion to the bloodstream of British thought, but the characteristically British fear of contamination has delayed the transfusion.

Shelley has been thrown into soaring passions, mindful as he has been of the powerlessness and vagueness of his conviction of the wrongness of the society into which he was born. He has often cried out, in the bitterness of his contempt, both for the tyrant and himself, leaving, in the process, some of the most humane and radiant poetry ever written. In 'Ozymandias', the poet grants even the pompous expectations of absolute power a tint of empathy:

> Half sunk, a shattered visage lies, whose frown,
> And wrinkled lip, and sneer of cold command,
> Tell that its sculptor well those passions read
> Which yet survive, stamped on these lifeless things,
> The hand that mocked them and the heart that fed.
> And on the pedestal these words appear –
> 'My name is Ozymandias, king of kings:
> Look on my works, ye Mighty, and despair!'
> Nothing beside remains. Round the decay
> Of that colossal wreck, boundless and bare
> The lone and level sands stretch far away.
>
>   – 'Ozymandias'

Tyrants come and go like the clouds above, and the greenery in and around, the ruins of Egyptian monuments, or Anglo-Norman castles. Rats are eaten during sieges of cities, but not when the sieges are over and *coq au vin* is back on the menus. Royalist and republican vocabulary fluctuates and goes through wide changes of meaning. The words on a pedestal dating from *circa* 2000 BC will now be in a context different to the one in which they were first inscribed. The threat of social revolution can seem larger or smaller than the threat of counter revolution, depending on where one happens to be situated on the arc of attitude running through the seven ages of short-lived man. Shelley's faith is in something greater than the confused, slippery, wily, panic-stricken life of the human animal. Shelley's persistent expression of his faith flashes afresh like the light of a coal, sensible of a commitment to burning despite having been isolated from the fire.

Conclusion

> This world is a contradiction – a shade, a symbol – and, spite of
> ourselves, we know that it is so. From this knowledge does all
> melancholy proceed. We crave for that which the earth does not
> contain ...
>
> – Hartley Coleridge, 'Atrabilious Reflections upon Melancholy',
> *Essays and Marginalia*, I, 58

BYRON, KEATS AND SHELLEY ALL WANTED respect from readers. They got some eventually. Like Hartley Coleridge, they had their exquisite sensitivities, but unlike Hartley Coleridge they also had the boldness and crude insistence needed to achieve anything in 'this naughty world of ours' (*Don Juan*, I, xviii). They were creative and destructive, and they could contain the competing energies at least in the realm of ink and paper:

> But quiet to quick bosoms is a hell,
> And *there* hath been thy bane; there is a fire
> And motion of the soul which will not dwell
> In its own narrow being ...
>
> – *Childe Harold*, III, xlii

They searched for essences though they lived amid clutter.

My dear Shelley, -
I am very much gratified that you, in a foreign country, and with a mind almost over-occupied, should write to me in the strain of the letter beside me. If I do not take advantage of your invitation, it will be prevented by a circumstance I have very much at heart to prophesy. There is no doubt that an English winter would put an end to me, and do so in a lingering hateful manner. Therefore, I must either voyage or journey to Italy, as a soldier marches up to a battery. My nerves at present are the worst part of me, yet they feel soothed that, come what extreme may, I shall not be destined to remain in one spot long enough to take a hatred of any four particular bedposts ... You, I am sure, will forgive me for sincerely remarking that you might curb your magnanimity, and be more of an artist, and load every rift of your subject with ore. The thought of such discipline must fall like cold chains upon you, who perhaps never sat with your wings furled for six months together. And is this not extraordinary talk for the writer of Endymion, whose mind was like a pack of scattered cards?

– *Letters*, II, 323

They were, as it seemed to turn out, orphans of Wordsworth and Coleridge. They were also orphans of the revolution. But they were orphans with a pedigree. They could be supermen. They could also be sickly, consumptive, neurotic and perverse. They were bookish and otherworldly, and they were often wounded, humiliated and in retreat.

They were at once unprecedentedly innovative and profoundly indebted to other writers, including Wordsworth and Coleridge. The paradox is perhaps central to the continuing power of their work. Contradictory views could be held simultaneously, and sometimes by the same poet. The self was often a goal, but it was also often somewhere the poet could fly to for sanctuary when the world got the better of him. The self could be his monastery.

As Keats put it, 'My imagination is a monastery and I am its monk'
(*Letters*, II, 323). The self could be the poet's pleasure dome. It
has been handed over to us now:

> ... Thought
> Alone, and its quick elements, Will, Passion,
> Reason, Imagination, cannot die ...
>
> – *Hellas*, 795-7

The three poets in this study are the principal avatars of a
'Romantic' sensibility that is supposed to have 'had its day'. On
the one hand, they are unlike us enough to be looked at with
alien fascination. Most of us have been trained to collude in the
construction and maintenance of a comfortable mediocrity – our
attempt to prevent life from inconveniencing us with a superior,
and therefore often more joyous (and often more painful), quality
of consciousness. This is why, when not 'on the make', we devote
so much of ourselves to essentially absurd activities, from weeding
the garden to reading the *Guardian*. On the other hand, the three
poets are enough like us to be recognised as appealing to something
deep in our nature. We are insubstantial, cloudlike and connected.
We are part of something eternal. It's not necessarily the eternity
promised by Christianity (or by any other literalising system of
thought with a history of violence), but it is eternity, and deep
down we know it:

> I am the daughter of Earth and Water,
>   And the nursling of the Sky;
> I pass through the pores of the ocean and shores;
>   I change, but I cannot die.
> For after the rain when with never a stain
>   The pavilion of Heaven is bare,
> And the winds and sunbeams with their convex gleams
>   Build up the blue dome of air,

I silently laugh at my own cenotaph,
  And out of the caverns of rain,
Like a child from the womb, like a ghost from the tomb,
  I arise and unbuild it again.

– Shelley, 'The Cloud'

Further Reading

Byron

The Poetical Works of Lord Byron, edited, with a memoir, by Ernest Hartley Coleridge (John Murray, Albemarle Street, London, 1905)

Byron's Poetry, selected and edited by Frank D. McConnell (Norton, 1978)

Caroline Franklin, *Byron: A Literary Life* (Macmillan Press Ltd., 2000)

Phyllis Grosskurth, *Byron: The Flawed Angel* (Sceptre, 1997)

Fiona MacCarthy, *Byron: Life and Legend* (Faber, 2003)

Jerome J. McGann, *Fiery Dust: Byron's Poetic Development* (University of Chicago Press, 1968)

Doris Langley Moore, *Lord Byron: Accounts Rendered* (John Murray, 1974)

Peter Quennell, *Byron: The Years of Fame* (Penguin, 1954)

Jane Stabler, *Byron, Poetics and History* (Cambridge University Press, 2002)

Keats

John Keats: The Poetical Works, edited by H.W. Garrod (Oxford University Press, 1958)

The Letters of John Keats 1814-1821, edited by H.E. Rollins (Harvard University Press, 1958)

Keats's Poetry and Prose, selected and edited by Jeffrey N. Cox (Norton, 2009)

John Barnard (ed.), *John Keats: The Complete Poems* (Harmondsworth: Penguin, second edition, 1976)

Walter Jackson Bate, *John Keats* (Harvard University Press, 1963)

George H. Ford, *Keats and the Victorians: A Study of His Influence and Rise to Fame 1821-1895* (Yale University Press, 1944; reprinted 1962)

Robert Gittings, *John Keats* (Penguin, 1967)

Donald C. Goellnicht, *The Poet-Physician: Keats and Medical Science* (University of Pittsburg Press, 1984)

John Spencer Hill (ed.), *Keats: Narrative Poems* (Palgrave Macmillan, 1983)

G.M. Matthews (ed.), *Keats: The Critical Heritage* (Routledge, 1971)

Andrew Motion, *Keats* (Faber, 1997)

Christopher Ricks, *Keats and Embarrasment* (1974)

Nicholas Roe, *John Keats: A Life* (Yale University Press, 2012)

Aileen Ward, *John Keats: The Making of a Poet* (Viking Press, 1963)

John Whale, *Critical Issues: John Keats* (Palgrave Macmillan, 2005)

Shelley

The Poetical Works of Shelley, edited by Newell F. Ford (Houghton Mifflin Company, Boston, 1974)

The Letters of Percy Bysshe Shelley, edited by Frederick L. Jones, 2 volumes (Oxford: Clarendon Press, 1964)

John Buxton, Byron and Shelley (Macmillan, London, 1968)

Paul Foot, Red Shelley (Sidgwick and Jackson, 1980)

Richard Holmes, Shelley: The Pursuit (Harper Perennial, 1975)

Thomas Medwin, The Life of Percy Bysshe Shelley, edited by H.B. Forman, 1913 (Oxford, 1847)

James A. Notopoulos, 'Shelley and Thomas Taylor', PMLA vol. 51, no. 2 (New York, 1936)

Walter Edwin Peck, Shelley: His Life and Work, 2 volumes (Houghton Mifflin Company, Boston, 1927)

Neville Rogers, Shelley At Work (Oxford University Press, 1967)

Mary Shelley, Frankenstein, 1818 (Penguin Classics)

Mary Shelley, Journal, edited by Frederick L. Jones (University of Oklahoma Press, 1947)

Stephen Spender, Shelley (Longman, Green & Co. Ltd., London, 1960)

Francis Thompson, Shelley (Burns Oats & Washbourne, London, 1923)

Timothy Webb, Shelley: A Voice Not Understood (Manchester University Press, 1977)

Ann Wroe, Being Shelley: The Poet's Search for Himself (Jonathan Cape, London, 2007)

General

Marilyn Butler, *Romantics, Rebels & Reactionaries: English Literature and its Background 1760-1830* (Oxford, 1981).

Rupert Christiansen, *Romantic Affinities* (Vintage, 1994).

Daisy Hay, *Young Romantics: The Shelleys, Byron and Other Tangled Lives* (Bloomsbury, 2011)

Thomas De Quincey, *Complete Works*, edited by Grevel Lindop, Volume 15 (Pickering & Chatto, London, 2003)

William Hazlitt, *Spirit of the Age* (1825), edited by E.D. Mackerness (Northcote House, Plymouth, 1991)

Leigh Hunt, *Selected Writings*, edited by David Jesson Dibley (Fyfield Books, 1990)

Francis Jeffrey, *On English Poets And Poetry* (Routledge, 1900)

Paul Johnson, *Intellectuals* (Phoenix, London, 1988)

E.V. Lucas, *The Colvins and Their Friends* (London, 1928)

Tom Paulin, *The Day-Star of Liberty: William Hazlitt's Radical Style* (Faber, 1998)

Plotinus *Collected Writings*, translated by Thomas Taylor (Prometheus Trust, Somerset, 2000)

Alexander Pope, *Selected Poetry*, selected by Douglas Grant (Penguin, 1985)

Mario Praz, *The Romantic Agony* (Fontana Library, 1960)

Bertrand Russell, *History of Western Philosophy* (Routledge, 1995).

Duncan Wu, *30 Great Myths About the Romantics* (Wiley Blackwell, 2015)

Eighteenth-Century Verse, edited by Roger Lonsdale (Oxford, 1984)

INDEX

JOHN KEATS

Against All Doubtings

Andrew Keanie

978-1-906075-75-0 (pbk)
110pp

Having identified him as a sort of semi-educated little cockney chancer, Keats's contemporary reviewers savaged him in the pages of Britain's most influential magazines. High ambition, unaccompanied by high birth, and radical affiliations and liberal inclinations, made him an object of contempt to those of, or aping the opinions of, the literary Establishment. In the short term, he never stood a chance.

Long after his death, his reputation was eventually brightened by much more enthusiastic – if, as some have since argued, misguided – appreciations for his beautiful and powerful otherworldliness.

Later still, in reaction to Keats-lovers' gushing admiration, a much more worldly Keats has been written up – including some bracing insights that seem to owe something to his first reviewers. As Martin Seymour-Smith has said, 'Many privately regard [Keats] with a condescension that is more smug than they would like to admit.'

This largely text-focused study promotes the best energies of a more Romantic view of a key Romantic figure. Keats was inspired and ill. By the time of his death, his genius and tuberculosis had pressurised him into poetry. The best he had to offer – including searching and scintillating confidences concerning how to live one's life in this world of suffering, 'the Vale of Soul-making' – are more accessible to the reader with a taste for poetry than they are to the consumer of ideologically appropriate journalism or ostentatiously unemotional academic analyses.

WORDSWORTH AND COLERIDGE

Views from the Meticulous to the Sublime

Andrew Keanie

978-1-871551-87-7

For a long time the received view of the collaborative relationship between Wordsworth and Coleridge has been that Wordsworth was the efficient producer of more finished poetic statements (most notably his long, autobiographical poem *The Prelude*) and Coleridge, however extraordinary he was a thinker and talker, left behind more intolerably diffuse and fragmented works. *Wordsworth and Coleridge: Views from the Meticulous to the Sublime* examines the issue from a number of different critical vantage points, reassessing the poets' inextricable achievements, and rediscovering their legacy.

OTHER TITLES OF INTEREST

STORY
The Heart of the Matter
Maggie Butt (editor)
978-1-871551-93-8 (pbk) 184pp

W.H. DAVIES
Man and Poet: A Reassessment
Michael Cullup
978-1-906075-88-0 (pbk) 146pp

MILTON'S *PARADISE LOST*
Peter Davies
978-1-906075-47-7 (pbk) 108pp

JOHN DRYDEN
Anthony Fowles
978-1-871551-58-7 (pbk) 292pp

RAYMOND CHANDLER
Anthony Fowles
978-1-906075-87-3 (pbk) 206pp

POETRY MASTERCLASS
John Greening
978-1-906075-58-3 142pp

SWEETLY SINGS DELANEY
A Study of Shelagh Delaney's Work, 1958-68
John Harding
978-1-906075-83-5 (pbk) 204pp

DEREK MAHON

A Study of His Poetry

Christopher Steare

978-1-910996-08-9 (pbk) 232pp

BETWEEN TWO WORLDS

A Survey of Writing in Britain, 1900-1914

Hugh Underhill

978-1-906075-55-2 (pbk) 188pp

To find out more about these and other titles visit
www.greenex.co.uk
www.greenexeducational.co.uk